RELIGION, FUNDAMENTALISM, AND VIOLENCE:

AN INTERDISCIPLINARY DIALOGUE

T0351369

RELIGION, FUNDAMENTALISM, AND VIOLENCE:

AN INTERDISCIPLINARY DIALOGUE

ANDREW L. GLUCK, EDITOR

UNIVERSITY OF SCRANTON PRESS
SCRANTON AND LONDON

CREDIT FOR COVER IMAGE
The Fall of the Rebel Angels, from Book I of 'Paradise Lost' by John Milton
(1608–74) c.1868 (engraving) by Gustave Dore (1832–83) (after)
Private Collection/ The Bridgeman Art Library
Nationality / copyright status: French / out of copyright

Library of Congress Cataloging-in-Publication Data

Religion, fundamentalism, and violence : an interdisciplinary dialogue / Andrew L. Gluck, editor.
    p. cm.
    ISBN 978-1-58966-204-9 (pbk.)
    1. Violence--Religious aspects. 2. Religion. 3. Fundamentalism. I. Gluck, Andrew Lee.
    BL65.V55R4625 2010
    201'.76332--dc22

                                                              2010010571

Distribution:
University of Scranton Press
Chicago Distribution Center
11030 S. Langley
Chicago, IL 60628

PRINTED IN THE UNITED STATES OF AMERICA

In Memoriam

Richard Antoun

3/31/32 — 12/4/09

On December 4, 2009 Richard Antoun, one of the contributors to this volume, was murdered. Professor Antoun was a friend of the Islamic world, as his many writings will attest. He was also an extremely gentle, charitable, and helpful person. This volume is dedicated to him.

CONTENTS

FOREWORD

To illuminate a set of issues that have become increasingly vexing in our time, Andrew Gluck gathered a group, at once informed and sensitive to global affairs, "capable of critiquing their respective traditions but who are also appreciative of them and understand them from the inside." Their plural perspectives remind us that the terms *religion, fundamentalism,* and *violence* embrace vast complex domains and will require sustained collaboration even to begin to clarify the issues involved. What are we speaking of in each case? What varied and often contradictory faces have religion, fundamentalism, and violence displayed in response to historical and cultural shifts over the centuries? Can a concerted exchange — like the one laboriously executed here — offer any illumination to realities daily bowdlerized by a sound-bite media in an ostensibly enlightened world?

The answer to this last passionate question is evident in the work itself, which promises to equip readers with a set of tools to begin to untangle the issues involved. Andrew Gluck's own introduction displays how exasperating the questions are, then his interlocutors employ anthropological tools (Richard Antoun, Carol Delaney), philosophical and theological strategies (James Cary, Craig Nichols, Seyyed Nassir Ghaemi), and intercultural legal perspectives (Sai Ramani Garimella) to try to unscramble the complexities of the related issues. The way contributors interact with one another testifies to the sheer human interchange needed to solve our shared problems in these areas.

With all this, we have the further poignant reminder that the lead contributor, Richard Antoun, gave his life for just such nonviolent inquiry into the conundrum of religious violence. As the editor communicated to us in December 2009:

> To you and all my other friends of the Christian faith who have been involved in [this] book on religion and violence, I cannot

IX

> help but think of Richard Antoun, another Christian involved in the book, who was brutally murdered a couple of weeks ago. May this holiday usher in peace on earth and an end to ethnic and religious strife.

His brutal stabbing reminds us of the import of inquiries of this kind and the potential cost of intellectual probity. The lines of demarcation between religious groups can easily become hardened, but one of the gains of this inquiry is to more clearly differentiate the authentically religious from the belligerently ideological.

Under the early tutelage of the Canadian theologian, Bernard Lonergan, S.J., I learned to identify the signal difference while maintaining a capacity for self-criticism. As he liked to put it, the world divides between those who seek understanding and those who need certitude. Note the telling difference between an intentional verb (*seek*) and a psychological one (*need*), and reflect that this bifurcation can cut right down the middle of each of us. Craig Nichols's foray into orthodoxy from a rich Christian perspective, redolent of both eastern and western traditions, displays the valence of this distinction as Christian tradition manifested its best side in developing doctrines. Other contributors lay bare the darker side of one or another of the Abrahamic faiths (Carol Delaney), and still others mine the spiritual dimensions to offer substantial illumination of a religious tradition's capacity for criticism and renewal (Seyyed Nassir Ghaemi, Sai Ramani Garimella). A bonus is an especially clear presentation of the Christian "just war" tradition, underscoring its striking ethical demands — just when new modes of combat seem to have rendered it passé (notably in distinguishing combatants from noncombatants) or regimes intent on war have moved to co-opt it for their own purposes.

This engaged group of inquirers, operating (more or less explicitly) from diverse religious traditions, employ discriminating and discerning human intelligence in such a way as to engage our own, and help us find a way forward. Much that could be said about that way forward is better illustrated by their collaboration here.

David Burrell, C.S.C.
Uganda Martyrs University, Nkozi

About the Contributors

These are scholars, knowledgeable about religion and other areas, who can look at this problem in novel ways. Some are observant members of their respective faiths; others are not.

Richard Antoun (1932–2009) was professor emeritus of anthropology at SUNY Binghamton. His scholarly interests focused on comparative religion, Islamic law and ethics, and the sociology of dispute with respect to tribal law in the Middle East.

James Carey teaches philosophy at St. John's College, Santa Fe, NM. Since 2004 he has also been Distinguished Visiting Professor of Philosophy, United States Air Force Academy. His teaching focuses on Thomism, Natural Law theory, and the Catholic Just War Tradition.

Carol Delaney teaches anthropology and sociology of religion at Stanford University. She specializes in the Abrahamic faiths and their impact upon women and violence.

Seyyed Nassir Ghaemi teaches psychiatry and public health at Tufts University. He has a masters' degree in philosophy and is working on a book on Islamic philosophy. He is particularly interested in Sufism and in the philosophy and methodology of psychiatry.

Andrew L. Gluck taught philosophy at Hofstra University and St. Johns University. He has published in the areas of medieval philosophy, philosophy of education, consciousness studies, and forensic economics.

Craig Nichols teaches philosophy at the University of Rhode Island. He has specific interests in Christian theology (Roman Catholic, Greek Orthodox, and Protestant) and modern existentialist philosophy.

Sai Ramani Garimella was a professor of law at the National Law Institute in Delhi, India. She is currently an associate professor of law at IILM Institute for Higher Education, Gurgaon, India.

INTRODUCTION

ANDREW GLUCK

THE RATIONALE FOR THIS BOOK

Is there a connection between violence and religion and if so what is the nature of that connection? That is the question that will be addressed by this inquiry. The various experts assembled, who are knowledgeable regarding Judaism, Christianity, Islam, Hinduism, philosophy, anthropology, sociology, psychology, and psychiatry, will be looking at this question from a number of angles and commenting on one another's essays. Some of them are religious adherents (in the traditional or conventional sense) and some are not. We have attempted to choose scholars who are capable of critiquing their respective traditions or the traditions of others but who are also appreciative of them and perhaps understand them from the inside. We also included one rather strong critique of the Abrahamic religions (Judaism, Christianity, and Islam) in general. That contributor is hardly unique in considering those religions peculiarly intolerant and prone to violence, but that belief will also be discussed critically. This book is not meant to be a critique of fundamentalism.[1] There is, however, an implicit assumption, shared by many, that when religion contributes to violence (or even contempt for other humans) it is a matter of great concern. I will attempt to frame the discussion in this introductory essay. But each participant will then be free to address the question as he or she sees fit.

This book is not meant to be a comprehensive treatment of the subject. It certainly does not purport to be a comparative study of religious traditions. I am not even sure if such a thing is possible given our present state of knowledge (or lack of it) regarding the effects of religion — as opposed

I

to those of general culture, power politics, and so on — as related to violence. There may be more comprehensive works as well as ones that focus more intensely on particular traditions. What I wanted to achieve — and I think we have — is a lively discussion and critical debate on the subject such as I have not seen in print.

There are also great religious traditions (such as Buddhism) that this book does not deal with at all. Perhaps some will view it as unbalanced because we might seem to focus on Christianity and Islam more than on other traditions. This deserves an explanation. We assume that most readers will be Christians of some sort and that one of their major concerns will be Islamic terrorism. That is simply the fact of the matter and we want this book to be of interest to a wide range of such readers. But we have also attempted to look both appreciatively and critically at Judaism and Hinduism — traditions which many view (perhaps wrongly) as largely lacking in religiously inspired violence.

Perhaps a more comprehensive study will emerge from this conversation. Nevertheless, there is always need for dialogue, and that is what this project aims to be. It is also meant to be interdisciplinary and to avoid the kind of thinking that could be called "tunnel vision." We were even interested in airing ideas that are relevant but that might not be entirely germane to the question at hand in the hope that they would shed light on the topic. For example, we included a chapter on the just war tradition in Christianity but no correlative treatments of other "just war" traditions. The author of that chapter quite deliberately avoids the word *violence* in favor of *force*. This is obviously an important distinction and a more comprehensive book would not only compare just war theories in the various traditions but also address the important normative distinction between violence and force. We, however, have not attempted either. We assume that, within various traditions, levels of force are tolerated and justified — levels which outsiders might consider unacceptable violence. We leave that normative judgment to the reader.

If the book seems tilted towards the Abrahamic religions, that was no accident and will explain why we even bothered to include a chapter on Judaism despite the fact that the number of people in the world who actually practice that religion is relatively miniscule. But we wanted to look at this subject in a large number of ways in order to elicit a currently relevant conversation without having to be encyclopedic. We also do not deal specifically with the kind of religious or quasi-religious stupidity that may do violence to human beings without really meaning to — for example, the vegan couple who were recently arrested for starving their child to death unintentionally. Undoubtedly, some religious people are guilty of such irrational negligence and fanaticism, but it is not the focus of this book. We mean to deal with deliberate violence committed with religious motives.

Readers may be particularly interested in the comment sections where one author comments on another's work. We did not want this to turn into an interminable debate, however, and therefore only allowed one reply to the original comments. This unfortunately prevents the authors from replying to some additional criticisms or misinterpretations. But we have also made every effort to eliminate uncharitable criticisms that could be easily refuted and are therefore superfluous. We hope that this book will clarify issues even if it does not provide definitive answers. Such clarification may be just what we need right now.

FRAMING THE PROBLEM

It has been suspected for some time that fundamentalist religion and violence have some affinity for one another, and the general tendency is to view it as a causal relationship with fundamentalism as a direct efficient cause.[2] This may cohere with a more general bias towards imputing all statistical correlation between two variables to direct causal connections between them as well as the common intuition (imbedded in our folk psychology) that our ideas influence our actions. Both of those biases or intuitions surely need to be subjected to critical investigation, but this has been done elsewhere to no small extent and interested readers need only peruse the literature in philosophy of social science and philosophy of mind. But those epistemic biases are not all that needs to be investigated.

Even if we were to grant that religious fundamentalism contributes causally to violence (itself a controversial assumption), is it the fundamentalism or the underlying religious beliefs that are doing the causal work? This will require some attempt at differentiating fundamentalism not only from religion in general but also from general cultural motifs that may or may not originally have been religiously inspired. We recently lost one of our most influential historians, Norman Cohn, who attempted to show in *The Pursuit of the Millennium* how messianic ideas have inspired animosity and violence. He also argued that those messianic ideas were infectious and ultimately came to influence even purely secular ideologies. But the unveiling of a number of historical examples is not sufficient as evidence of a universal law. Perhaps the real culprit behind violence that is not chaotic, and not confined to the level of the individual, is spiritual/cultural ideals in general, religion being only one example. The following quotation from Charles Taylor may be instructive.

> From all these examples, in my view, a general truth emerges, which is that the highest spiritual ideals and aspirations also threaten to lay the most crushing burdens on humankind. The great spiritual visions of human history have also been poisoned chalices, the causes of untold misery and even savagery. From the very beginning of the human story religion, our link with the highest has been recurrently associated with sacrifice, even mutilation, as though something of us has to be torn away or immolated if we are to please the gods. . . . But the sad story doesn't end with religion. The Kharkov famine and the Killing Fields were perpetrated by atheists in an attempt to realize the most lofty ideals of human perfection.[3]

So perhaps the reactive nature of violent fundamentalism has been overemphasized. Is there really a statistical correlation between fundamentalism and violence? Perhaps such intense and naïve religiosity or quasi-religiosity decreases intra-group violence to a greater extent than it increases inter-group violence (assuming it does the latter). This would be a result of the oft-cited function of religion, namely increasing group solidarity. Perhaps such solidarity is needed more in periods of radical change or crisis but not as much in other situations and is one of those phenomena (like nationalism) that have both good and bad effects depending upon the circumstances.

In an age that is not particularly hospitable to religion (at least in academia and some other sectors), the many peaceful fundamentalists may often be overlooked, while those who advocate or even engage in violence may reinforce the suspicion that fundamentalist belief does indeed cause violence — or, at least, is associated with it. As Jeff Gainey, the Director of the University of Scranton Press, pointed out to me, there are Christian fundamentalists who interpret the Sermon on the Mount quite literally and may be quite nonviolent — unwilling to use force. This leads to another suspicion, that such concepts as fundamentalism may not really be transferable from one tradition to another. While appreciative of these important questions, we have proceeded on the assumption that there are indeed commensurable aspects of the various traditions and that we will be capable of discussing them across denominational divides.

There is indeed much anecdotal evidence to suggest (if not to substantiate) some link between religion (in general) and violence: religious wars, inquisitions, current Islamic terrorism, and the like. On the other hand, the real culprit may be something even more deeply rooted in the human psyche than religious belief, and perhaps that real underlying cause may be responsible for both violence and the religious beliefs. Many of those who are antireligious do not believe in free will or in folk psychology. It is, therefore, not exactly coherent for them to assume that adoption of religious belief (by itself) makes people violent.

We are, after all, animals, and many if not most species of mammals exhibit some violence towards one another. This should be apparent to anyone who has been around stallions and bulls, both of which are members of relatively peaceful herbivorous species. And we are an omnivorous species, presumably a bit more aggressive than cattle and horses. Therefore, whether we believe in free will or not, most of us might acknowledge some deeply rooted violent impulses that are operative in our species. Is it also possible that some deeply felt anxiety is another cause of both violence and the need for religious certainty? This more deeply rooted cause might be masked by the apparent correlation between fundamentalist belief and violence. In a secular age, it might express itself in political belief and violence.

Or perhaps a deeply rooted human tendency towards violence has the power to infect religion in a peculiar way since people are more willing to die (and perhaps kill) for religion than they are for most other concerns. Psychoanalysts, following Freud, have sometimes hypothesized the existence of a death instinct (*Thanatos*) in humankind, which might explain both violence and the willingness to die and kill for one's beliefs. But one could certainly imagine other deeply rooted tendencies that would fulfill similar functions. For example, if humans completed their basic psychological evolution in the Pleistocene age as members of small closely related groups, it is at least plausible that they are hardwired by evolution to both die and kill for *group* survival in general.

I recognize that natural selection for purely group survival is not accepted by all evolutionary biologists. Some of them deny that traits injurious to individuals but adaptive for the group would have survived the rigors of evolutionary selection. But since those early human individuals could only have survived in a small group, violent protectiveness of that group might have had individual survival value as well. An individual who was useful as a fighter against the group's enemies might have had high status even if he were quite annoying within the group. That is because even proto-humans might have had the mental capacity to value such individuals for their long-term instrumental value. We may be able to see this phenomenon in the modern world as well. In a similar way, the group might have also protected particularly altruistic individuals, even if they were otherwise uniquely vulnerable to the competitive strivings of others. That might also seem to have required some foresight or innate principle of reciprocity, but perhaps not. Archaic humans might have reasoned that such individuals either deserve protection or should be protected because they may be useful in the future.

On the other hand, we find passive (apparently altruistic) individuals (*omegas*) in wolf packs that coexist with the more dominant ones (*alphas*). Only aggressive males are allowed to breed, but the "altruistic" ones survive nonetheless. That presumably can be explained by viewing altruism as a natural response to weakness. So perhaps evolution equipped some humans to be aggressive and violent and others to be altruistic (by virtue of their weakness) by nature. And human religion, presumably, would have to address both of those impulses. Perhaps there is something about humans that evolutionary theory does not explain. But in any case, there seems to be confirming evidence for the hypothesis regarding the need for religion to address both aggressive and passive impulses in the radically differing motivations of members of the exact same religious groups. But as is the case with the domestic dog, some of which were bred to be vicious and others tame, perhaps some human societies (and religions) favored pacifism and others activism.

Evidence for a basic violent propensity infecting both religion and politics would include such things as Stalinism, the regime of Pol Pot in

Cambodia, and tribal or clan violence in Africa. These are all nonreligious movements that are every bit as violent as religious fundamentalist ones. As far as I know, the horrible massive killings in Rwanda were not basically inspired by religion. Perhaps religious fundamentalism is therefore just one specific manifestation of a more general human propensity for violent defense and/or oppression.

One could perhaps plausibly argue that in certain environments (such as ancient or primitive nomadic conditions) there is no real distinction between defense and aggression. So perhaps tribalism as a cultural phenomenon (sometimes disguised) lies behind the violent excesses that are sometimes associated with both religion and politics. If the basic cause lies within the human psyche, the solution might seem to be some kind of personal transformation or growth. But if the basic problem is tribalism, then the solution might well be political and/or cultural.

Perhaps we should conceptualize the relationship between violence and fundamentalism in a Weberian manner, as one of mutual selective affinity but essential independence. Those who are prone to violence (at least psychologically) might gravitate towards fundamentalist religion as it allows for a *justification* for their innate tendencies. And the religious adepts who might not be prone to violence may nevertheless ignore (and sometimes even encourage) the violent tendencies of some of their followers since they represent both a useful constituency and a potential defense force. Despite this meaningful relationship between the two psychological profiles (the spiritual and the aggressive) we would be dealing with two essentially independent phenomena, and we could not really say that one causes the other.

It is also possible that religion actually deters or puts a damper on violence. And it is conceivable that some kind of fundamentalist or at least orthodox belief is the default religion for most of the human race. We will try to distinguish orthodoxy from fundamentalism, but such an attempt may be fraught with difficulties. Without some such standard religious beliefs, many people might be even more violent than they currently are. Recently we witnessed the takeover of Somalia by a fundamentalist Muslim group that, despite employing ideas and methods that we deplore, actually decreased the violence in that country. We will now see what occurs when that group is ousted and more moderate or secular forces take control.

The usefulness of religion for deterring violence must of course be tested over extensive periods of human history because in some snapshot views this may or may not appear to be the case at all. One could at least envision a study that would correct for other relevant factors such as education, personality variables, cultural propensities, and so on, but even such a study would not correct for historical factors. For example, previous studies suggested that capital punishment did not deter violent crime and more recent studies suggest that it actually does, but the methodology does not seem to have changed. In the same way, religion might have different effects in different epochs. But even those beliefs that may be effective in deterring violence may not be sufficient to deter the violent tendencies of some people. And even if religion is such a violence-inhibiting belief, in some unusual cases a religious belief system — in some way, like those effective anti-depressant drugs that occasionally cause suicide — might even make a peaceful person violent.

DEFINING FUNDAMENTALISM

Most people are fairly certain about what religion and violence are but less certain regarding what fundamentalism is. Since we are not yet ready to draw conclusions regarding the relationships between religion, fundamentalism, and violence, let us turn to the phenomenon of fundamentalism itself. We would like to know whether it carries within itself some seeds of violence that might be distinguishable from religion in general, from deeply rooted universal psychic tendencies, or from tribalism. We would also like to know whether it is useful to distinguish between religious orthodoxy and fundamentalism in terms of their effects on violent ideation and behavior.

We have seen that the answers to those questions are somewhat independent of the question regarding whether religion also deters violence — because it could possibly do both, in varying settings or with different people. And if that is the case, we might ultimately want to compare the two effects quantitatively. I don't expect that such quantitative studies will occur within this project, but their contemplation may make us less sure of ourselves as we discuss our views or findings.

A good place to begin is with a definition. We will not attempt to define *religion* or *violence* since most people know what is meant by those words, although this may become worthwhile in the study of specific traditions. But the definition of *fundamentalism* is another matter entirely. What is fundamentalism? The dictionary definitions do not help us much because they generally refer to certain Christian (usually Protestant) beliefs involving literalism in biblical exegesis and rejecting "modernist" interpretations. Undoubtedly, that is the etiology of the word, which began with a return to "fundamentals." This may have involved a rejection of what one may broadly call "orthodox tradition"[iv] and then evolved into opposition to more modern, empirically based accretions to Protestant thought.

Yet most of us are quite capable of and even prone to extend the term *fundamentalism* to include Jewish belief systems that are not literalist at all and Islamic religious phenomena that are not particularly concerned with the Bible. The term is also now used for certain Hindu groups. Eventually the dictionaries may catch up to popular usage, but in the meantime we must deal with the word as it is currently being used. It seems to me that all of those religious phenomena that I mentioned involve what some would term a naïve belief in certain authoritative sources such as the New Testament, church teachings, the Talmud, or the Qur'an. And they all tend to reject or ignore more modern critical scholarship regarding their respective religions as well as more moderate traditional compromises. The latter is particularly significant because it may differentiate fundamentalism from a more broadly based orthodoxy or traditionalism.

This "rejectionism" may stem from attitudinal factors more than it does from belief. More moderate coreligionists may have similar beliefs without the deep commitment to them that characterizes fundamentalism. Perhaps fundamentalism even defines itself by this active and virulent rejection of liberal and tolerant belief systems. In Protestant Christianity, we have witnessed the decline of Unitarian and other liberal belief systems and the rise of Evangelical Christianity, which defines itself by a literalistic interpretation of scripture. In Judaism, we witness a phenomenon often called "Torah True Judaism," but that appellation really betrays its rejection of modern liberal ideas. In Islam we have seen the almost total eclipse of philosophy and liberal ideas that were so prominent in the Middle Ages and the dominance of a more narrow-minded theology.

Is it possible that fundamentalism has a relationship to violence between groups that is more than casual? That is to say, perhaps at the very root of some orthodox religiosity lies a conception of the other that could indeed spill over into violence under the right conditions. What I am tentatively suggesting is that it is not simply the case that religions carry with them contemptuous ways of thinking of outsiders but that this way of thinking is in some sense a fundamental or foundational aspect of those religions. I am not, however, suggesting that all religions are like that. It does seem plausible that most primitive tribal religions would be like that, but I do not claim to know enough about them to decide. I am willing, however, to tentatively suggest that the Abrahamic religions share that quality. It is one that must be carefully distinguished from violence, but it seems to bear a relationship to it.

To rationally suggest this requires a mental exercise — a thought experiment that would allow us to refute it. Keep in mind that we have not yet distinguished between orthodoxy and fundamentalism, and therefore we are really considering types of religiosity that might also be called orthodox but would certainly include fundamentalists. Let us briefly examine the three Abrahamic religions in terms of their belief systems, excluding moral or ritual prescriptions. We know that Orthodox Jews are able to interpret many biblical passages allegorically and can even understand how various rabbinic opinions in the Talmud may be understood in terms of particular discussions taking place within a particular historical context. Therefore, even such apparently fundamental beliefs as the six days of creation could theoretically be set aside. But what of the doctrine regarding the chosen people? If that were set aside, would we still be speaking about Orthodoxy or fundamentalism?

Likewise, it is conceivable that liberally minded Christian fundamentalists could set aside the literal belief in the six days of creation. But could they be willing to admit that non-Christians are "right with God" in the same manner as Christians and still be called orthodox or fundamentalist? Orthodox Muslims can perhaps investigate the various passages in the Qur'an and Hadith in a scholarly fashion and come to conclusions that may be somewhat untraditional. But what if they came to believe that Islam has no peculiarly decisive role to play in the world, at least in comparison with Judaism and Christianity? If they were to come to the conclusion that these are all perfectly acceptable forms of monotheism, each adapted to a particular people, culture, and history, what would we call such a belief system? Would it still be orthodox Islam?

I have deliberately answered the questions with questions because I am unsure of the answers. Nevertheless, it remains a suspicion of mine that there is a meaningful connection here that has not yet been sufficiently explored and it may explain why some beliefs and not others are truly "fundamental."

We could perhaps further extend the term to include Marxism and certain fascist phenomena. They also seem to rely at times upon certain authoritative or canonical sources. Having emerged from Western civilization, those nonreligious political/economic phenomena may also share some of the messianic features of the Abrahamic religions. If a Communist were to come to the conclusion that capitalism can evolve into a benign social and economic system by itself, perhaps he or she would no longer be a real communist. While discussion of those secular movements may emerge in the book, we have not specifically recruited anyone to discuss nonreligious ideological movements. It was feared that stretching the term *fundamentalism* to include nonreligious ideologies might make the discussions too amorphous. Nevertheless, it is obvious to me that those ideologies contain something significantly analogous to fundamentalist religion, especially regarding the psychological needs of their adherents and their commitment to changing the world.

But one could also find other equally naïve religious and nonreligious belief systems that do not involve the same fervent and urgent desire to change the world, have other people view things in the same way as the true believers do, and actively reject more liberal beliefs. For example, theosophists or naïve psychoanalysts might be termed fundamentalist in terms of their beliefs, but they are rarely violent or even coercive. Furthermore, even those in the mainstream of those movements are willing to expand their belief systems.[5] In addition, practitioners of certain primitive religious cults might or might not qualify as fundamentalist depending upon one's definition. They don't generally seek to impose their views on outsiders and are relatively unconcerned about opposing beliefs. But they are certainly naïve and dogmatic in their beliefs without a great deal of critical and/or argumentative tradition, and they might practice their own forms of violence.

These are all legitimate considerations. I would like to suggest, however, that we not get bogged down in such gray areas but concentrate on movements that almost everyone would accept as fundamentalist. Even as we attempt to do that, though, there seems to be an important intuition (which not everyone shares) that will affect our classifications. Some religious believers are quiet and passive and seem to adapt well to a secular world. Others are extremely uncomfortable with that world and seek to aggressively confront secular society, destroy it, damage it, or at least alter it significantly. And it does seem to be that very desire to extend one's worldview (or at least radically solidify its locus of control) that is behind so much religious violence today. Professor Richard Antoun, for example, while using the term *fundamentalist* to refer to those more militant groups, views fundamentalism itself as an ideal type that exists widely — but not usually in an extreme form. This would explain the fact that it is not always easy to distinguish between the two shades of religion on the basis of statements of belief.

I think there is indeed a meaningful distinction to be made between those religious groups that are militant and expansionist and those that are merely passive or defensive. We might be well advised, therefore, to restrict the bulk of our inquiry to forms of religiosity that seem to constitute a problem to the modern world. But this distinction is not always easy to maintain. For example, the Wahabi movement in Saudi Arabia is not particularly aggressive (although it practices draconian methods of social control at home that could be called violent and has missionary tendencies abroad), but it gave birth to Osama bin Laden and the al Qaeda movement. If we were to examine the core beliefs of both, there might not be significant differences — even though in their relationship to the outside world there are immense differences. In order to know to what extent we want to link those two movements we need more information about them. We also need more clarity regarding our own goals because systems of classification are almost always related to human motivations.

The key question is this: Should the term *fundamentalism* apply primarily to a staunch faith in a belief system or to an assertive attitude toward outsiders? And that leads to these questions — one factual, the other motivational: Do movements like Wahabism usually give birth to such externally violent offspring and to a greater degree than other cultures? Is our goal the tracking of violence to direct causes only — or also to more indirect ones?

It might indeed be useful to distinguish fundamentalism from orthodoxy (in the broad sense). Both rest upon trust in authority and it may be easy to confound them. Perhaps orthodoxy evolves out of some early kind of fundamentalism or perhaps fundamentalism is a later phase of religious belief. There may be no general rule regarding that or perhaps there are general historical tendencies. Be that as it may, orthodoxy generally involves some kinds of historic compromises that allow the religion to adapt to the world, while fundamentalism often challenges such adaptation as inauthentic. Fundamentalism as we know it in the modern world may also result from relative powerlessness and the feeling of being threatened by modernity.[6] That assessment, however, may be proven false as such movements gain power, as they have in Saudi Arabia and Iran.

In terms of doctrinal belief, orthodoxy and fundamentalism may not be that different. This leads to speculation that what really constitutes fundamentalism is not so much belief as attitude. All orthodox Christians believe in a life after death but few show the willingness to die that characterized either the early martyrs or later extreme believers. The same distinction can surely be made regarding Judaism and Islam and perhaps other religions as well.

It is often argued that Hinduism and Buddhism do not have the disease of violence to nearly the same extent as the Abrahamic religions. We have not in fact, throughout the histories of Hinduism and Buddhism, seen the same degree of violent aggressive actions as we have in Christianity and Islam. Is that because the more extreme elements in the former have tended to be quietist? (The caste system in India might have been imposed by force by invading Aryans. Is that an example of religiously inspired violence?)

Two distinguishing fundamentals of the Abrahamic religions are the belief in one jealous God and a very strong condemnation of idolatry, variously defined. Judaism is an interesting case because it is the root of both Christianity and Islam. Throughout most of later Jewish history, we have not seen a great deal of violent aggression against outsiders, but the fact of Jewish dispersion and minority status might constitute the simplest and best explanation for that. And in fact we do have many examples of ancient Jewish aggression such as the forced conversion of the Idumeans and the violence perpetrated by the Hasmoneans. Even the concept of holy war itself may well have originated with the Jews in the biblical period. And one should not ignore more recent violent actions of some individuals under the influence of Zionism and/or Judaism.[7]

The problem of violence also seems to have crept into the more peaceful religions, as recent events in Asia have shown. Hinduism has become somewhat violent on the Indian subcontinent and we have the very interesting phenomenon of Hindu-Buddhist violence in Sri Lanka. Are these a result of Western and/or Islamic influence or is our notion of peaceful Eastern religions somehow flawed?

We should beware of calling every fervent expression of religiosity fundamentalism, even when they show a propensity for irrationality — and even violence. For example, there are instances of mass hysteria — sometimes fueled by strong charismatic leadership and exploiting underlying religious beliefs — that might not qualify as fundamentalism because the belief systems are not sufficiently crystallized. What this line of questioning seems to suggest is the difficulty in fully defining fundamentalism despite the fact that it seems to be a useful category, at least as an ideal type. Perhaps, however, fundamentalism (like pornography) is something largely indefinable, but most of us know it when we see it.

THE ROLE OF THE BIBLE

Biblical religion has sometimes been blamed for the almost ubiquitous state of human violence. That, in my opinion, is an exaggeration. As I mentioned previously, it is possible that they share something with many other religions that is essentially connected to suspicion of others and is, therefore, potentially violent. Biblical man is told by God to subdue the created world. The Hebrew word that is used for subdue (*cavash*) could also mean rape. And there are indeed examples of divinely ordained violence in the Bible that make many of us cringe.

So, to be fair, we must admit that the biblical tradition does seem to be an activist one that certainly has great potential for violence. This is magnified by what I have suggested is a type of exclusivism that all the Abrahamic religions share to a certain extent. On the other hand, the Bible recalls a pristine and nonviolent state of humankind where even the eating of animals was forbidden. It also records the initial divine dissatisfaction with humankind stemming from human disobedience (in the Garden of Eden) and then violence (prior to the flood). But it was only violence (according to the Bible narrative) that prompted God's decision to destroy the world.

To many modern people, God's flood may appear to be an unjust, disproportionate response and one that sets a bad example for us humans. Few of us would destroy our children because they became violent towards one another. But, looked at another way, this may reflect an essential biblical abhorrence of violence. The continuation of violence and other crimes prompted God to intervene again by choosing Abraham (a fairly peaceful person) to become the father not only of the Jews but of Christianity and Islam as well. Therefore, despite certain difficult episodes and the obvious propensity for biblically influenced religion to become violent, the Bible has deep affinities to peace and nonviolence, which emerge again in the great prophecies regarding the messianic age when warfare will end.

Even more radical, perhaps, was the admonition to the Jews to give their cheek to those who smite them, traditionally attributed to Jeremiah (book of Lamentations) and most likely the source of Jesus' more famous saying regarding turning the other cheek.[8] Those were quite radical notions in the ancient world. The evidence of archeology points to warfare as a continuous feature of ancient and primitive human life, and the Bible must be viewed in that context. One could surely argue that biblical religion has restrained those human passions more than it has inflamed them.

Yet there does seem to be a connection — often unacknowledged — between religious belief and violence (at least in negative terms) that I will now attempt to articulate. Such a connection, while not pertaining specifically to biblical religion, may affect those belief systems more than others because of their activist nature. Perhaps any lack of cultural or intellectual sophistication leads to violence — at least by those who are otherwise prone to it (most often, young males under stress). But what of those who are not otherwise so predisposed to violence? Perhaps they *need* religion in order to become violent.

If you were to ask the average secular Westerner what the worst imaginable sin is, almost all would say murder or some other extremely violent act. But if you were to ask the same question to religious people, a rather significant number might say heresy, blasphemy, idolatry, apostasy, or atheism. This points out a rather interesting psychological phenomenon that might indeed be behind certain examples of institutional violence instigated not by the vulgar masses but by more intellectual or cultured elites. One tends to be more constrained by the values that are uppermost on one's list of priorities.

There surely are people who would rather kill than eat pork, even if that prioritization is not endorsed by either Judaism or Islam. For some secular people, who have shed most religious beliefs and taboos, violence may remain as the major, if not the only, thing that is really ultimately forbidden.[9] But for religious people, it may be just one of many activities that are forbidden by their faiths. Is it possible that for two equally nonviolent people, religious affiliation might actually increase the propensity to take violent action? Could this explain the abhorrence of capital punishment in relatively secular Western Europe and its somewhat enthusiastic reception in the more religious United States? But even if this suspicion were to be confirmed, it is still possible that it is not the Bible that is the causal factor but the various fundamentalist belief systems that emerge from it.

The physicist Steven Weinberg was reported to have observed that good people tend to do good and evil people tend to do evil, but for good people to do evil, "that takes religion."[10] There is a great deal of truth in that, but I would caution him and other secularists that perhaps it takes a certain *kind* of religion and that it can also be accomplished by secular ideologies, such as Marxism.

There is another feature of religion that might tend to allow for violence against those who are not believers. The Bible states unequivocally in the story of creation that all humankind was created in the image of God. But there seems to be a deeply rooted tendency in religious thought to distinguish between different *kinds* of human beings. This even turns up in Genesis with the reference to the sons of God cohabiting with the daughters of men. We can perhaps assume that the former were more heavenly beings and the latter more earthly or physical beings. This seems to be consistent with other Near Eastern mythologies. There also seems to be a tendency among primitive tribes to believe that they are the only *real* humans.

We must be cautious in interpreting those "primitive" beliefs but many more "advanced" religions create similar dichotomies. What is perhaps most interesting for our purposes is the fact that this may tend to strip the lower kind of human beings of their essential dignity. It is well known that some Christian thought considers those who are not saved through Jesus Christ as being slaves to sin, condemned to eternal damnation. This reduces the unsaved in certain respects to an animal level or, even worse, demonizes them by viewing them as enemies of God and objects of His wrath. We have seen similar ideas expressed by Muslims. It is perhaps less well known that similar ideas crop up in Judaism as well. Maimonides in the Mishneh Torah (at least according to one interpretation) states that non-Jews, in order to insure a place in the world to come, must obey the moral law out of a conscious knowledge that it was given to Moses on Mount Sinai. If they act morally out of any other kind of knowledge or belief, it is not accounted by him (and presumably God) as righteousness. That particular passage has been challenged and given an altogether different meaning by some scholars. But in *The Guide for the Perplexed*, Maimonides surely says that heretics quite often need to be killed, and that primitive people without an advanced religion can also be killed with relative impunity (though they rarely need to be).[11] These examples ought to alert us to the dangers inherent in all exclusivist claims to religious truth.

Perhaps the following examples will flesh things out even more. I have heard of a family of formerly secular Jews in Brooklyn who became more religious, moved to Israel, and then to the West Bank as settlers. So far, the story seems rather commonplace. At some point, however, they converted to Islam and were heard on a National Public Radio broadcast chanting, "Kill the Jews," in Arabic. This is a very extreme and unrepresentative case, and we can surely assume that the parents are well outside the psychological norm. The following example, however, is more instructive because it is less extreme and perhaps more common. I heard of a man who at one time was attempting to convert Jews to Christianity. Later on, he converted to Judaism. Now he believes (in accordance with some ancient Jewish legends) that God offered the Torah (five books of Moses) to all of the nations, but they rejected it because of their evil predilections; only the Jews (due to their virtuous nature) accepted it.

Why do I offer these examples? I think they illustrate two essential ingredients of fundamentalism that may be shared by orthodox religiosity in general. The first is what can only be called a naïve and unenlightened reliance upon traditional opinions, legends, and doctrines. Given the wide range of such traditions, why do fundamentalists latch on to certain legends and not others? When we examine more closely those traditional beliefs that seem to win out, we see something very interesting, which is the second feature. They tend to exalt one particular religion or people over others. And even when there is another authentic tradition that is less exclusivist or triumphalist, it seems that the more extreme form tends to win out. There may be good historical (or even evolutionary) reasons for that. It reminds me of many nationalistic claims and it may have a distinct survival value — or perhaps it may be more accurate to say they *had* such value in the past.

Perhaps counterexamples do exist of religions that could be called fundamentalist (or at least naively traditional) yet are zealous of the civil rights and dignity of all humans. Such examples (if they exist) would surely be worthy of intense study. But even in such cases, I suspect there may be a modest and secret pride in being in possession of a truth that others do not have. Such pride can easily spill over into violence when certain restraints are lifted.

I will now attempt to make some distinctions between the three Abrahamic faiths, all of which share an ideological affinity and find their roots in the Hebrew Bible. I do not know enough about other religions to make further comparisons, but it should be obvious from the chapter regarding Hinduism that the dynamics of that religion are rather different even though they also experience problems with fundamentalism and violence. Therefore, I do not mean to imply that other faiths are necessarily nonviolent. The Abrahamic faiths, however, all seek to change the entire world for the better in accordance with the promise that God made to Abraham. This is somewhat different from philosophically based religions that only seek to change the individual believer or perhaps a single society.

In this process of providing a blessing to all the nations of the world, some violence (or force) may result. In all those three religions, the world is radically divided between "us" and "them," but all three also foreswear violence against innocent outsiders to a great extent. Nevertheless, the potential for violence clearly exists. What is really needed, however, is to look more deeply behind authoritative statements regarding violence in order to find underlying trends.

In Judaism, a feeling of superiority coexists with the clear resignation that Jews will remain in the role of a relatively weak minority at least until the coming of the messiah (who never seems to come). Therefore, the use of violence against the more powerful majority is almost a practical impossibility (but messianic movements may be a matter of some concern in this regard). There is one significant exception to this, however, and that involves the Holy Land. There is clearly a biblical tradition of a kind of holy war to conquer that land. This tradition is interpreted in various ways, however, by different Jewish thinkers and jurists.[12] Furthermore, Jews are a clear majority in Israel. Hence, violence against outsiders in Judaism tends to be a geographically circumscribed phenomenon. History in fact confirms that trend.

In Christianity there is a tradition, stemming from Augustine, of dividing the world into *civitas terrenae* and *civitas dei*. The former has a loose connection with the Roman Empire while the latter has a similarly loose connection with the Church. Violence was a common motif of Roman imperial rule and has become internalized in Christianity to an extraordinary extent — but mostly in terms of martyrdom. It should be noted that both the history of earliest Christianity (as a Jewish sect), and even at the time of Augustine, is that of a relatively powerless group against much larger, better organized powers. Yet, since the messiah has already come for Christianity, the achievement of coercive earthly power by the Church is a conceivable scenario even if Christianity is essentially uncomfortable with the wielding of such power. This combination of the glorification of martyrdom with the possibility of coercive power is of great interest and may help explain certain historical events and trends.

In Islam as well, the world is divided between two realms: *dar al-harb* and *dar al-islam*. The former is (literally) the lands of warfare and the latter the lands of peace (literally submission to God). This dichotomy is extremely significant. In both Christianity and Judaism, peace and safety is provided by the corrupt powers that be. Therefore, compromise with those corrupt earthly powers comes easily to them even if fundamentalist elements sometimes reject such compromises. In Islam, on the other hand, only submission to God through Islam can truly bring peace. Therefore, the goal of peace may only be achievable through warfare or submission of non-Muslims to the rule of Islam.

This vision of the world may emerge from historical circumstances when neighboring tribes were quite literally at war with one another until the coming of Islam. Based on those historical circumstances and on the fact that Mohammed was a political and military leader as well as a prophet, Islam may be more comfortable with the exercise of coercive power and/or violence than are Christianity and Judaism. In many varieties of Islam, martyrdom and the promise of heavenly reward also plays a role in the motivation of holy war (jihad). Nevertheless, Islamic thought in many of its authoritative expressions rejects coercion in religion and/or aggressive warfare. Therefore, the differences that I am describing should not be interpreted as essentialist necessities but only as trends that are subject to change. Religions, like people, do change, but it is not at all an easy matter and often takes a great deal of time.

FURTHER REFLECTIONS

Our discussion has suggested a possible distinction between people with a propensity for violence (who might be deterred from it by religion) and those not disposed to violence (who might at times be encouraged towards it by religion). The presumption often seems to be that young uneducated males are a particular threat to the peace of society. We may also have tacitly assumed that rationality and cultural sophistication can act effectively as a brake upon what may indeed turn out to be a hard-wired propensity for violence in male human beings. If culture is an effective brake, and if some types of religion might provide justifications or psychological motivations for violence, then perhaps religious fundamentalism is indeed a candidate for blame.

That certainly seems at times to be the case, but a close look at Nazi Germany might tell a different story. There, intellectually and culturally sophisticated people, many of whom lacked strong religious beliefs, perpetrated the greatest imaginable crimes. Perhaps any strongly held belief system, religious or not, can sometimes lead to violence. Or perhaps the roots of violence go even deeper and are more pervasive than was initially suspected; perhaps it will eventually find an outlet unless it is constrained by an equally *nonrational* force. This was what Spinoza seemed to think, and, though no personal fan of institutionalized religion, he concluded that a beneficent religion (and not reason) was the most effective cure for the passions of the masses.

Fifteen of the twenty chapters of Spinoza's *Theological-Political Treatise* are devoted to religion. And yet it is rationality for Spinoza that provides the only freedom that humans can ever really know, and no one can accuse him of disrespecting rationality. In keeping with a distinct trend in Jewish thinking, Spinoza restricts the power of state-sponsored religion to human actions, leaving the inner life relatively free from coercion. Hence, he anticipated modern functionalist sociological interpretations of religion as essential to social control. At one time, such control was seen as at least theoretically extending to ideas as well as actions, and even now there is some reason to think that ideas are an important component of social adhesion. In retrospect, we can view Spinoza's liberal attitude towards religious freedom as an extension of Maimonides's fight against superstition. However, unlike Maimonides, who was quite concerned with doctrinal issues and explicitly justified violence against heretics, Spinoza feared religious violence above all the ills that can be attributed to an organized social state. Perhaps the extremes of the Iberian inquisition and his own bitter experience had drawn a red line beyond which social control was no longer acceptable to him. Ironically, this essentially heretical thinker may now be the torchbearer for those who desire (or recognize the need for) some beneficent societal influence of religion, yet reject a strictly theocratic state.

Today we tend to think more in cultural than religious terms, but a similar conclusion could encompass both if we were to argue that it is the *general* cultural climate and not individual cultural achievement that restrains violence. For example, North America has been largely spared the religious and ethnic warfare and persecutions of the Old World, despite a much lower level of cultural sophistication. This is one of the apparent paradoxes of American society. But the disconnection between a beneficent society and cultural sophistication should not really surprise us. There are many examples of culturally sophisticated societies that had bad political or economic systems. The question that needs to be answered, however, is how American society avoided many of the evils often associated with religious persecution. Perhaps that is a result of the confluence of various religions in a mélange that eventually exerted an influence on the general culture. This should not necessarily be interpreted as a melting pot but rather as recognition of difference while seeking common values. While not perfect by any means, North American society is indeed a model for peaceful relationships between multiple religious and ethnic persuasions. On the one hand, it welcomes a diversity of religious and ethnic communities, but on the other hand it seems to blunt their more extreme manifestations, allowing for a general allegiance to American cultural and political ideals.[13]

A good example of the interactions between various religious, cultural, and historical factors is the uproar regarding Mel Gibson's movie *The Passion of the Christ*. It was feared (for valid historical reasons) that it might inflame anger and even violence against Jews. Yet, despite the vocal opposition of many prominent Jewish spokespersons and organizations, no such result seems to have occurred. In fact, both the movie and the opposition to it seem to have improved Christian-Jewish relations in the United States by forcing people to confront their lingering suspicions and prejudices. Ironically, this may even have applied to Mel Gibson's own attitude towards Jews, as more recent events may have shown.

Perhaps the fear of fundamentalism is overblown in certain societies, while not in others. We in the United States have difficulty understanding why countries like France and Turkey would feel threatened by external religious observances. We tend to extol all manifestations of freedom of speech and religion — unless they are state-sponsored, and even then they are sometimes allowed. But other societies have witnessed the disastrous results of religious warfare that we have been relatively immune from. Perhaps there is an optimal amount of religion in society while either excess or deficiency might lead to frequently unanticipated problems.

Could there be a connection between the relative lack of concern for religion in France and the rise of militant and violent Islamic rage there? In the United States, on the other hand, the relative religiosity (much of it quasi-fundamentalist) of the general populace is also associated with a much *less* militant Islamic population. Or should we attribute this difference only to the relative numbers of Islamic citizens in France or to their closer proximity to their homelands? Perhaps the implicit French assumption that all minorities will give up their ethnicities creates more resentment than does the American assumption that ethnic and religious identities will be maintained over time. In fact, it may be that latter assumption that fuels much of the anti-immigration sentiment in the United States today and therefore keeps immigration down to what many consider manageable levels. So we seem to have a paradoxical situation where a nation that has traditionally welcomed immigrants and celebrates ethnic differences now feels threatened by both. But such an apparent paradox would dissolve if one were to recognize the need in every society for a certain degree of conformity and orthodoxy.

There is another element of religion that we have not yet discussed and that I suspect is somewhat significant. In all three Abrahamic religions (and perhaps for others as well) the concept of blood sacrifice is prominent. Why is blood such a persistent element in those religions? Does it alleviate a psychological propensity for violence or does it inflame it? Surely we have witnessed examples of violence against innocent people that do resemble sacrificial rites. And for much of human history such sacrifices did indeed involve innocent human beings.[14] I would be very interested to hear the opinions of the participants on this issue as well as the others that I have discussed. Professor Antoun has already alerted me to the fact that researchers differ on the effect of sacrificial rituals. There is also a notion of the blood of the covenant that begins with the Jewish commandment regarding circumcision and is continued with the Christian New Covenant. Why does a covenant (an ancient near eastern juridical concept) with God require blood?

There is yet another aspect of fundamentalism that may be connected to violence, but in some ways it may be even more closely connected to tribalism. By this I do not mean the kind of tribalism that exists today under the overarching authority of Islam or other universal religions. I am referring to the belief that one's own religion or group is the only truly correct one. Perhaps such a belief in one's own superiority is also characteristic of primitive tribes. We certainly find this to be a prevalent view in many religions. Professor Antoun (in a personal correspondence) indicated that it is a prominent belief only in the three monotheistic religions. I must claim a lack of first-hand acquaintance with the other religions, but we may have some legitimate reasons to suspect that at least under certain conditions they can also be quite intolerant. For example, Montesquieu drew an analogy between the cruelty of the Iberian inquisitors (which for many is the paradigm of religious intolerance) and the equally cruel Japanese attitude towards alien religions.[15]

Perhaps there is some truth to the widely held belief that the Abrahamic religions are in general the most intolerant. Sometimes, however, this belief in one's own superiority is connected to a "charitable" view of other religions as containing a part of the truth but at other times it is connected with a demonization of other religions as the "anti-Christ", infidel, or some similar characterization. It is probably true that every classical exposition of Abrahamic religion contains some implicit or explicit assumption that other religions are inferior, if not evil. But we also find such views in other cultural fields. Everyone thinks that his or her scientific theory is superior to other contenders, but not everyone thinks that his or her preference in art is — it could just be a matter of taste. But such a relativistic attitude in religion seems somehow inconceivable even when one doesn't really care what religion other people practice. In fact, such relativism is usually associated with lukewarm religiosity or none at all.

And when the question regarding others' religious beliefs is linked to the ultimate destiny of the creation, it seems unrealistic or even cruel for believers not to care. Hence the historical struggle between Christianity and Islam may seem somehow inevitable since each conceives of itself as the ultimately valid religion that will bring salvation or peace to the world. But need this competition entail violence? We don't generally see contending scientific theorists or their followers confronting one another violently. Yet it must be admitted that there is more likelihood of violence when each side views itself as possessing an exclusive truth.

Perhaps it is possible to believe in one's own religion as the best one but still acknowledge that another religion is superior in certain respects. But that would probably not be fundamentalism or orthodoxy; if it were, it would be of great interest indeed. Recently there was a story in the New York Times (March 11, 2006, front page) about an "Islamic" psychiatrist who believes that Jews have responded better to persecution than Muslims. At first I thought this would be extremely interesting. I was rather disappointed, however, to read later on in the article that this individual had actually abandoned the Muslim faith. I had been hoping to find a refreshing kind of religiosity but what emerged was a complete lack of it.

One sometimes does encounter believers who extol other religions. For example, Christians frequently admire the more intellectual and participatory aspects of Judaism. Both Christians and Jews have admired the unself-conscious way that Muslims pray in public. The Jewish thinker Franz Rosenzweig found much in Christianity that was favorable in comparison to Judaism, such as its strength of conviction and power to change the world. But it must also be admitted that these are somewhat rare exceptions.

Religious belief in those three faiths tends to demand (at least psychologically) a belief in the inferiority of other religions. In the case of Judaism, there is a possible escape from this dilemma, albeit an option that has rarely been exercised. Since the Jews consider themselves the chosen peo-

ple, it is possible to emphasize the special status of the *people* and not necessarily the religion. It is at least conceivable to consider Judaism the correct religion for this *particular* people only, with other religions being just as good — but only for non-Jews.

Another interesting mental experiment might be to imagine a fervently religious person believing that his or her religion is at least as good as any other but that it might be superseded in the future. Could we call such an attitude towards one's religion fundamentalist or even orthodox? And what if a religious person is critical of his or her faith even while practicing it? I think the answer to such questions is that we would not consider such individuals fundamentalists and probably not orthodox either, but I would be very interested to know what others think.

Here is another question I find interesting: Is a nonfundamentalist attitude towards religion really feasible for most people who suddenly become religious. If the answer to that question is also no, we may have to put up with a certain amount of religion-related violence in order to reap the benefits of acquiring religion (if such benefits exist). This should not surprise us since most good medicines have some bad side effects.

CONCLUSION

It is widely believed that some religions are more violent than others — just as violence is more likely to break out at a rock concert than at a classical performance. But that analogical explanation does not prove that rock and roll makes people violent. If you put symphony orchestra patrons at a rock concert, they would probably not become violent, even if violence erupted around them. In order to substantiate any causal conclusion, we would need controlled experiments. We would, for example, need to look deeper and investigate the *kinds* of people who are attracted to various kinds of religious and cultural genres. Nevertheless, it would be strange if religion did not have *some* effect on human behavior.

This leads us to the investigation of specific religious traditions and how they are used or misused in the modern world. It could be that essentialist notions about religions are largely misplaced and the real onus should be placed on human use of religious traditions. That having been said, it is still conceivable that some religions have this problem to a greater extent than others. Few would expect Jains to be as violent as Muslims even though the vast majority of the latter are surely not violent either. Furthermore, the more fundamentalist expressions of the various faiths seem more inherently violent, at least most of the time.

It is also possible that religions that follow a single prophet or leader are more prone to fundamentalism and violence than those with a broader base of sacred writings. That might have been true of early Christianity even though their belief system encouraged martyrdom (which is a kind of violence against oneself) but certainly not violence against others. It might also be true of varieties of Islam. It is certainly not true of normative Judaism where the role of Moses was downplayed and there are even legends that he himself would not recognize the religion that the rabbis inferred from his teachings. It is true, however, of some fundamentalist versions of Judaism that revere certain rabbis and writings to an extraordinary extent. Of course, this is only a tendency, and in fact no religion really follows the teachings of only one individual — though some may think they do.

I certainly suspect that many people have a great need for religion and that some kind of orthodox or fundamentalist religion is needed by most of those believers. This may be unwelcome news to those who hope for some vague modernist religious feeling that could unite humankind in a spirit of brotherly love. Few people get their religions individually tailored; they usually buy them off the shelf with a conspicuous label and then make minor (and inconspicuous) adjustments. This tendency towards orthodoxy or even fundamentalism when people acquire or re-acquire religion can be seen in many different historical contexts. It is obviously the case in the Muslim world and places where Muslims constitute a substantial proportion of the population. It can be seen in the rightward trend of Orthodox Judaism where its numbers are substantial. It can also be seen in the growth of the Evangelical movement in America and the decline of more modernist Christian churches. But such a tendency towards fundamentalism in religion does not necessarily translate into violence.

I suspect that much of the violence associated with such religion has other causes but that some of it may indeed be caused by religious beliefs. Although I am not overly enamored with depth psychology, I would like to make one suggestion along those lines. Perhaps some people force themselves to espouse religious propositions about which they actually harbor serious (but often unconscious) doubts. There may be a tendency to balance such inner turmoil with external conflict. The inner psychological act of repressing those doubts may therefore be accompanied by an external opposition to the heretic, infidel, and apostate that could easily spill over into violence.

I certainly don't want to sound like those public intellectuals who are finding it increasingly profitable and convenient to bash religion as an irrational belief system that can only have baneful consequences. As a matter of fact, I am convinced that many if not most human beings need religion and that nonrational faith commitments are not necessarily irrational or harmful. But we must be willing to acknowledge undesirable side effects of good things, whether they are medicines, religions, or freedom. I certainly hope that future research concerns itself with these more subtle relationships and avoids the simpleminded tendency to either blame religion for the ills of the world or absolve it of all such responsibility.

Until such definitive research emerges, we must content ourselves with more tentative conclusions. We have assembled here seven separate essays which I consider to be laden with valuable suggestions. The first, by Richard Antoun, takes advantage of many years of anthropological research in the Middle East and elsewhere. He views violent fundamentalism in its most problematic form to be tied to the Abrahamic faiths and their tendency to insist upon one final truth. He views fundamentalism as a radical and atypical expression of faith and at the same time as an ideal typical constituent of even the more moderate expressions of those faiths. In other words, he both absolves normative Abrahamic religion (particularly Islam) of responsibility for violence and at the same time points out some quite disturbing underlying essential elements.

The second essay, by Carole Delaney, also utilizes social scientific research. Her conclusions are in a sense far more radical than those of Antoun since she views the Abrahamic faiths, even in their more common and normative expressions, as peculiarly and dangerously violent and anti-feminine.

The third essay, by Sai Ramani Garimella, attempts to survey Hinduism as basically a nonviolent philosophy which has for peculiar historical reasons evolved into a much less tolerant religious system — which, nevertheless, manifests itself (because of its philosophical roots) as far less intolerant and less violent than the Abrahamic faiths.

The fourth essay, which I authored, attempts to distinguish between Jewish fundamentalism and Orthodoxy. I find deep similarities but also subtle differences. I acknowledge problems with violence against both outsiders and "heretical" internal elements while at the same time attempting to place those violent tendencies in correct perspective.

The fifth essay, by Seyyed Nassir Ghaemi, views Islam and its problems with violent fundamentalism in a nuanced fashion that could only be accomplished by one with a background in psychiatry, philosophy, and religion. His interest in nonviolent Sufism and other nonviolent strands in Islam allow us hope for an eventual resolution of the perennial struggle (sometimes violent) between Islam and the West.

The sixth essay, by Craig Nichols, is from the perspective of orthodoxy in Christianity. Unlike the first study by Richard Antoun, he views fundamentalism as *essentially* distinct from orthodoxy despite the fact that the two have been historically linked from the very beginning. In fact, he views fundamentalism as a form of Gnosticism that is essentially incompatible with his view of a more enlightened, philosophically based religion. Like Ghaemi, he sets forth the possibility of a truly tolerant and nonviolent, yet authentic, expression of the Abrahamic faiths.

The seventh essay, by Anthony Carey, takes a good look at just war theory in orthodox Christianity and its impact upon questions regarding the use of force. He stresses the universal nature of natural law, yet insists on a much more dogmatic expression of orthodox faith than do some of the other authors. This is an interesting combination of what some others would see as incompatible worldviews. Could such a rational and universal code of conduct and belief (transcending and indeed ignoring confessional differences) lay the foundation for a less violent world? Or do we need to reform religions from within in a more philosophical and less fundamentalist direction if we are ever to live in peace?

The first possibility seems the simpler one and might be feasible right now since most major religions agree on a large number of moral issues, though there are surely technical ones (When does human life begin?) regarding which they don't always agree — and which are not insignificant. But we must ask ourselves why this has not already occurred; the suspicion is that something deeper is required. We currently have examples of deep splits within particular religions over belief, liturgy, and even ethics, yet the respective groups are not at each others' throats. A counter example, of course, is Northern Ireland, but that may be more of a political struggle than a religious one. Perhaps if all humans could become thoroughly convinced of the fact of universal brotherhood, just as they currently experience solidarity within their own religious communities, religion might lose whatever deleterious effects it currently has in terms of inciting violence. If that is to occur, the doctrine of human brotherhood must become the most important or at least one of the most important components of those particular religious belief systems.

Notes:

1. For a well-reasoned but less than dispassionate critique of fundamentalism, see Solomon Schimmel, *The Tenacity of Unreasonable Beliefs: Fundamentalism and the Fear of Truth* (Oxford: Oxford University Press, 2008).

2. A glance at the Internet (which may reflect popular opinion) indicates a common assumption that fundamentalism is a significant cause of violence. Martin Marty and R. Scott Appleby consider fundamentalism (whether violent or not) a reaction to threatening secular or religious beliefs. See Marty and Appleby, *The Fundamentalism Project*, 5 volumes (Chicago: University of Chicago Press, 1994). Karen Armstrong has also stressed the uniqueness of modern fundamentalism as a religious cause of violence. See Armstrong, *The Battle for God: A History of Fundamentalism* (New York: Ballantine, 2000). This strong distinction between modern religious movements and traditional ones has also been approached from an opposing perspective. Max L. Stackhouse and his contributors to *God and Globalization* (Harrisburg, PA: Trinity Press International, 2000–2002) have argued that globalization will make traditional religion more tolerant due to the infusion of new ideas and cultural motifs. We have indeed seen fundamentalist or at least orthodox religiosities become more tolerant in the United States, but we have also seen what appears to be the opposite reaction in parts of Asia. We also need to disaggregate the effects of secular toleration of all beliefs, including religion, from *religious* toleration of other religions.

3. Charles Taylor, *Sources of the Self: The Making of the Modern Identity* (Cambridge, MA: Harvard University Press, 1989) p. 519.

4. By *tradition* I mean a living body of beliefs and practices that evolve over time but never completely sever the connection with the source. It is certainly not an unchanging belief system.

5. We actually do sometimes find fundamentalist thinkers expanding their belief systems in accordance with more modern psychological teachings. Often they attempt to integrate those teachings with orthodox principles of faith. This, however, is characteristic of those religious thinkers on the fringe of fundamentalism rather than in the mainstream.

6. James Turner Johnson argues that this is the case with Islamic fundamentalism and gives it a far less tolerant complexion than Islam in the classical period of its expansion. See J. T. Johnson, *The Holy War Idea in Western and Islamic Traditions* (University Park: Pennsylvania State University Press, 2001) p. 68.

7. I am referring to events such as the killing of Prime Minister Rabin by a fundamentalist, the killing of Muslim worshippers in Hebron by Baruch Goldstein and the subsequent justification of that horrible event by some, and similar though less publicized occurrences, but not to Israeli defense activities regarding which reasonable persons might disagree.

8. See Lamentations 4:30

9. An interesting example of this phenomenon was reported in *The New York Times*, August 25, 2006, pp. A1, A8. The Iranian government has exhibited a group of cartoons depicting Jews, Israel, and the Holocaust as a kind of art exhibit. One purpose of the exhibit is to point out the inconsistency of certain Western societies allowing cartoons of Muhammad but forbidding certain forms of hate speech, Holocaust denial, and so on. As detestable as this rationale is, it points out something profound. In the secular West, religion may, almost without exception, be ridiculed, but speech or writing related to violence may often be banned. That shows a prioritization that is obviously not shared by certain fundamentalist groups or societies and which they may even find incomprehensible.

10. *The New York Times*, Tuesday, July 25, 2006, p. F4.

11. See *The Guide for the Perplexed*, III: LI. The views of Maimonides will be dealt with in much greater depth in my essay on Judaism.

12. Some say that this is a commandment for all time; others say that it pertained only to the time of Joshua. This tradition of holy war should not be confused with legal discussions among rabbis regarding the ethics of various types of wars. These discussions are to a large extent theoretical and have no bearing on current practical decision making or on past conflicts to any great extent. The question regarding a Jewish right to wage war in order to re-conquer Palestine is a much more pressing issue.

13. A quite similar situation seems to exist in the United Kingdom, Canada, Australia, and New Zealand, and this may actually be a characteristic of the English-speaking peoples rather than America per se.

14. We saw this noting of the significance of sacrifice in the quotation from Charles Taylor and this should be fairly obvious to all those who are acquainted with primitive or archaic religion. Some, however, develop a more crystallized theory around it. For René Girard, the original sacrifices were fellow humans, and Girardians tend to view human society as fundamentally violent. This view has a great deal to teach us if interpreted widely enough. Recently, Girard admitted that his theory was not dependent upon the actual historical accuracy of the human sacrifice preceding animal "scapegoating." See *The Bulletin of the Colloquium on Violence & Religion,* No.33 (October 2008) p. 7. I fear, however, that the more narrow Girardian perspective may indeed be another example of a particularistic religious view possibly promoting contempt for other human beings. As an example of this, I submit the following depiction of an event from the same *Bulletin* (pp. 6–9). It describes a "diatribe" delivered against René Girard by Richard Cohen (a Levinas specialist) who accused Girard to his face of "Gnosticism and Christian heresy." The publication makes an issue over Cohen acting "rudely" in the presence of "Girard, now nearing his eighty-fifth birthday" and calls Cohen a "non-Christian." From an academic perspective, as well as from a modern humanistic one, it makes no difference what one's religion is when it comes to evaluating ideas, and such *ad hominem* arguments strike me as falling into what Girardians themselves see as an essentially violent and "scapegoating" approach to one's fellow human beings.

15. See book 25 of Montesquieu, *De l'esprit des lois.*

Religious Fundamentalism and Religious Violence: Connections and Misconnections

Richard T. Antoun

The common disposition among many journalists, scholars, and laypersons, more so after the events of 9/11, is to link religious fundamentalism with religiously motivated violence, particularly in discussing the Islamic world. This essay challenges that notion and points to a more complex view of both fundamentalism and religiously motivated violence. Its three sections discuss, successively, fundamentalism, religiously motivated violence, and, briefly, what we (the public) can and should think and do about them.

Fundamentalism

It is not profitable to discuss religious fundamentalism only as a commitment to scripturalism — that is, to a literal belief in an inerrant holy scripture — as most scholars and journalists tend to do. Nor is it profitable to discuss fundamentalists/nonfundamentalists as mutually exclusive categories of people. It is much more profitable and accurate to view fundamentalists and nonfundamentalists as on a continuum, and to view fundamentalism as an ideal type.[1] All of us share some attributes of fundamentalism to some degree, and no one, not even Ayatollah Khomeini or Jerry Falwell, possesses all such attributes.

What is fundamentalism, then, in this broader view? It is a worldview and an ethos as well as a protest movement. A worldview is our broadest intellectual construction of the world, and our ethos is the emotional attitudes with which we view that world. The two are usually linked.[2] The worldview of fundamentalism, if I have to compress it into one phrase, is the struggle between good and evil; and its ethos is outrage, protest, certainty, and fear. Outrage and protest are directed against the rapid economic and social change that has swept the world since the end of the eighteenth century at an ever more accelerating pace. Think of the changes with which we have had to cope since the attacks of 9/11. Who can board a plane with the same attitude now?

Fundamentalism is a protest against the relative political weakness that has been foisted on the whole world — excepting only the one superpower that has benefited most, the United States — by these rapid technological, economic, and social changes. It is a protest against the progressive secularization of society — that is, the withdrawal of religion from arenas where it was dominant not so long ago: schools, universities, courts, markets, the state, and leisure activities (the Puritan blue laws that forbade listening to baseball games on Sundays were lifted in Massachusetts only after World War Two). And it is a protest against the ideology of modernism which values quantity (the mass production of goods or services — in American academia, "publish or perish") over quality, change over continuity, and commercial efficiency over human sympathy for traditional values (such as the cultivation of interpersonal relations among family and friends).[3]

Certainty is part of the fundamentalist ethos because the selective reference to scripture (the Hebrew Bible, the Christian Gospels, or the Muslim Qur'an) provides clear-cut everyday guiding norms for social behavior in all aspects of life. But fear is part of the ethos because fundamentalists are a majority in no country of the world; in most countries, they are a distinct (though often vociferous) minority.[4]

What are the attributes of religious fundamentalism?

(1) The quest for purity in a corrupt world. This quest can be achieved either through flight from the world (the Boers of South Africa in the nineteenth century), physical separation from it (the ultra-Orthodox Jews or *haredim* of Jerusalem), or institutional and symbolic separation (sectarian Christian academies in the United States). Or it can be achieved by the alternative strategy of confrontation (through electoral contests, demonstrations, boycotts, legal action, and so on).

(2) "Traditioning," a particular way of thinking about time and the past.[5] Traditioning is the process of collapsing the primordial, the ancient, the heritage of the golden age (here scriptural time) with present time, making them one and the same; therefore, ancient events (of Biblical and

Qur'anic times) become immediately relevant for daily life in the contemporary situation.

(3) Scripturalism, not simply the belief in an inerrant scripture, but reference to and dependence upon the emotional power of scripture and its numinous qualities which inspire both awe and dread, but in any case, transform the believer who comes in contact with it. Scripturalism also has the important pragmatic function of providing everyday guiding norms of behavior.

(4) Activism, the belief that religion should be applied in the world and particularly in its political institutions, and should not be confined to the worship center. Fundamentalist leaders are generally laymen (almost exclusively, men), men of the world, engineers, pharmacists, journalists, teachers, lawyers, and technicians.

(5) Totalism, the belief that religion should be taken out of the worship center and applied to all social institutions and arenas: the television studio, marketplace, school, court, battlefield, and the streets (graffiti on the walls).

(6) Millenialism, the belief that history will end on judgment day when a general accounting of human actions will take place and the individual's eternal destiny will be decided. Many fantastic apocalyptic events will occur at the end of time.

(7) Selective modernization and controlled acculturation. Selective modernization is the process by which fundamentalists accept only those aspects of technology and modern social organization (such as bureaucracy) that enhance their own religious movement. Fundamentalists of all stripes use radio broadcasts, television, and web sites to proselytize and raise money. Indeed, they don't just accept modern technology and social organization, they have been innovative in developing them to far outstrip their competition, whether in election campaigns (computerized voting lists helped elect Ronald Reagan in 1980), or the fundraising of evangelists. The other side of their innovation is controlled acculturation, that is, accepting changes from the modern world, but tailoring them to promote fundamentalist values. Christian televangelists in the United States promote social traditionalism (the "traditional" family) and economic libertarianism (laisse faire) on their programs.

RELIGION AND VIOLENCE

The scriptures of the monotheistic religions are not dominated by verses pertaining to violence. Most verses deal with ethics, law, prophecy, history, and personal life crises — verses from which believers draw comfort, solace, insight, wisdom, and inspiration. Moreover, religiously motivated violence is only one, and not nearly the dominant mode of violence in the world today. Again, with respect to terrorism — and by terrorism I mean public acts of destruction committed without a clear-cut military objective (usually against civilians) that arouse an overpowering sense of fear — religiously motivated terrorism is only one and not nearly the dominant mode of terrorism in the world today. Politically motivated terrorism (of nationalist movements), criminal terrorism (of drug lords), pathological terrorism (of isolated individual extremists), and state terrorism dominate the contemporary scene. State terrorism is by far the most lethal because states possess the most destructive weapons (artillery, tanks, planes, and missiles).[6]

Yet nested in certain verses of the Hebrew and Christian Bibles are calls for violence, even terrorism. Resorting to violence against the opponents of God's chosen people and brutal retaliation for wrongs done are actions justified time and again in the scriptures: "When the Lord your God brings you into the land which you are entering to occupy and drives out many nations before you — Hittites, Girgashites, Amorites, Canaanites, Perizzites, Hivites, and Jebusites, seven nations more numerous and powerful than you — when the Lord your God delivers them into your power and you defeat them, you must put them to death. Make no covenant with them and show them no mercy" (Deuteronomy 7:1–2).

In one verse, God commands Joshua, "You shall not leave any creature alive" (Deuteronomy 20:16–17). And scripture records Joshua's response: "So Joshua massacred the population of the whole region — the hill country, the Negeb, the Shephelah, the watersheds — and all their kings. He left not survivor, destroying everything that drew breath, as the Lord the God of Israel had commanded. Joshua carried the slaughter from Kadesh-barnea to Gaza, over the whole land of Goshen as far as Gibeon" (Joshua 10:40–41).

Such verses have been used to justify violence against opponents in the contemporary world. Indeed, one author has argued that the master religious images in the world religions depict a "cosmic war" with metaphysical conflict between good and evil. In this cosmic struggle, disorder and death can be overcome through images of the afterlife, the raising of the dead, purgatory, karmic cycles of reincarnation, and martyrdom.[7] Martyrdom is exalted in both Christianity and Islam. In both religions, suicide is condemned, but martyrdom is witnessing to God's truth.[8] The Muslim term for martyr is literally, witness (to God's truth), *shahid*.

It is enlightening to move for a moment to a brief account of how one scripture, the Bhagavad Gita, in a nonmonotheistic world religion, Hinduism, deals with the question of the justification of the use of violence. In the long dialogue between the god, Krishna, and the prince, Arjuna over whether Arjuna should go to war against his cousins who have usurped the throne and oppressed the people, Krishna urges Arjuna to follow his destiny/duty (dharma) as a warrior and go to war. But a procedure is stipulated with several conditions before Arjuna can resort to violence. First, he must attempt to persuade his enemy to desist from violence/oppression; if that doesn't work, he should offer him gifts, that is, bribery or appeasement is called for to avoid violence; if that fails, the threat of violence should be used; and only in the case of the failure of diplomacy, appeasement, and threat should violence be used.[9]

In the Muslim case, the justification for violence (and here I am simplifying a very complex set of opinions over a long historical period) has a minority and a majority scholarly tradition. The minority tradition is endorsed by many fundamentalists. Before describing these traditions, it should be pointed out that the term *jihad,* is not translated as "holy war" except by non-Muslims (mainly Christians) and a minority of Muslim scholars. Rather, for most Muslim scholars, jihad is struggle, striving, persevering towards a fixed goal, fighting to defend one's life. That striving takes place in many different contexts: against oppressive rulers, against unbelievers, but also against the evil in oneself — for example, against miserliness and jealousy.

THE MINORITY TRADITION

The minority tradition of Islam regards jihad as "the neglected duty." This is the title of an essay written by Abd al-Salam Faraj, the spokesman of Islamic Jihad, the movement responsible for assassinating Anwar Sadat, the president of Egypt, in 1981. In this tradition, the establishment of an Islamic state is necessary for the establishment of an Islamic society and the living of a Muslim life. The establishment of that state is, furthermore, commanded by God.

An Islamic state ceases to exist when people are ruled by other than Islamic laws, when Muslims no longer feel safe, and when unbelief prevails in society. According to this tradition, so-called Muslim rulers (or ordinary lay Muslims) are not Muslims when they fast and pray but do not enforce Islamic law and ethics — fail to pay the alms tax (incumbent on all Muslims), and indulge in the drinking of alcohol, gambling, and fornication /adultery — even though they have recited the profession of faith.[10]

Many contemporary Muslim scholars in this minority tradition cite Ibn Taimiyya, a prominent thirteenth-century Muslim scholar. He rejected the Mongols as Muslims even though they professed Islam and made some attempt to observe some of the pillars of Islam (prayer, fasting) because they drank alcohol and governed Anatolia by a mixture of legal codes — including some Muslim laws but also many Mongol (tribal) and Christian norms.[11]

The minority tradition generally argues that propaganda and missionary activity — that is, education — cannot establish the Islamic state because mass communication is controlled by the (evil) state. Moreover, they argue that Islam does not triumph by attracting the support of the majority (through political party activity) and that those who "follow the straight path" (an oft-repeated Qur'anic phrase) are always a minority.[12] Their conclusion is that if a state can only be established by war, then war is a religious obligation. Some fundamentalists are generally comfortable in this minority tradition and quote numerous proof-texts from the Qur'an to justify their views: "Fight them (unbelievers) until there is no dissension and the religion is entirely God's" (Qur'an 8:39). "Fighting is prescribed for you, though it is distasteful to you. Possibly you dislike a thing, though it is good for you, and possibly you may love a thing, though it is bad for you" (Qur'an 2:216). "Then when the sacred months have slipped away, slay the polytheists, wherever you find them, seize them, beset them, be in ambush for them everywhere" (Qur'an 9:5).

THE MAJORITY VIEW

The majority scholarly interpretation of the religious justification for violence is quite different. Followers of this view cite the Qur'anic verse, "Let there be no compulsion in religion" (2:256), as a clear-cut condemnation of holy war for the purpose of forceful conversion. They point out that calls for holy war, jihad, by secular rulers violate prophetic precedence. The absence of a single religious authority in Islam allows any cleric with a following to claim authority and proclaim aggressive jihad. For the majority of scholars, these calls for war lack any semblance of legitimacy.

But the strongest argument against aggressive jihad is the practice of the Prophet, Muhammad, during his career as Messenger of God, founder of the first Muslim community (*ummah*), and political leader. For the first thirteen years of his prophecy in Mecca, Muhammad was neither a political activist nor a militant. When his followers were oppressed, he recommended flight (*hijrah*), first to Ethiopia and later to the oasis of Medina, two hundred miles to the north, in the year 622 CE. He was not called to Medina to be ruler or prophet, but rather to be an arbitrator (*hakam*) between the disputing tribes, a role for which he had become known in Mecca.

Once in Medina, he waged a war of attrition against the Meccans for eight years (622–29) rather than an aggressive war. Numerous raids occurred, mainly small-scale with few casualties. This was a war to preserve the vulnerable new religious community. In the year 629, Muhammad appeared before the gates of Mecca for the first time with a large army that could easily have taken the city by force.[13] The Meccan leaders told him they would not allow him to enter the city, but if he returned to Medina and came the next year they would allow him peaceful entry. Muhammad advanced his cause by mediation, as befitted his role as *hakam*. He returned to Medina with his sizeable army, and the following year he came to Mecca, entering the city and performing the first Muslim pilgrimage at the Kaaba.

It is important to note that he did not destroy the Kaaba, the previous center of polytheistic tribal worship, which he had denounced. Rather he emptied it of its idols and made it the center of the Muslim pilgrimage — the hajj. He did not allow his army to take revenge against the Meccan leaders who had derided his message, hounded him, and oppressed his followers. Rather, he declared a general amnesty for the population, including those who were in the forefront of his opposition. His entrance into Mecca in 630 is recorded in the history books as "the conquest of Mecca." But it was not a military conquest. Rather, it had been achieved through negotiation and a peace agreement. This culminating event of his political career marks Muhammad as a man of peace, reconciliation, and compassion, rather than as a militant seeking revenge.

The majority view, then, is that jihad is just war not holy war. Jihad is struggle, striving, and perseverance toward a fixed goal: to do good deeds such as serving one's parents, giving to one's kinsfolk, opposing oppressive rulers, defending one's country against aggressors, performing the pilgrimage, or striving to help others with one's wealth.

POLICY IMPLICATIONS: WHAT TO THINK, WHAT TO DO

This essay is about the connections between a religious ideology and a religious movement — fundamentalism — and the propensity to use violence in the public and increasingly transnational arena. What do we think and what do we do about these connections?

First, research on fundamentalism and violence should be cross-cultural. Cross-cultural research is, however, the most difficult kind. Historians are most comfortable studying historical cases within cultural and class traditions, and even social scientists such as sociologists and anthropologists who preach the merits of cross-cultural comparisons seldom pursue them. But to study single traditions (such as Islam) apart from their apposite cases is to miss the general nature of the phenomenon and to seriously misinterpret it, usually in a self-serving way; this can lead to major policy errors. Only by cross-cultural comparisons can we identify similarities and differences (which are also important).

Second, a nondichotomous view of fundamentalism is necessary in order to avoid the kind of oversimplification that divides the world into "us" and "them." Viewing fundamentalism ideologically and behaviorally as a continuum of attributes in which all of us participate to some degree — and which none of us embrace completely — allows us to interpret events, contemplate groups, and assess ourselves in the more complex and realistic way that befits our increasingly global civilization. The practical result of defining the world as an opposition between "us" and "them" is lack of communication and, ultimately, conflict — sometimes violent conflict.

Third, we have a question and an answer. Are fundamentalists violent people? Only a tiny minority of fundamentalists resort to violence, not to speak of terrorism. Fundamentalists pursue strategies of flight, radical separation, spatial separation, and institutional separation — none of which are violent — as well as confrontation. The great majority of confrontational acts are nonviolent: contesting elections; staging demonstrations; boycotting products, services, and entertainments; propagandizing over radio and television; acting as pressure groups; and pursuing legal action. The overwhelming majority of fundamentalists are law-abiding people, like the general population.

Fourth, how do we communicate with fundamentalists when they are ideologues? If we repudiate the dichotomous notion of fundamentalism and embrace it as a continuum of attributes, we have the basis for dialogue —that is, we begin the conversation by assuming we are on the same ideological and behavioral planet. Engaging a fundamentalist, like any other individual or group with strong views, is better undertaken in a more private one-on-one situation rather than in public meetings or lectures where individuals on both sides grandstand to their audiences for effect.

Fifth, ideologies, that is, programs of action in the world guided by set principles, can — in spite of their absolutist claims and principles — manifest flexibility and compromise when a particular situation promises them the possibility of realizing at least some of their goals. The history of the world is filled with former terrorist leaders who became respectable heads of state. When absolute principles clash with other staunchly held principles within the same ideology (often the case) some reinterpretation and compromise is necessary. In Europe and North America, the widely held beliefs in liberty and equality, followed to their logical implications, are incompatible; yet societies must and do accommodate them.

The holy scriptures of Christianity, Islam, and Judaism themselves juxtapose a wide variety of often incompatible norms which believers must accommodate — usually by prioritizing them according to the immediate situation. Absolutist ideologies are still open to interpretation and compromise in order to achieve peace or obtain a desired goal.[14] In the end, even states and powerful political movements that use terrorism usually conclude that the continuous resort to violence leads to counter violence, and does not achieve the political ends desired.

NOTES

1. The discussion of fundamentalism that follows is a simplification of a more complex argument. That argument is detailed in Richard T. Antoun, *Understanding Fundamentalism: Christian, Islamic, and Jewish Movements* (New York: Alta Mira, 2001).

2. For an interesting discussion of this relationship, see Clifford Geertz, "Ethos, World View, and the Analysis of Sacred Symbols," in Geertz, *The Interpretation of Cultures* (New York: Basic Books, 1973).

3. See Bruce Lawrence, *Defenders of God: The Fundamentalist Revolt against the Modern Age* (New York: Harper and Row, 1989); and Antoun, *Understanding Fundamentalism* (see note 1 above), chapter one for the more detailed argument.

4. I would argue that this is the case even in the Islamic Republic of Iran where fundamentalists rule, but where they are a minority of the population. The Iranian revolution of 1979 was brought about by a wide coalition of forces — workers, peasants, students, bazaar businessmen, and religious leaders — though the latter filled the prominent leadership positions afterwards.

5. For an elaboration of the concept, see Samuel Heilman, *Defenders of the Faith: Inside Ultra-Orthodox Jewry* (New York: Schocken, 1992).

6. This insightful breakdown of different motivations and forms of terrorism and their lethal effect was made by the Pakistani social scientist, Eqbal Ahmed, in an address given in Boulder, Colorado on October 12, 1998.

7. For an elaboration of the theme, see Mark Juergensmeyer, *Terror in the Mind of God: The Global Rise of Religious Violence* (Berkeley: University of California, 2000).

8. For an elaboration of the theme, see Mahmoud Ayoub's essay, "Martyrdom in Christianity and Islam," in Richard T. Antoun and Mary E. Hegland, *Religious Resurgence: Contemporary Cases in Islam, Christianity, and Judaism* (Syracuse, NY: Syracuse University Press, 1987).

9. For details, see Steven Rosen's essays in Steven Rosen, editor, *Holy War: Violence in the Bhagavad Gita* (Hampton, VA: Deepak Heritage Books, 2002).

10. Historically, it is important to note that the first caliph, Abu Bakr, Muhammad's political successor, fought the first war after the Prophet's death against certain Arabian tribes labeled apostates because, though they were self-identifying Muslims, they refused to pay the alms tax.

11. For details of the argument, see Abd al-Salam Faraj, "The Creed of Sadat's Assassins," in Johannes J. G. Jansen, *The Neglected Duty* (New York: Macmillan, 1986).

12. In the middle of the twentieth century, Sayed Qutb, the most authoritative Egyptian fundamentalist scholar of the time, argued in his work, *Milestones* (Cedar Rapids, IA: Unity, 1988) that the majority of Muslims in Egypt were not the Muslims they professed to be, but rather *jahilis*, ignorant people, living in the *jahiliyya*, the time of ignorance — before the Prophet, Muhammad. This, because they drank alcohol, gambled, caroused in the nightclubs of Cairo, dressed immodestly, and committed adultery. Their prayer and their fasting, then, was irrelevant to their living a Muslim life.

13. All of the above-mentioned events and many others in the Prophet's life are recorded in detail in his famous biography by Ibn Ishaq. See A. Gillaume, *The Life of Muhammad: A Translation of Ibn Ishaq's* Sirat Rasul Allah (Lahore: Oxford University Press, 1955).

14. For Ian Lustick's analysis of the absolutist pronouncements of the Jewish fundamentalist movement, *Gush Emunim* (Bloc of the Faithful), and their accommodation to such values as saving life, see Lustick, *For the Land and the Lord: Jewish Fundamentalism in Israel* (New York: Council of Foreign Relations, 1988).

COMMENTS ON RICHARD ANTOUN'S ESSAY

SAI RAMANI GARIMELLA

Jihad (root: JUHD): struggle or striving; referring to exhortation to follow the right path.

Some Islamic scholars have mentioned that the word *jihad* has never been used in the Qur'an in the context of an armed struggle. They mention that the Qur'an uses the word in the context of self-struggle to remain on the right path. Many of the verses of the Qur'an using this word were revealed in Mecca when the small Muslim community was persecuted and just trying to have sufficient strength to retain their faith.

The mainstream Muslim discourse has understood *jihad* as "struggle" or "striving." The Islamic philosophy of jihad has been derived from the meaning of *jihad* as "struggle" — that is, struggling to follow the right path. But in non-Muslim discourse, it has been mostly translated as "holy war."

Jihad has held a sacred meaning in Islam. For Muslims, it has been traditionally understood as a worship of God and something that spiritually elevates the believer. This struggle has been understood on two levels, most prominently, based on the Hadith — oral traditions relating to the words and deeds of the Prophet, Muhammad, collected and recorded much later. The chain of transmission is not strong: "Some troops came back from an expedition and went to see the Messenger. He said, 'You have come for the best, from the smaller jihad (*al-jihad al-asghar*) to the greater jihad (*al-jihad al-akbar*).' Someone said, 'What is the greater jihad?' He said, 'The servant's struggle against his *nafs* [ego, soul, psyche, self, or mind].'"

The wider meaning of the jihad is further clear from many other Hadiths. A few are as follows: "The strong one is not the one who overcomes people; the strong one is he who overcomes his *nafs*" (Majma al-Zawa'id). "A man asked, 'What kind of jihad is better?' The Prophet replied, 'A word

45

of truth spoken in front of an oppressive ruler'" (Sunan Al-Nasa' I:4209). "A man asked, 'Should I join the jihad?' The Prophet asked, 'Do you have parents?' The man said yes. The Prophet said, 'Then do jihad by serving them!'" (Bukhari: 5972). "On another occasion he said, 'The *mujahid* is he who makes jihad against his *nafs* for the sake of obeying God'" (Ibn Hibban: I624).

Based on these Hadiths and various Qur'anic verses, the Sufis did an elaborate study of controlling the *nafs* (ego, soul, psyche, self, or mind). This jihad, which is *jihad-al-Nafs* (also *jihad al-akbar*), has resulted in an elaborate study of the spiritual heart and the spiritual diseases of the heart (envy, miserliness, malice, arrogance, ostentation, hatred, treachery, covetousness, lust, and so on) with various methodical treatments devised over the centuries for healing it.

The other jihad, which is armed struggle and the more commonly understood one, is also a part of the same philosophy of struggle. It is in no way a wanton destruction of life but a means of self-defense or of opposing oppression (as a prerequisite). The approach is well summarized in this Hadith — when the Prophet was sending an expedition for war: "Do not betray, do not get carried away, do not backstab, do not disfigure, do not kill an infant, nor the old; do not kill a woman, do not harm a palm tree or burn it. Do not cut a fruitful tree; do not slaughter a sheep, cow, or camel, except for food. You will encounter hermits on your way; let them be, and let them pursue their dedications."

It is clear that jihad does not mean "holy war" in the traditional Islamic discourse but has a much broader meaning. It is also true, however, that historically the word has often been misused for various reasons by some conquerors and even by nonreligious people. One may also find some medieval texts influenced by the political context of those times that can give the same "holy war" narrative. The nineteenth-century view of jihad was very much along those lines.

Sir Syed Ahmed Khan, the most well-known Islamic educator and theologian, subscribes to the view that jihad, in the sense of battles fought from the time of the Prophet, was defensive in nature and an attempt to establish peace. They were not intended for converting people to Islam by force, as is usually alleged. Forcible conversion is strictly prohibited in Islam. The Qur'an clearly says, "There shall be no compulsion in the matter of professing a religion." Sir Syed says that Islam does not allow deceit, anarchy, fraud, or mutiny. It instructs Muslims to obey and feel obligated to those who have given them security and peace, whether they are Muslims or non-Muslims. Moreover, all pacts or treaties, whether with Muslims or non-Muslims, are to be followed faithfully. Islam forbids Muslims from invading any country to conquer it and forcibly spread Islam. Even a single person is not to be forced to convert to Islam.

Sir Syed emphasized that a true religion must be compatible with the law of nature and human nature. His views on some social laws of the Qur'an were quite unorthodox, however, and ran contrary to the traditional understanding of the Qur'an. His more modern understanding of these issues made him realize the importance of looking at them from the rational standpoint. But while we do have a few instances of such egalitarian views of Islam, unfortunately the region of South Asia did not find such a broad interpretation in the minds of the common men subscribing to this religion, with the result that such thoughts have not been able to make inroads in the face of increasing religious indoctrination by the seminaries.

In South Asia, the idea of a political state did not have a foundation beyond religion. The result was that states have always been Islamic in countries with a Muslim-majority population. In some countries, like Malaysia, religion and economic development were viewed as two different standards, but in other countries, like Pakistan, Afghanistan, and other South Asian countries, religion was seen as a cloak that they held onto with great zeal and protectiveness. This was also more of a politico-religious movement, religion meaning only what was given out to the congregation at the Sabbath prayers. In fact, most of the communities with a Muslim population are highly insulated within their religious denominations — the sermons of the leader being the Qur'an for them.

The Deobandi School, which gained prominence in Asia especially after the Iranian revolution, has a huge following in South Asia, including India. This school's activities aim at opening seminaries (*madrasas*) devoted to teaching puritan and extremely orthodox theology. It is an ultra-orthodox Sunni school and rejects the Shia thought. Its aim is to promote a return to Islamic values and adherence to the Shariah and the Tariqah or the Right Path. Madrasas of this school have been known to produce fiercely fanatic zealots who would rather go to paradise fighting a jihad (holy war ordained by the Qur'an and the Shariah according to the interpreters of the school) than to live out their lives. The standard syllabi of this school — in addition to learning the Shariah — include, among other subjects, the *tabligh* (spreading of the word of God), the *fiqh* (Islamic jurisprudence), and the *tajweed* (recitation of the Qur'anic verses). It's the *tabligh* that acted as an instrumentality in the training of many militant groups, by exhorting them to perform acts of militancy in the name of God. The school usually bases itself on verses like "fight them (the nonbelievers) so that Allah may punish them at your hand. . . . And put them to shame." So much is the fear element attached to these institutions that students in some *madrasas* in Pakistan run by the Deobandis are made to practice recitation of Qur'anic verses — while chained, lest they escape. Some of them are forcefully kept there and attempts to bring the schools under check are answered with violence.

The strict interpretations of Qur'anic verses and the Shariah law are not limited to education alone. We see these interpretations dominating the personal lives of individuals too. Strict gender-based segregation, special codes and edicts issued to women, deciding upon familial relations, and the banning of media of mass communication are a few examples of Deobandi influence in everyday life. They preach an uncritical and unquestioned acceptance of the religion as preached in sermons by the ulema of the school. Such habitual uncritical acceptance is passed down the generations to children through teaching and indoctrination. The beliefs preached in these sermons are accepted as self-evident truths, which a pious Muslim is taught to preserve and protect at any cost. Doubts become difficult, and the pious are made to realize that obligation is a sacred activity, including the obligation to spread the faith (*tabligh*) and to compel others to join in the faith. There is an economic and social angle to this, too. While affluent Muslims hardly ever respond religiously to these *madrasas* and view their gifts to them as acts of charity, these places have become the refuge for the poor, orphaned, and destitute.

I would ask Professor Antoun to comment on the Islamic institutional role in the face of such professedly inerrant views preached by schools like the Deobandi School. While it is heartwarming to hear a Western academician take such a rational interpretation as against the current views that are being circulated in the Muslim countries, I suggest that he talk about the moderate Islamic intelligentsia's role, if any, in countering these violent

interpretations of Islam. He might dwell more upon this reverential acceptance of the interpretations of "inerrant and self-evident" truths.

While he suggests that the majority view of jihad was condemnation
of forcible conversion, I wonder what he is referring to by using the word
majority. The Shias accept jihad as a part of their twelve religious ordain-
ments, and the Sunnis have accepted it as the sixth pillar of their religion
even though the word never before found a place in their denomination. For
a long period since the inception of Islam, the word *jihad* has been interpreted as armed struggle to establish the name of God and to fight the in-
fidels. In fact, verse 2:190 ordains the establishment of the supremacy of
Islam over the world. Here is an authoritative ordaining of the rule of Islam.
While the Sunni intelligentsia of the medieval period subscribed to a very
enlightened meaning of the word, what came to be practiced by the rulers
and the common folk was jihad by the sword — armed fighting in the name
of God. There haven't been many examples in recorded history of a general
acceptance of the intelligentsia's views on jihad.

RICHARD ANTOUN'S REPLY

Professor Ramani gives a more nuanced explanation of the historical usage of the term *jihad* than I did. Her comments are very valuable. I agree with much of what she says. Her request that I preach against the Deobandi School and its violent norms and practices, however, is beyond my ken. I am a scholar, not a missionary. Moreover, I am not deeply conversant with the Deobandi School, as she seems to be. Therefore, she would be the likely person to take on this mission. Again, although I have my own personal beliefs, and religious and political preferences, my scholarly work has been to understand fundamentalism. I do not treat fundamentalism in any of the traditions as a pejorative term. As my chapter makes clear, I do not equate it with violence, which I do condemn.

Ramani is right in questioning my referring to a "majority view of jihad." I do mean the majority of Muslim scholars and jurists rather than the majority of the Muslim population. My best guess about the latter is that their views of jihad change with the times and the strengths of various religious and political movements and leaders.

The Fundamental Violence of the Abrahamic religions

Carol Delaney

Judaism, Christianity, and Islam are collectively called the Abrahamic religions because they all derive from the story of Abraham. Despite the different revelations of Moses, Jesus, and Muhammad, the three religious traditions go back to the Abraham story, specifically the one told in Genesis 22 of the Hebrew Bible and in Sura 37 of the Qur'an. In this story, Abraham is willing to sacrifice his son because God commanded it. This story cannot be relegated only to the ancient past—something that might have happened a long time ago—nor is it just one story among others. It is central to these religions, theologically and liturgically. Jews recite it during the services of Rosh Hashanah, one of the most holy days in their liturgical calendar, and devout Jews recite it every day. Christians believe that it prefigured the Crucifixion, when God the Father sacrificed his only begotten son, and the story is traditionally recited during the services of Easter Week. Muslims reenact the story on their most holy day, the Feast of the Sacrifice, when every male head of family sacrifices a ram or other animal in Abraham's stead, and each male child can think, "There but for the grace of God, go I." All three have used the story to justify and give moral authority to certain actions, most commonly, to war.

But it is not this conventional type of violence nor its justifications that I address in this essay. Instead, I suggest that all three religions are fundamentally violent. Fundamentalism is not fundamentally different from more moderate or mainstream versions of each religious tradition, but it is a literal and very intense version of each. It brings to the fore their violent underpinnings. The violence is inherent; fundamentalists merely enact it. Here, I spend a bit more time on Islam, since that is currently the focus of most attention. For this, I rely heavily on my experience from my anthropological fieldwork in a Muslim village in Turkey. But I will also draw parallels with Judaism and Christianity.

The Abrahamic religions share a great deal: all are monotheistic, that is, they share the primary, important belief in one God; they also share many of the same stories and figures, similar concepts and values. If these religions share these fundamental elements, why then can't their adherents get along?

A major problem is that, although they share a great deal, they are each mutually exclusive of the others. It is not possible to be both Muslim and Christian, Christian and Jew, or Muslim and Jew. One way to think about the problem of exclusivity is to imagine the three religions as sibling faiths fighting over the patrimony. Which "son" will inherit the promises given in the beginning to Abraham? Basically, it is a contest concerning which tradition has the correct interpretation of God's will and His plan for human society. Thus, the antagonism; thus, the internecine fights. Will it be Ishmael, Abraham's first-born, and thus all Muslims—or Isaac, and the Jews? Or is it Jesus, and thus only Christians?

Because they are fighting over surface differences, they have never explored the roots of their strife. However, unlike many others, I do not mean to imply that, if they could just get over their particular differences and focus on what they share, they could get along. Quite the contrary, I think the violence is inherent in the things they share—especially, monotheism, the Abraham story, and views about gender. These are the issues I will discuss in the rest of this essay.

Let me begin with the Abraham story since it encapsulates the other issues. The sacrifice story is performative, for it is Abraham's action that gives shape and substantive reality to the God to whom the action was directed. Regardless of whether he ever lived, Abraham is symbolically the person through whom a new conception of the divine, namely monotheism, entered human society. Although that conception entered history at a particular time, it was projected back to the beginning—a vision, not just of the way things are, but of the way things had always been. Thus, although the Bible begins with Creation, it is through Abraham—or, at least, through his story—that the theological notion of the one and only God enters into human consciousness. This is yet another reason why the Abraham story is foundational. Many theologians believe that the earlier stories in Genesis were ancient Near Eastern stories reworked to provide a frame for the new ideas put into action by the story of Abraham's faith.

We have been brought up to think that monotheism is a good thing, that it is an advance over polytheism or "primitive" traditions that endow earthly things with sacred significance. Yet polytheism could be seen as a model for a more democratic system where differences of opinion struggled for dominance, and monotheism could be considered a model for a hierarchical and authoritarian system. In addition, and just as important, monotheism is inherently exclusive and, thus, inherently violent. Any faith that claims only *its* adherents are the chosen, the saved, or the elect excludes those who are *not* of that faith. Any religion that claims to have the one true path automatically excludes those who take another path.

For centuries, the Abraham story has been taken as the foundation and model of faith in all three traditions. If God commands, how can a mere mortal refuse? While there are volumes of commentary on the story, there has been little attempt to get behind it to ask what concepts and values make the story possible? Since I have written a book about this story, *Abraham on Trial: The Social Legacy of Biblical Myth*,[1] I will try to summarize my argument.

At the crucial moment when Abraham lifts the knife to slay his son, an angel calls out, "Lay not thy hand upon the lad, neither do thou anything unto him, for now I know that thou fearest God, seeing thou has not withheld thy son, thine *only* son, from me" (Genesis 22:12). Of course, that son is *not* the only one. Thus a first violence is the exclusion of the first-born son, Ishmael. At the same moment, in the Qur'an account, a voice calls out, "Thou hast already fulfilled the vision. Lo! thus do We reward the good. Lo! that verily was a clear test." (Sura 37:105–6). In the Islamic version, the father seeks the collusion of the son. Abraham/Ibrahim tells the son, who is not named, what he has been asked to do. The son responds, "O my father! Do that which thou are commanded. God willing, thou shall find me of the steadfast." In the biblical version, the son is deceived. Abraham says, "God will provide, himself, a lamb for the burnt offering" (Genesis 22:8). Both versions do violence to the son's innocence and love.

Although the angel/voice indicates that the human sacrifice is unnecessary, Abraham is extolled because of his willingness to do it. That is what makes him the model of faith we should all aspire to, for he puts love of God above all else. Perhaps what is sacrificed in this transaction is human emotion, human attachment, human love for one's child and, by extension, one's fellows, for it is surely true that some adherents of these sibling faiths are at each others' throats, literally.

Regardless of the fact that Abraham did not kill his son, he is revered as the "*father* of faith" because of his willingness to do it. His name (as *Abram*) means "exalted father" and (as *Abraham*) "father of many nations." The story involves a father, a son, and a male-imaged God. I began to wonder whether gender was accidental or precisely the point. Although the story is usually interpreted in terms of faith, I began to see that it is also about fatherhood.

As anthropologists, we know that gender definitions and roles vary considerably across cultures, and kinship terms do not always reflect what *we* consider biological roles. It is even more difficult for many of us to realize that the terms *father* and *mother* are conceptual rather than naturally given—that the terms are *concepts* that arise from a very specific *theory* of procreation, a theory that is neither universal, nor, historically, the one we believe today.

A clue to this theory is in the word *seed*. The story of Abraham is all about his *seed*; he was promised, "Nations will come from your seed." The word *seed* occurs more times in Genesis than elsewhere in the Bible, and many of the chapters are really only lists of the seed-line—that is, *patrilineages*. In this theory, the male is the one thought to have the seed; if he can ejaculate, it is assumed he is capable of producing a child. Females, on the other hand, are construed as *fertile* or *barren*—terms that also apply to the soil; in other words, they are imagined as the medium in which the seed-child is planted. The Qur'an is quite specific. It tells men, "Women are given to you as fields, go therein and sow your seed as you will" (Sura 2:223). In numerous Christian Bibles, Jesus is referred to as the true "seed" of Abraham.

You may think these are merely metaphors, but words can be more powerful than visual images, for they color our thought. Recall, too, the biblical idea that God created with the Word. In any case, in the absence of modern medical knowledge, the seed-soil theory of procreation represented the way people thought about the process and is still used in nonmedical parlance.

In this theological/folk theory, men *beget* and women *bear*, while men give the life and identity, women merely give birth. Men are allied symbolically with the Creator, and women with the Earth—the created material. The seed-soil theory of procreation in the Bible and the Qur'an is what I have, elsewhere, called a monogenetic theory.[2] It is, I believe, the human analog of monotheism, for the principle of creation comes only from one source—the male or a male-imaged God.

A prominent Muslim scholar has said, "The Muslim family is the miniature of the whole of Muslim society. . . . The father's authority symbolizes that of God in the world."[3] And Turkish villagers told me that the father is the second god after Allah.

In some modern versions of the Hebrew Bible and New Testament, the word *seed* has been changed to *children* or *progeny* which implies that these words are equivalents, that they all mean the same thing—but that is deceptive. Such attempts to make the language more gender inclusive actually work to conceal the reasons for women's exclusion in the first place. The same can be said for notions of God. Today, people claim that the use of *he* and other epithets such as *Lord, King,* or *Master* applied to God do not really *mean* God has been conceptualized as male. Such attempts do violence to the word; they discount the power of language to conceptualize the world. Instead, I agree with Swedish theologian, Anders Hultgard, who said, "By projecting the modern image of a genderless and sublimated God back into the biblical times, it becomes possible to reinterpret a massively patriarchal body of text in more 'favorable' directions. This appears to me to be but an attempt to save the Bible as the canon of church and synagogue." The same applies to the mosque.

Let me return to procreation. Today we believe that both men and women provide the same kind of things to the creation of a child, namely genes. In other words, both contribute *half* of the essential ingredients, *half* of the generative "seed" in the formation of a child.[4] Of course, women do much more by also gestating, giving birth, and breast-feeding. But, symbolically, women are still seen as nurturer—not as creator.[5]

What we forget is that the genetic theory of reproduction is relatively recent, did not become widespread in Europe and America until the 1930s and '40s, and is still not known to most of the world's peoples. Yet even in the West, this knowledge has not been assimilated symbolically, for references to the older folk theory can be heard all the time—in songs, poems, literature, and common speech. And it is further indicated by words such as *inseminate*, which means, literally, "to put the seed in"—or by the notion of "seminal ideas." Although women may have such creative ideas, the implication is that these are masculine in character. The scientific/medical theory is rarely put in conjunction with the folk theory, and thus the old attitudes and practices continue in numerous ways.

In Providence, Rhode Island, where I now live, I came upon a church billboard with the following statement announcing the 2006 Christmas season: "God walked down the stairs of heaven with a baby in his arms." Where is the mother? Even if Mary is imagined primarily as the pure vessel for the divine seed—the nurturer who contributed the physical aspects to Jesus—she is still at least present in the Christmas story. But the minister of that particular church perpetuated, perhaps unwittingly, the age-old theory of procreation. For whether it is God the Father or a human father, it is fatherhood that is imagined as generative.

In this theory of procreation, Father and son are one—they are of the same essence. This is, of course, the Christian definition of the Godhead. On the human plane, it is essential to produce a son for he is the *only* one, in this theory, who can continue the line. As the Turkish villagers told me, "A boy is the flame of the line, a girl the embers." And women will continue to bear children until a son is born. Inability to bear a son is a legitimate reason for a man to divorce or to take another wife.

If men, through their seed, are imagined as the creators/authors of children, as God is imagined as Creator/author of the world, is it any wonder that children are imagined to belong to them? Fathers have traditionally been given custody of children. With the nature/nurture debate in the 1920s, women, at least in the United States, began to gain this privilege, although in recent years the tide seems to be turning back. In the Turkish village where I conducted anthropological fieldwork, knowledge of the modern medical theory of procreation was absent. Children were said to belong to their father because they were his seed. Because children belong to their father, a woman tended to endure a violent or destructive marriage rather than seek divorce, for if she divorced her husband, her children would remain with their father.

If the seed-child is believed to come from the man, it follows that a woman must be controlled so that a man can be assured that a particular child is his. Virginity of women, but not of men, is a primary value. Women must be kept under wraps—literally, in the case of headscarf and *hijab*. In the Turkish village, girls and women are under the "protection" of their fathers, brothers, and husbands, and the headscarf symbolizes that protection. A girl or woman is *kapali* (covered, closed) if she wears the scarf, but *acik* (open) if she does not. To be open is to be promiscuous—open to the advances of men. Girls and women were thought not to have the power to refuse such advances. Given the social pressure in the village, the scarf was NOT optional. They did not have the luxury of choice. (Urban women who say it is their choice to cover rarely consider the fact that in so many Muslim countries, girls and women have no choice.) At social puberty, which is reached at the end of mandatory schooling—at that time, sixth grade—girls had to don the headscarf and most of them did not continue their schooling; instead they sat at home working on their trousseaux.

During that time, they were also enclosed in the house and not allowed to mix with unrelated boys or men. If a girl was seen talking to an unrelated boy, and especially if there was any suspicion of sexual relations between them, she stained the *honor* of the whole family and that must be avenged. In order to wipe out the stain, the girl could be killed by a male relative, sometimes her own father. More recently, girls are being coerced into committing suicide so that the male relative will not face a jail sentence. I recently learned that such an act occurred in "my" village, something that had never happened in the twenty-five years since I lived in the village (which I still visit frequently).

These shocking deeds are occurring not only in Muslim countries but also with some frequency in Europe,[6] due in part to the inevitable mixing that occurs on the street and in school—and because there are few who can keep watch. Since girls are married off in their teens, they have little opportunity to become further educated or to work outside the home. Their lives are constricted to their home and village. In Belgium, where I also conducted fieldwork, many Turkish (and Arab) girls were kept at home—generally a small, crowded apartment—precisely because their parents could no longer count on village surveillance. Not surprisingly, many developed serious health problems due to the lack of friends and outside activities. In both cases, their education was sacrificed and they learned little about the wide world around them.

This violence against women is hardly specific to Islam. We should not forget that, until fairly recently, women in the West were thought to be "under the wing" (*coverture*)—of their fathers or husbands. Furthermore, people of my generation are well aware that virginity of girls was also prized—girls were categorized as either virgins or whores. While it was unlikely that a girl would be killed by her family, she got a *reputation* and was often ostracized or abandoned. Girls who became pregnant out of wedlock were often hidden away and some did commit suicide. While some of these harsh treatments have ameliorated in recent years, they have not disappeared. The realities of public welfare in the United States are evidence of this. Single mothers, whether ever married or not, are excoriated and enlisted in a punishing regime of low-paying jobs without adequate childcare. Despite the rhetoric, the fathers of these children are rarely called to account or expected to help shoulder the burden—as the dismal record of child support attests.

Let me return to the seemingly minor but actually quite illustrative issue of hair and the headscarf. Why does Muslim identity rest on women's heads? Why *women's* hair? To answer this, one needs to consider not only the gender definitions but also head hair versus body hair, women's hair versus men's hair, and the changes in treatment of hair over the life cycle. The issue entails far more than human rights and freedom of religion around which the headscarf debate has revolved. Anthropologists who have studied the phenomenon of hair in a number of cultures conclude that hair often symbolizes beliefs about sexuality and gender, and I agree.

Villagers' comments and my observations in Turkey suggest that women's hair symbolizes the physical entanglements by which men are thought to be ensnared, entanglements that distract them from their focus—which should be on spiritual things. Women's hair is said to arouse men's uncontrollable lust. Pubic hair is removed and head hair is covered. In contrast, men exhibit their hair; after puberty they begin to wear a mustache—a symbol of virility. Beards were the prerogative of men who had made the hajj. In short, the sexual symbolism has been displaced from the genital area to the head—a sign that anyone can read.[7]

Similar beliefs and practices about hair exist in both Judaism and Christianity. Upon marriage, some Orthodox and ultra-Orthodox Jewish women shave their heads and wear a wig as covering. Women in some of the other Jewish sects also wear head coverings. Not that long ago, Christian women were required to wear veils, hats, or other head coverings when entering a church. This goes back to the passage in I Corinthians 11:4–9:

> Every man who has *something* on his head while praying or prophesying disgraces his head. But every woman who has her head uncovered while praying or prophesying disgraces her head, for she is one and the same as the woman whose head is shaved. For if a woman does not cover her head, let her also have her hair cut off; but if it is disgraceful for a woman to have her hair cut off or her head shaved, let her cover her head. For a man ought not to have his head covered, since he is the image and glory of God; but the woman is the glory of man. For man does not originate from woman, but woman from man; for indeed man was not created for the woman's sake, but woman for the man's sake.

And, like their Muslim counterparts, fundamentalist Christians demand that girls and women dress modestly, though the particulars vary in practice.

From these few examples, I think it is clear that the basic gender definitions in each of the Abrahamic religions are the same or very similar. Fundamentalists, whether Jewish, Christian, or Muslim, intensify and reinforce them. They are opposed to the secularizing influences that have been embraced by most moderates in each tradition.

In this section, I consider some of the forces that led to or allowed for the growth of secularism, more moderate forms of the religions, and the promise of the emancipation of women. Without presuming to be comprehensive, I very briefly mention four things: beliefs within the religious traditions; the Protestant Reformation, the Enlightenment, and education.

Within Christianity, there is the idea of rendering "unto Caesar the things that are Caesar's and unto God those that are God's" (Luke 20:25). It is an acknowledgment of a difference between God's realm and human government; there is a *space* for the development of an earthly, secular government. While Jews in the Diaspora rendered taxes and other services unto the host governments, within their own communities they followed the Law as set down by their religion. These laws are not abstract; they detail every aspect of daily life.

In Islam, good government is supposed to follow from God's rules. Muhammad, according to one influential Muslim scholar, called all people "to the submission of the one God and rejection of the lordship of other men."[8] He goes on to say, "To establish God's rule means that *His* laws be enforced. . . . All those systems and governments which are based on the rule of man" should be abolished.[9] First, this demands that one believe these laws actually came from God, but more importantly, as in Judaism and Christianity, it has been only men who are authorized to interpret and adjudicate the Law.

The Protestant Reformation might be seen as a response to the papacy usurping jurisdiction over secular as well as spiritual concerns. But those who became protestant were also reacting against what they perceived as the corruption of the Catholic Church and against its hierarchical structure. They declared that each individual could maintain a personal relationship to God without the mediation of priests and pope. The individual, alone, became the locus of moral behavior and accountability. The religious and social system was still patriarchal to be sure, but the ascendancy of the individual over and above family and community as the locus of value and rights is very different from the identification and submersion of the individual—especially women—in the family, ideas that one encounters in parts of Judaism and Islam.

A friend conducting anthropological research in Turkey about Muslims who convert to (protestant) Christianity told me that one of the things they valued about Christianity was the guarantee of forgiveness. If one accepts Jesus as Savior, one's sins can be forgiven. They believe that the notion of "hate the sin but not the sinner" is uniquely Christian and implies a distinction between one's deeds and one's inner person or soul. It should be noted that, in some Muslim countries where fundamentalism is predominant, such conversion is considered apostasy—a crime punishable by death, even though Muhammad said there should be no coercion in religion. In Islam, at least as I encountered it in the Turkish village, punishment seemed almost automatic. For example, people told me that for every strand of hair that showed from under a woman's headscarf, she would burn so many days in hell. Not surprisingly, hell was imagined to be filled mostly with women. Women are thought to be less able to control their behavior because they lack that core of identity (autonomy) that men are thought to have naturally, and this is related to their "seed"—the essence of their identity.

Within Christianity, only in certain of the Protestant churches are women permitted to become ministers and preach. In the Roman Catholic Church, they cannot become priests, bishops, cardinals, or Pope. Recently, I read that some women are being secretly ordained as priests. The rationale against the ordination of women has to do not only with the fact that the apostles were all male, but also with notions of impurity during menstruation. It is thought that women, at that time, are impure and thus not in a state to administer the Eucharist.

In Judaism and Islam, women are also considered impure during menstruation, but in certain Jewish sects, women are now able to become rabbis, lead prayers, and touch the Torah scroll during menstruation. Muslim women cannot become heads of congregations, imams, or ayatollahs, and cannot lead prayers in the mosque; nor are they allowed to touch the Qur'an or participate in religious rituals at the hajj during their menstrual periods. Beliefs about the impurity of menstruation are not universal, however. There is nothing pure or impure about menstruation except as the religion and culture say so.[10]

The mood engendered by the Protestant Reformation was not picked up by European Jews until the nineteenth century. Then, the Jewish reform movement led to religious splits, widespread changes in acceptable practices, and more moderate social views. But there has not yet been a reform movement in Islam. Instead, there seems to be a return to more orthodox interpretation and rigid implementation of rules.

Another important factor in secularization was the Enlightenment. The Enlightenment furthered the idea of the individual by an emphasis on reason rather than faith. Reason was considered an essential attribute of human nature, endowed by the Creator for the purpose of being able to investigate his divine Creation. Early modern scientists believed they were discovering God's laws, but in so doing they developed scientific, experimental methods. Muslims had been great scientists, particularly in the area of astronomy and mathematics—but that burst of creative energy seems to have been channeled into religion. A few years ago, Turkish television broadcast public service announcements saying, "Reading is the path to enlightenment." Villagers scoffed and told me that "the only path is Islam."

Of course, in the West, there have been endless debates over whether women have the same kind of reason, or to the same extent, as men, or whether women are too much under the sway of emotion. This erupted most recently when Harvard University President Lawrence Summers declared that women were not as good at scientific reasoning as men. It cost him his job. Nevertheless, reason as the defining attribute of being human has had repercussions on notions of education.

In all three religious traditions, the education of girls was considered a waste except when it related to what was considered their primary role in life—as mother and housekeeper. Not until the late nineteenth century was there a call, at least in the United States, for the education of girls. Ideally, education has meant the "drawing out" not the "putting in." Students are encouraged to be *open*—to new possibilities, new experiences, and new people and perspectives. This idea is hardly encouraged in Islam, given that tradition's definition of *open*. Except in elite urban schools (even in the secular state schools in Turkey), education is still conducted in the style of religious instruction, that is, mostly by rote—memorization of information with little or no concern for understanding—the goal being to learn the right answers.[11] I was told that innovation and creativity—especially prized in the educational systems and ideologies in the West—are not valued in Islam. Creativity is an attribute only of God; it was considered blasphemy to suggest that humans also be creative.

In the United States, compulsory education became the rule during the twentieth century, and, as girls excelled and went on to college, they began to question their allotted roles. This became acute in the 1960s when many educated women began to be afflicted with the "problem that has no name." Highly educated women were still expected to get married and perform their supposedly "natural" roles—and many of us rebelled. Following in the steps of our nineteenth-century foremothers, many of us saw religion as the source of oppressive gender definitions and began to enter divinity schools and seminaries—to challenge, critique, and change the institutions, the texts, and the practices. Some of us, like myself, think they are not redeemable.[12]

While groups of Muslim women have begun meeting privately to study the Qur'an and the traditions, my sense is that this movement, if it can be called that, is not really critical. To be sure, they are reading and interpreting the texts themselves, but—as with similar groups of ultra-Orthodox Jewish women or conservative Christian women—the purpose seems to be to become better Muslims, better apologists. Women of Muslim background who are outspoken critics of Islam receive death threats, are put under house arrest, or flee to Europe, Canada, or the United States.[13] Yet they never really escape the possible repercussions due to the diffusion everywhere of radical Muslims who wish to silence them.

In this time of cultural relativism, there has developed a critique of Western values—the individual, human rights, women's emancipation, and secularism. I understand the charge of ethnocentrism, but do we need to go to the other extreme? I have been shocked by the way some of my students have picked up and reinterpreted notions of cultural relativism. They say things like this: "It's their culture, their religion. Who am I to object to their beliefs and practices?" They are afraid to make moral judgments, but taking no stand is equivalent to relinquishing morality. It is a very lazy response and an easy way out. People who respond in this way need to be encouraged to investigate who is representing that culture, that religion. They need to ask, "Just who has the right to interpret, to adjudicate, to make laws, to impose punishments?" What they do not realize is that cultural relativism is not the same as moral relativism.

Secularism is often conflated with atheism, which is considered unacceptable to many Muslims, Jews, and Christians. Somehow, *secular* has come to mean devoid of moral values or even morally depraved. But the conflation between secularism and atheism needn't be the case, as the United States so vividly demonstrates. In addition, people do not consider that atheism has meaning only in relation to the Abrahamic, monotheistic religions; nor do they consider that there are other ways to live an ethical and spiritually meaningful life that do not depend on belief in God or an afterlife.

In summary, let me recapitulate the major points of this essay. First, it is my belief that the Abrahamic religions are inherently exclusive, thus inherently violent. The model of faith extolled in each of them is a person who puts love of God before and above love of fellow humans—including those nearest and dearest. This has been exemplified throughout the ages in the actions of martyrs, including today's Muslim suicide bombers. Indeed, they call themselves martyrs for the faith, and their deaths are celebrated as the epitome of faith. Second, monotheism is inherently exclusive, hierarchical, authoritarian, and patriarchal. A mother Goddess religion could not, by the very definition of *mother*, merely be the inverse of the patriarchal religions. And while a "mother-father" deity would no longer be monotheistic, it would not resolve the problem of the definitions of what it means to be a male or female parent. The gender issue is neither accidental nor peripheral. It is central to the theology of these religious traditions and the social structures and values they have inspired. Until this is recognized and dealt with, the fighting will continue.

Despite my pessimistic view, I would like to end on a somewhat more positive note. Religion, especially its more fundamentalist forms, has come to the forefront of public awareness and discussion. I believe this is a good thing. Rather than ignoring religion or relegating it to the private sphere, its resurgence creates the potential for public debate. It creates a venue for people to reflect on their own beliefs and to compare them with those of others. We should take advantage of this opportunity.

In the global village in which we live today, all of us need to know about different religious traditions and different cultures. More information about different traditions could lead to greater understanding and appreciation of other religious traditions as well as to a critical discussion of what is shared and worth saving and what can and must be changed. Alas, this rarely occurs. In keeping with the separation of church and state, held to be so important in the United States, it is not possible to teach about religion in public schools. Those who wish their children to have a traditional religious education are expected to send their children to private, denominational schools.

In either case, the absence of knowledge among American youth about religious traditions other than their own is appalling. Without such knowledge, they remain ignorant of what motivates millions of people in the world; or insular, taking whatever their preacher claims is "true religion"; or susceptible to the recruiting strategies of fundamentalists and a variety of cult-type organizations. I think it is important to begin to teach *about* religion beginning at the high school level. This is not the same as teaching religion. There is a huge difference between teaching religion and teaching about religion, but it will take very gifted teachers trained in the study of a number of religious traditions to do the job properly. Of course, many Americans would reject such a project, but—strangely—a community in New Jersey did not object when they learned that a public high school teacher was intimidating his students with his evangelical beliefs and telling them that they would go to hell if they did not accept Jesus as their savior (*The New York Times*, December 18, 2006).

Although instruction *about* religion is not, generally, taught at the high school level, it has long been available at Western colleges and universities. While these institutions have fostered the study of other religions (interestingly, anthropology and comparative religion emerged together in the nineteenth century), this is not the case in Muslim countries. I know of no courses about other religions or comparative religion in any Muslim country, not even in secular Turkey. Increasing the academic study of religion at home and abroad—rather than missionizing, proselytizing, and killing in its name—might be a good place to start.

Parts of this work were presented at the plenary session, "Secularism, Diffusion, and Religion," at the meetings of the European Association of Social Anthropologists in Bristol, England, September 18–21, 2006. A major topic of discussion was how Europeans, and by extension, Americans, should respond to the influx of millions of Muslims into Western societies. While the focus was mostly on Islam, the issues, I feel, are much broader and involve all three of the Abrahamic religions—Judaism, Christianity, and Islam. While there are fundamentalist and moderate versions or interpretations of each of the traditions, what is too often missed is the violence inherent within them.

NOTES

1. Published by Princeton University Press, 1998; finalist for the National Jewish Book Award, 1998.

2. See Carol Delaney, "The Meaning of Paternity and the Virgin Birth Debate," *Man* 21:3 (1986): pp. 494–513; *The Seed and the Soil: Gender and Cosmology in Turkish Village Society* (Berkeley: University of California Press, 1998); *Abraham on Trial: The Social Legacy of Biblical Myth* (Princeton, NJ: Princeton University Press, 1998).

3. Seyyed Hossein Nasr, *Ideals and Realities of Biblical Myth* (London: George Allen & Unwin, 1985 [1966]) p. 166.

4. Muslims sometimes claim that they have a two-seed theory of procreation which is based on the ancient theories of Galen—as opposed to those of Aristotle. What they fail to realize, however, is that Galen did not believe the female "seed" was generative; instead, it was merely a lubricating material.

5. But to change the term for God to *mother-father God*, as some have suggested, does not solve the problem; instead it perpetuates the conventional meanings of *father* and *mother* and projects them onto the cosmological plane.

6. It also occurs in Israel among Muslims. See *The New York Times*, April 20, 2007.

7. For further discussion of the meaning of hair, see "Untangling the Meaning of Hair in Turkish Society," *Anthropological Quarterly* 67:4 (1994): pp. 159–72.

8. Sayyid Qutb, *Milestones* (Indianapolis, IN: American Trust, 1990 [1960]) p. 101.

9. Sayyid Qutb's book (in English rendered either *Signposts* or *Milestones*) became an influential text for Muslim fundamentalists.

10. See Thomas Buckley and Alma Gottlieb, eds., *Blood Magic: The Anthropology of Menstruation* (Berkeley: University of California Press, 1988).

11. President Bush's education campaign, "No Child Left Behind," which has instituted annual school testing, seems to have adopted this notion of education, for a standardized test compels teachers to make sure that students learn/memorize the facts considered standard.

12. My book on the story of Abraham and its implications is one product of my education at Harvard Divinity School and it led to my doctoral work on the theory of procreation in Turkey.

13. I think here of Irshad Manji, Noni Darwish, and Ayaan Hirsi Ali—among others.

COMMENTARY ON CAROL DELANEY'S ARTICLE

While Professor Delaney's essay is undoubtedly based on careful anthropological research and much divinity-school-based discussion (and further is laid out in more detail in book length elsewhere), to a nonspecialist reader, her essay seems to rely on a few basic claims:

(a) What is male is bad (or at least not as good as what is female);
(b) Exclusion entails violence; and
(c) The Abraham-sacrifice myth provides the key to all Abrahamic religions, revealing (a) and (b) above.

It seems that in much of academia today it is sufficient to label something as paternalistic or patriarchal for it to be deemed unworthy. An extensive discussion of the concept of "seed" is conducted, for instance, to show how Abrahamic religions ignored women in their creation stories. Further, this is tied to a general male dominance in those cultures, such as Turkey, and in their customs, such as in covering female hair. Yet, such customs existed before Islam (to take the main object of critique); women always covered their hair, and males always dominated, even in the (not so golden) age of polytheism.

Is it Islam that is to be shunned for its masculine bias, or is that masculinity part of the culture of the world where Islam came about? (In fact, Islam rejected and fought against much of the anti-female customs that had existed in pagan Arabia, such as the practice of burying unwanted girl babies). Further, as to the presumed violence-equals-male equation, I wonder, as a nonspecialist, what anthropologists have found in regard to mother-goddess-oriented cultures. Are they indeed less violent than patriarchal religious cultures? (One wonders about rather warlike Native American cultures whose religious symbolism was primarily maternal).

We are also told that these religions ("inherently") exclude and thus are ("inherently") violent. They exclude, granted, but this *inherence* which links the exclusion to violence is never demonstrated. Is it not possible to exclude and not be violent? I can certainly imagine a case where a religious group might say to the rest of the world, "Too bad, you're unlucky, we are saved," and go along its way without wanting to violently harm others. Is exclusion *the same as* violence? Where is the inherence of it all? Does inclusion imply nonviolence? (One might argue that the Christian Crusaders were among the most inclusive persons in the world: they wanted to include everybody—voluntarily or not—in their religion of salvation.)

This brings us to the core myth which reveals all: the Abraham-son sacrifice attempt. Besides the fact that it might be debatable why this myth, and not another, was chosen as key to all three religions—or whether these complex religious systems can be reduced to any single myth (or group of myths for that matter)—let us take up the myth and see whether it reveals the paternalism and exclusion that ultimately entail violence. The exclusion, we are told, comes from Abraham's willingness to kill, irrespective of the fact that in all versions of the tale, his son is spared. Abraham, the violent father of all three religions, puts murder at the core of his religion.

But could not the story be interpreted differently? What if we think of that classic Oedipal myth, which a not-too-shabby (but, alas, sexist) thinker once thought was central to all human psychology. The other myth has it that the son wants to kill the father, so Ishmael (or Isaac) should be killing Abraham, not the other way around. Why are the Abrahamic religions suggesting the reverse? This seems like an essential question. If Freud would be allowed to speak despite his misogyny, one might imagine him seeing the Abraham myth as a cultural reaction to the biological pull of the Oedipal instinct. We want to kill our fathers; instead, we imagine our fathers want to kill us. And of course we love our fathers, and they love us (though we also hate each other), so we don't kill them, and God stops our fathers from killing us. Altogether a wonderful compromise so we can all go on living with each other—with God getting all the credit.

In other words, the myth can be seen as a way to acknowledge the aggressive impulses of all humans (not just men, by the way), while showing us that these impulses can be controlled, that they need *not* end in violence—if we believe in a just and forgiving God.

If anything, those pre-Abrahamic cultures could be argued to have been much more violent before these three religions came along than afterwards (or at least more violent than they might have come to be, had not our violent biological instincts led us to use these religions in the interests of our own aggressive wishes).

It could be that the violence that we see, if it is inherent anywhere, is inherent in us, in our human nature, in our biological roots, in that 99.9% of our genes that we share with chimpanzees and gorillas, rather than in that patriarchal myth that forces us to exclude and (almost) kill.

I will end by suggesting attention to another storyline: Jesus famously preached peace and nothing else; Muhammad pardoned the entire city of Mecca, and all of his most implacable foes, when they were at his mercy; and Moses peacefully took his people out of Egypt rather than violently rising up against the Pharoah's armies. One can find what one wants in these religions: peace if we wish, war if we like. The choice, perhaps, is inherent in us, not in them.

CAROL DELANEY'S REPLY

There are two main issues I wish to respond to in Dr. Ghaemi's comments—gender and exclusivity. He has grossly misinterpreted and misunderstood my argument. I never claim or even imply that "what is male is bad," nor that what is female is good. If he had read my article more carefully he would have realized I am saying nothing of the kind. My article, and my work more generally, focuses on gender—which has to do with the cultural construction of anatomical differences between male and female. My focus has been on the *meaning* of father, not maleness, and that meaning is interrelated with an entire theory of procreation. Gender definitions, and even understandings of male and female roles in procreation, vary across cultures and across time, and ideas about gender are tied into other concepts and values in a culture—the most powerful influence being religion.

I focus on the word *seed* because it was (and still is, in some places) believed that the male, by means of his "seed," was the creator of a child and, to follow the analogy, the female was imagined as the nurturing soil. In giving birth, she brought forth the seed-child, but was not co-creator. While the seed-soil theory is also found in ancient Greek and Hindu cultures, but hardly in all cultures, it has been most highly developed, and without any ameliorating factors, in the monotheistic religious traditions of Judaism, Christianity, and Islam.

I find it very odd that Dr. Ghaemi wonders why I chose the Abraham story rather than some other myth as key to all three of them. As I stated right at the beginning, it is precisely because all three trace their origins to Abraham, collectively they are referred to as the Abrahamic religions, and the story of that sacrifice is the model of faith revered in each. And I ask here again: Why is the willingness to sacrifice the child, rather than protection of the child, the model of faith? Dr. Ghaemi's answer, that it mitigates innate male aggression, is a facile way to try to reduce human behavior and culture to biology. We go to war not because of innate aggression, for if that were

73

so, all men would be rushing to join up to fight in the current wars. Soldiers have to be taught to become violent against people who are deemed the "enemy." We go to war because of certain humanly constructed reasons.

Regarding his comments about Freud, I refer him to the lengthy discussion in my book, *Abraham on Trial* (pages 187–230).

I do wonder where he gets the idea that "women *always* covered their hair and that males *always* dominated." It is true that women in some cultures cover their hair and did so before Islam, but hardly always and everywhere; the same goes for male dominance.

Considering exclusivity and its relation to violence, I am surprised that a psychiatrist would think of violence only in terms of physical violence, for surely he is aware that psychological violence can be just as devastating. One need only think about the exclusion of blacks from drinking fountains, toilets, and buses to realize the violence entailed. Consider the "untouchables" in India who are excluded from common social life, or the kinds of ethnic slurs that are still too common. There are many kinds of violence and, yes, I believe that any religion that claims that only *its* believers are the chosen, the saved, or the elect is violent in its exclusion (from their society or from salvation) of those who do not join. Furthermore, those who do not join or convert are labeled "infidel" or something comparable, which is just as denigrating and de-humanizing and tends to allow—if not encourage—physical violence or coercion against them.

HINDUISM AS A PHILOSOPHY OF LIFE
AND ITS RELATIONSHIP TO VIOLENCE

SAI RAMANI GARIMELLA

Hinduism, like all religious phenomena is historically conditioned and has been influenced (for better and for worse) by external forces. What I am attempting to do in this essay is to extract what I consider the essence and genius of Hinduism and also to show where it has failed to live up to that essential genius. This method can be viewed as analogous to a Weberian ideal type, which nowhere existed in a pure form nor ever will. On the other hand, what one might call folk religion has a long involved history and is constantly changing. We will also attempt to show how that folk religion has sometimes deviated from those essential ideas and ideals.

Atmano Mokshardham Jagaddhithayacha means the effort of man toward achieving salvation and, more importantly, the duty of man to work selflessly for the betterment of the society as he endeavors to concentrate his mind or consciousness on the Supreme God. *Advesthaa Sarva Bhootanam maitrah karuna evacha* means that one should not hate anybody but should live with the basic traits of friendship and compassion.[1] These two prescriptions, from one of the most sacred texts of Hinduism in the Mahabharata era, encapsulate the Hindu philosophy of benevolence and tolerance as the ideal way of life. Hence, we could say that Hinduism, at its core, is a nonviolent religion. Nevertheless, problems with violence do exist.

From mythological times till today, India is called *Bharatavarsha Bharata. Bha* means divine illumination and *rata* means engrossed. Thus *Bharata* means being engrossed in divine illumination. The land derived its name from the Vedas, which essentially are divine revelations, and, according to the Rig Veda, the principal priests who engaged in rituals are referred to as *Bharatas*. Other legends abound regarding the source of the name. One such legend says that India was named after the famous king of the Mahabharata period, Bharata, son of King Dushyanta and his wife Sakuntala. King Bharata was a very noble ruler, credited with sowing the seeds of democracy (people choosing the ruler) during the mythological period.

This land is also called *Bharatavarsha* for a very spiritual reason.[2] According to the Smritis (revelations of God concerning human conduct) there is undoubtedly One Transcendental Eternal Power; everything has originated from it, and all must merge into it again. This tenet is the hallmark of *Bharatiya*; he who has not acquired this belief is not entitled to that name.[3] The *Bharatiya* philosophy (or religion) explained that the self is no other than the Over Self or God. It directs men and women on a long journey through varied paths, to be confronted by circumstances and encouraged and enlightened by various types of faith — moving toward the goal of the Splendor of God Consciousness (Consciousness of the Divine). He who does not endeavor to achieve this end is not entitled to the name *Bharatiya*; he does not even deserve to be called a Hindu.[4]

That brings us to the question: What does the word *Hindu* mean? The word is sometimes etymologically explained thus: *Hin* stands for *himsa* (violence) and *du* means *doora* or "staying away." *Hindu* then would mean anyone and everyone who has shunned or moved away from the path of violence in thought, word, and deed. For centuries, millions of Hindu voices have been praying daily: *Loka Samastha Sukhinoh Bhavanthu* (May all the worlds be happy)! The prayers end with the *Santhi* mantra — *Om Santhi, Santhi, Santhihi,* meaning "Peace, Peace, Peace"— after every invocation in Sanskrit. Every child born in India is taught to respect God in human forms: mother, father, preceptor, and — equally as important — the guest of the house.

THE HISTORY OF HINDUISM

It is generally believed that the basic tenets of Hinduism were brought to India by the Aryans who settled along the banks of the Indus River about 2000 BCE. According to at least one scholar, the evolution of Hinduism may be divided into three periods: the ancient (650 BCE to 1000 CE), the medieval (1000 to 1800 CE), and the modern (1800 CE to the present).[5] Hinduism is commonly thought to be the oldest existing human civilization, but Hinduism as a religion is of recent origin. It took the shape of a religion towards the later half of the first millennium after Christ.

The first use of the word *Hindu* in a religious sense was by Alberuni in his work *Kitabu-ul-hind* (1030 CE). At one place in that book, he used the word to distinguish between Hindus and Buddhists. But actually he cannot be completely credited with chronicling the religious history of the word as his use of *Hindu* referred only to the Brahmins.[6] Lack of clarity around the religious meaning of the word continued even into the fifteenth century, when *Zia-ddin Barani*, the first Muslim to write a history on India, *Taarikh-e-Firozshahi*, took an ambivalent approach to the word in his references to the Hindus both as a religious and as a political community. What added to the ambiguity regarding the word was that neither the rulers nor the ruled designated themselves consistently as Hindus until the fourteenth century. The development into a religion of what began as a philosophy was initially prompted by the desire to erect a common front against invaders from West Asia. The practices that formed the life of the community living beyond the Indus River took concrete shape as religious orders and small kingdoms/principalities became organized societies.[7]

Reference to the word *Hindu* was also very vague during the *Bhakti* movement and in its literature, which was more concerned with raising a voice against some Brahmin practices and traditions which were seen as going against the spirit of Hindu thought. Even the very few references in the medieval *Bhakti* literature used the word to refer to the caste-centric Brahmin traditions rather than to a homogenous national religious community. Thus the pre-colonial period to a large extent lacked a Hindu religious identity, as we know it.[8] The British borrowed the word *Hindu* and gave it a new meaning and significance for the categorization of the community of the Indian people, thus paving the way for a global religious Hindu identity.[9] Thus *Hinduism*, as the name for a religion, is largely of colonial origin, not of great antiquity, and in a sense connotes the youngest of the great world religions.

HINDUISM—A SPIRITUAL PHILOSOPHY

The spiritual content of the religion, however, is of a much more ancient origin. It is variously described as eternal law, *sanatana dharma*, and culture, *bharatiya.* In India, culture, spirituality, and religion are conceptualized together, as none can be explained without reference to one or more of the others. Culture is understood as essentially derived from spirituality. A true understanding of religion also concerns spirituality. Therefore, culture is a part of an all-inclusive spirituality[10] and is evident as discipline, a way of life. What we call the Hindu way of life encompasses the fundamental tenets of love and compassion explained in the Bhagavad Gita.[11]

The English word *religion* has its root in the Latin word *religio.* It is commonly understood as the recognition of a supernatural authority or a supernatural spirit. This recognition expresses itself in man's behavior and his attitude. The Sanskrit approximation of the word *religion* is the word *mathamu,* which means "holding an opinion," "a thought process," or "a branch of thinking." Both the English *religion* and the Sanskrit variant emphasize an activity that finds its origin in man's mind. Thus we can say that the word *religion* in Indian (Hindu) thought emphasizes the mind and its basic activities, and man's religious leanings also depend upon his mind and his reasoning. In fact, there is really no exact translation for the word *religion* in the Indian languages since, from the Hindu perspective, the purpose of any religion would essentially be regulation of the mind, rather than temporal ordinances regulating behavior alone. The Hindu religion, then, involves the understanding of human consciousness or self-realization.

Culture is the complex of ideas, developed qualities, organized relationships, and courtesies that exist in a society. The difference between a cultured and a civilized society is that the latter is organized under conditions ministering to the welfare of the community while the former emphasizes the ideals, conduct, relationships, aesthetics, and so on that are cherished by the society. As with most other cultures, Indian culture relates directly to religious ordinances, both ritualistic and philosophical. But apart from preaching nirvana, it also emphasizes ethics, which — though founded on religious beliefs — need not be regulated by religion.[12] Thus, Indian culture is a combination of a religious background with secular practices.

While renunciation as a method to achieve self-realization has indeed been preached in this culture, it does not necessarily mean inaction. Renunciation, according to Indian culture, has to be achieved through the *Purusharthas,* the objectives of life. It is a widespread misconception that Indian culture emphasizes renunciation but not action. The truth is that renunciation and self-realization have to be achieved through fulfilling the physical responsibilities which the individual cannot shrink from. In India today we witness cultural cosmopolitanism. Buddhists, Parsees, Muslims, and Christians coexist with Hindus in a secular India that is Bhaarath.[13] This is the practical translation of the Vedic adage: *Sahanaa Vavathu; Sahanaa Bhunakthu; Sahaviryam Kara Vaava Hai* — meaning, "Let us live together; let us struggle together; let us grow together in joy and harmony."[14]

At the heart of Hinduism is the monistic principle of Brahman, meaning that all reality is a unity; the entire universe is one divine entity. Deity is simultaneously visualized as a triad: Brahman, the Creator who is continuing to create new realities; Vishnu, the Preserver; and Siva, the Destroyer. Whenever dharma (eternal order, righteousness, religion, law, and duty) is threatened, Vishnu travels from heaven to earth in one of ten incarnations; Siva, the Destroyer, is alternately compassionate, erotic, and destructive. Simultaneously, many hundreds of Hindu Gods and Goddesses are worshipped as various aspects of the divine unity. Depending upon one's view, therefore, Hinduism can be looked upon as a monotheistic, trinitarian, or polytheistic religion.[15] It lacks any unified system of beliefs and allows for a broad spectrum of beliefs and practices, some of which are akin to paganism, and others that are very profound, abstract, metaphysical speculations.

In Islam and Christianity, the history of the religion is more easily chronicled because of their founding thinkers and monotheistic structures, but it is difficult to point to any one order as Hinduism. It does not have a singular deity or a prophet-based system of worship and adherence;[16] it thrives on the multi-ordered structure loosely subscribed to under the name *Hinduism.* The Vedas (sacred Hindu texts) are not just religious and ritual ordinances but contain spiritual and temporal education. The Rig Veda says, "*Ekam Sath, Viprah Bahuda Vadanti,*" meaning that the truth is one and eternal, but is explained in a diverse manner by the learned men. A common manner of describing Hinduism among its adherents is as a way of life, as dharma. This tolerant quality is explained in another Vedic quotation: *Aano Bhadhraha, Krathavo yanthu Vishwatah* — meaning, "Let noble thoughts come to us from every side." That is why Hinduism is often described as a philosophy or a way of life. It defies dogma and seeks instead to align the human body, mind, and soul in harmony with nature.[17]

The Atharvana Veda, the last of the four books of the Vedas, utilizes symbolism to describe dharma's role. There, it says that we are bound by the laws of time, space, and causation according to finite reality, which itself is a limitation imposed by the self-projection of the infinite Brahman as the cosmos.[18] Dharma is the foundation of this causal existence, one step below the infinite. Indeed, dharma is the projection of divine order from Brahman — *Prithivim Dharmana Dhritam*, which means "This world is upheld by Dharma" (Atharvana Veda). The word *dharma* is of great importance in the history of Indian thought. *Dhaaranaath dharmam ityaahuh* means "what holds together." This is explained as *sanatana* dharma — the eternal tradition. The word *sanatana* is often used to explain the ancient characteristic of the Vedas that emphasize freedom of thought and worship as a unique feature of Hinduism. Swami Chinmayananda says that *dharma* is one of the most intractable terms in Hindu philosophy. Derived from the root *Dhri*, meaning "to uphold, sustain, or support," the term denotes "that which holds together" the different aspects and qualities of an object into a whole. Dharma is the Law of Being that makes a thing or being what it is.[19]

Perhaps one of the most beautiful aspects of this ancient spiritual path is its tolerance of other people's cultures, religions, and views. Followers of Yoga Spirituality believe that "God is one; though sages call Him by many different names" (Rig Veda). Within this nurturing framework is a tremendous spiritual freedom that encourages followers of Yoga to think, learn, explore, and look inside for the meaning of *sanatana* dharma and of life itself. Dharma encourages us to use both our heads and our hearts in making decisions and in how we approach God. We must use our God-given ability to discern truth from untruth in addition to using compassion and love in all important decisions.[20]

Yoga is a path of reason coupled with compassion. It is dharma that holds a society together. It has been said in the Vedic literature, *dharmo rakshati rakshitah*, meaning "Protect dharma and thou shall be protected." Such is the importance of dharma in society. Without it, there is chaos, confusion, and unworthiness.[21] But dharma is not just concerned with holding society together; it performs a more complex function. "Dharma is essentially a rule of interdependence, founded on a hierarchy corresponding to the nature of things, and necessary for the maintenance of social order. To break away from it is to violate one's destiny and expose oneself to the loss of one's salvation."[22]

Hinduism is actually an umbrella term for a collection of different theistic (and even agnostic) attitudes. The Hindu religion, therefore, is somewhat unique in that it retains a continuous link with its hazy origins in antiquity and, therefore, incorporates virtually all shades of human opinion. The aforementioned incarnations are only a few from the Hindu pantheon; there are many others, such as Ganapati, Shakti, Kartikeya, and Sheshnaga. The result of this is the great multiplicity of objects of worship that exists in this religion. The Hindu pantheon grew in an overlapping manner, with constant additions. Because of this, a follower of this religion may not even be aware that a particular deity forms part of the Hindu pantheon. Consequently, a Hindu's religious consciousness has been a relatively vague one, and his commitment to his religion has not been as fanatical as is seen among believers in the more monotheistic religions.[23]

The term *Hinduism* is similarly quite elastic. It includes a number of sects and cults, allied, but different in many important ways. Hinduism has, within its fold, various schools of Vedanta, Saivism, Saktism, Vaishnavism, and so on. It has various cults and creeds, and the mushrooming of innumerable local sects from a common system of beliefs has been an inevitable result. At times, the sects disassociated themselves from the main body and went their separate ways — as in the cases of Buddhism, Jainism, and Sikhism. But the pluralistic tendency they had inherited from their mother faith re-asserted itself, and the process of splitting continued in these offspring religious sects.[24]

The Upanishads declare that all these paths lead to the same goal, just as cows of variegated colors yield the same white milk. Lord Krishna says in the Gita: "Howsoever men approach Me, even so do I welcome them, for the path men take from every side is Mine." All these diversities are organized and united in the body of Hinduism.[25] It is interesting to note that though the concept of a formless and absolute infinite (Brahman) was floated by the Upanishads, the idea gradually changed and the concept of a personal god whom the average human could love and comprehend gradually emerged. This transition was easy and natural, and almost inevitable, because the human mind finds it difficult to establish a relationship with an impersonal godhead. The Upanishadic doctrine of an impersonal godhead was fused with the devotional worship of a personal god and a beginning was thus made which led to almost revolutionary changes.[26] Indeed, one of the most important traits of the Brahmanic religion is this spirit of reconciliation and harmony between orthodox and sectarian forms. Henceforth the Hindus came to be divided broadly into two classes: extreme sectarians who confine their devotion and worship almost exclusively to their sectarian deities like Vishnu, Shiva, Kali, and so on; and general followers of the Brahmanic religion who revere and worship all these and other gods, even though they might be specially attached to one sectarian deity and also follow some of the important Vedic rituals and practices. Thus the *Smartas* (experts in Hindu social law, the law of inheritance, and the like) prescribed the regular worship of the five gods Vishnu, Shiva, Durga, Surya, and Ganesh, but the rest of the Hindu pantheon are also freely worshipped by many.[27]

In addition to the purification of the Bhakti cult and its elevation to a high spiritual level, the Vaisnava teachers, together with Chaitanya, have made other notable contributions. These may be summed up as preaching in the vernacular, ignoring caste distinctions and admitting even the lowest castes to their fold, and (3) rejecting rites and ceremonials as useless while laying stress on morality and purity of the heart. While Ramananda and Chaitanya allowed some image worship, others carried this last feature to an extreme form, discarding all images. The eighteenth century was marked by the impact of Western thought, leading to the religious reforms of the nineteenth century and bringing back the rationalism of the fifth-century-BC Raja Rammohan Roywas, its great exponent. The new spirit led to the foundation of the Brahma Samaj (including Prarthana Samaj), the Arya Samaj, and the Theosophical Society on the one hand, and all-around reform in orthodox Hindu religion and society on the other.[28]

The close of the century saw the advent of Sri Ramakrishna who sought to reconcile not only the rationalist doctrine with the emotionalism and ritualistic orthodoxy of the earlier ages, but also the seemingly conflicting religions. His disciple, Swami Vivekananda, gave definite shape to his views. Formulating the teaching of his master into a creed, Vivekananda founded the Ramakrishna Mission, which is now a potent force in India as well as in other countries. He propounded the doctrine that all religions, if truly followed, are but different ways to salvation, and there is no inherent conflict between one and another. The Ramakrishna Mission synthesizes the varied cultures of India, combining the philosophy of the Upanishads and Shankara with theistic beliefs, the pursuit of abstract principles with meditation and devotion. While the rituals of the Vedic religion are performed with meticulous care, it observes no distinctions of caste and creed and honors Buddha, Chaitanya, Christ, Mohammed, and Zoroaster.[29]

Thus Hinduism is perhaps more a league of religions than a single religion with a definite creed. It is a fellowship of faiths and philosophies. It accommodates all types of people. It prescribes spiritual food for everybody, according to the person's qualifications and growth. This is the beauty and essence of this religion and there is no conflict among the various cults and creeds. Sanatana Dharmists, Arya Samajists, Deva Samajists, Jains, Sikhs, and Brahmo Samjists are all Hindus. Despite the differences in metaphysical doctrines, modes of religious discipline, forms of ritual practice, and social habits prevalent in the Hindu society (which might ordinarily define distinct religions), there is an essential uniformity in the Hindu conception of religion, and in the outlook on life and the world, among all sections of Hindus.

UNDERSTANDING THE ROLE OF RELIGION

It is necessary to understand the crucial role religion has played and still plays in the evolution of human consciousness. Man's quest for knowing the unknown Supreme Being is explained thus. Sri Aurobindo points out that "while it is difficult for man to believe in something unseen within himself, it is easy for him to believe in something which he can imagine as extraneous to himself." The spiritual progress of most human beings demands an extraneous support, an object of faith beyond his physical self. All religions and creeds are born from this intense inner need of the human being in his precipitous climb toward the Godhead. This takes the shape of rites, rituals, and creeds in accordance with the needs of the times and society. Consequently, all religions are marked by both eternal and temporal aspects. The eternal aspect of a religion embodies the aspiration of the individual and represents a living universal Truth of the Divine, while the temporal aspect formalizes the collective aspiration of a society by formulating codes, conducts, rites, and rituals of worship. The eternal or universal aspect of a religion comprises the mystical or psycho-spiritual experiences of the individual

seeker. The temporal aspect of a religion results in a social organization —
a practical, ethical, and legal framework — for its practitioners.[30]

Religion has often been looked upon as a vehicle of peace — both
inner peace and societal peace. With religion interwoven with cultural pluralism and freedom as we see it today, either of these is possible. Hinduism
might end up losing its significance as a ritualistic religion and become a
universalistic culture promoting a community of mankind.[31] Yet, looking at
world events, one tends to characterize this idea as too optimistic — as we
see ourselves in a world strife-torn (often, violently) on religious grounds.
Be it the 9/11 disaster, the terror unleashed by the Taliban regime, the seemingly never-ending Arab-Israeli conflict, the Tamil-Sinhalese dispute in South
Asia or the Hindu-Muslim ethnic conflicts in India (to mention only a few),
all have one common meeting point. Religion has been given as an explanation in all those conflicts. Does that mean religion has been interpreted violently? What is the place of violence in religion? To answer these questions,
we first have to attempt to understand the various facets of religion as understood by Hindu philosophy.

All religions evolve through three phases in their growth and development — the creed, the code, and the cult. The creed is constant and permanent and is spiritual in nature; the code is interpretive, changes somewhat
with time, and is moral in nature. The cult changes constantly from one society to another (even in the same country) and in modern times even from
one member of a family to another; it is religious in nature. Thus the spiritual
creed, the moral code, and the religious cult are the three different facets of
any religion. The differences are vital.

Man often ignores the creed, and conveniently forgets the code in
order to practice the cult as it suits him. In all the world religions, morality
is exemplified by God-men and Godly men, but morals are sometimes forgotten by modern man, who follows his religious cult only in its routine rituals. The cult tries to supplant the creed. The code is man's moral language
written on ice. In hoping to walk on that slippery ice, he tumbles down and
hopes to rewrite religion on water by the dictates of his compromising mind
according to the prevailing circumstances.[32]

The transformation of religion to the level of cult is often associated with violent outbreaks between and also within communities. On all
such occasions of violent behavior, the cult facet of religion is used as a jus-

tification. Thus, religion and violence have come to be interwoven historically. Despite the essentially peaceful nature of the creed and the code against violence, and even within the strengthened legal framework of modern political societies, violence as a method of cult interpretation has persisted within human communities. Yet though neither of them are strangers to one another, religion and violence cannot be woven into one piece.[33]

Violence is any diminishment or violation of *isness*, the quality of being that is intrinsic to all that is alive. Isness embraces form, essence, surface, depth, matter, and spirit. All living things — whether animate, like humans and animals, or inanimate, like stones — manifest their own isness. Violence, by definition, signals the loss, lapse, and negation of a spiritual way of being.[34]

Hindu philosophy is based on reasoning, but intuition is actually the only way to know the ultimate reality. Intellect is subordinated to intuition, dogma to experience, and outer experience to inward realization. Hinduism is not about either academic abstractions or ceremonies, but is a kind of life experience. This is the essential source of India's religious toleration and adaptability. Perhaps one of the most beautiful aspects of this ancient spiritual path is its tolerance of other people's cultures, religions, and views.

Followers of Yoga Spirituality believe that "God is one; though sages call Him by many different names" (Rig Veda). Within the nurturing framework of this path is a tremendous spiritual freedom that encourages and provokes followers of Yoga to think, learn, explore, and look inside them for the meaning of *sanatana* dharma and of life itself. *Isaa vaasyam idam sarvam* means God resides in every living and nonliving organism on this planet. *Eswarah sarva bhootanam* means God is omnipresent. For Hindus, even plants are seen as an incarnation of God. Even to this day, legends of the Bishnoi tribes of Rajasthan who sacrificed their lives to prevent felling of trees are told in each home to every succeeding generation. Every morning, oblations are offered to the Sun, who is seen as the primordial sustainer of life on earth.

Spirituality is attached to every aspect of creation and any act not in consonance with venerating that spirituality is seen as a sacrilege, for which penance is offered. The Bhagavad Gita, considered very sacred by the Hindus, equates anger, pride, arrogance, cruelty, slaying of enemies, and hatred as demonic qualities, in contrast to the divine qualities, which are nonviolence, absence of anger, peace, compassion, forgiveness, and absence of malice. From this description it becomes clear that the essential teachings of Hinduism do not support violence, especially when perpetrated for selfish or egoistic reasons.[35]

It is one of the little-known facts of Hinduism, however, that violence and nonviolence do coexist in it. The *Purusa Sukta* hymn in the Rig Veda, Hinduism's most ancient scripture, describes metaphorically the origin of humankind from the primordial sacrifice of the Cosmic Person (*Purusa*). From his mouth came the Brahmans (priest-teachers), from his arms the Ksatriyas (warrior-kings), from his thighs the Vaisyas (trader-craftsmen) and from his feet the Sudras (manual laborers). The respective duties of each group are defined and presented later on in the Bhagavad Gita (18:45–47) as conducive to the attainment of liberation. The Ksatriyas, the group from which kings and rulers are supposedly drawn, are the physical protectors of the community. They are custodians of justice and defenders of social and ritual order (dharma), by the force of arms, if necessary. Society could not survive without the might of the Ksatriyas, and Hindu tradition commends the ideal of the warrior who is prepared to fight in the defense of dharma. The ancient ideal of the Ksatriya is invoked and reinterpreted by militant Hindus today to justify their brand of violence.[36]

Vedic society in ancient India did not scrupulously adhere to ahimsa — reverence for all life, resulting in nonviolence and refraining from harming any living thing — as its highest value. Sacrificial rites involved the slaying of animals, and Indra, one of the most popular deities of the Vedic period, has many warrior-like attributes. While Manu (ca. 200 BCE–100 CE), ancient India's influential lawgiver, lists ahimsa among the general human virtues, the Ksatriyas are exempt from it. He permits killing in self-defense and for implementing the injunctions of the Vedas. In the Bhagavad Gita, modern Hinduism's most popular sacred scriptures, Krishna is revealed on a battlefield and advocates the position that participating in war may be, for a Ksatriya, a personal duty. We see quite clearly from the Gita that, while the tradition upholds the ultimate virtue of nonviolence, exceptions are made for the use of violence. The Mahabharata war is referred to in the Bhagavad Gita as a *dharma yuddha*, a war fought in defense of justice and righteousness and for the security and well-being of the community. Qualifying a war as a *dharma yuddha* means that it is used as a last resort after all peaceful methods of conflict resolution have been exhausted without success.[37] This distinguishes it from those forms of violence that are not sanctioned in Hinduism.

The Hindu value of ahimsa, praised as the "highest dharma" in the Mahabharata, is not passive masochism. Even so, ahimsa does imply a restraint on the use of violence. Force is sometimes necessary, as Krishna explains to Arjuna, but should not be resorted to lightly. Indeed, Krishna and the Pandavas exhaust all possibilities of compromise before they resolve to do battle. It is clear, therefore, that there are influential traditions within Hinduism which justify the use of violence under certain circumstances and which understand the use of violence to be consistent with the Hindu worldview. The use of force may not be altogether avoidable in the face of multiple aggressions, but to rely on force as a matter of long-term strategy to save India from its enemies would be contrary to Hindu ethics.[38] Leaving aside the influence of Gandhi, there are purely Hindu reasons for feeling uncomfortable with violent victories — namely, when violence is a wasteful and unnecessary method resorted to by those too lazy to try more subtle ways.[39] While the Upanishads refer frequently to ahimsa, they explain it to mean not just the antithesis of violence, but a complete cessation of violence from every facet of human life. These texts promote an ideal in which ahimsa is the first step for seekers of liberation. He who traverses that path passes through all the stages of life — celibacy, life of a householder, life of a recluse dedicated to seeking the Divine, and finally complete forsaking of worldly attachments as a final step toward the realization of the Self. Persons in the last stage were ritually freed from social and familial obligations and dedicated to the quest for liberation. They were expected to scrupulously adhere to nonviolence by not participating in wars and by nonresistance. In these circles, the value of the complex order of Vedic ritualism, including the sacrifice of animals, was questioned. The origin of Gandhi's nonviolence may be traced to this, as can Jain and Buddhist ascetic teachings, which share a great deal with those of the Upanishads.[40]

VIOLENCE IN HINDU/INDIAN CULTURE

Here we will look at the presence of violence in the Hindu society from two angles. The first approach to the subject is to look at practices within the creed, cult, and (to a lesser extent) code that involve physical and mental violence and curtailment of human freedom in the community. From the other angle, we look at how the cults that have taken their place in modern society use religion as an excuse to indulge in violence against other communities.

Religious Violence—Intra-community

In this section I explain a few practices indulged in by the community which are not a part of the creed of the religion, but have developed later as part of its cult stage, mainly because of aberrations introduced by cult and community heads in local areas. I will discuss a few of the practices that began during the later part of the Vedic period, which have been largely eliminated but still exist in scattered places all over the country. The first of these aberrations is the sacrifice of living beings — both animals and human beings. This is ritual violence. It involves various practices that were directed at inflicting harm on oneself or other beings for material gain and for self-expiation.[41]

These practices are a misinterpretation of the words *sacrifice* and *agni* (the holy sacrificial fire). Sacrifice, according to the scriptures, means offering one's demonic qualities in the sacred fire. Annihilation of demonic qualities in man by the virtuous traits in him is the correct understanding of sacrifice. But as with other tenets of the Hindu philosophy, this also suffered from misinterpretation by the code and cults that have developed in society. Sacrifice came to mean a violent end to a living being. In India, some semi-tribal Hindus, as well as some worship communities of *Shaktism* (which focuses on the worship of Shakti, the mother goddess) offer sacrifices of goats and buffaloes to the deity.

Some people in India are also adherents of a religion called *Tantrism* (not to be confused with Tantric Buddhism). Most either use animal sacrifice or symbolic effigies, but a very small percentage of them even engage in human sacrifice. These ritual practices crept into the religion, originating from practices of ethnic communities, initially as fanciful practices promoted by leaders of communities wanting to establish their hegemony and authority. Sacrifice in all its forms is now prohibited by Indian law.[42] Recent reports[43] of about 25 human sacrifices in an Indian state prompted the government to invoke strict sanctions against such activity. This brought renewed national and even world attention on *Tantrism*. Both ritual and military violence continue to be associated with Hindu goddess worship.[44] As recently as early medieval times, there were recorded instances of villagers, primarily pregnant women, offering themselves as sacrifices to the king if he promised to worship their heads. These human sacrifices were gradually replaced by animal sacrifices that are still regularly offered to Durga and Kali as a part of *Shaktism* — primarily in Northeast India and Nepal.[45]

VIOLENT RELIGIOUS PRACTICES AGAINST WOMEN — SATI

In certain areas of India the treatment of widows has extremely violent overtones. For example, the historic practice (sati) of a woman immolating herself at the funeral of her husband and the religious glorification of sati shrines, although outlawed at present, still remain a matter of concern.[46] In one celebrated case in Deorala, Rajasthan, Roop Kanwar and her 24-year-old husband had been married for less than eight months when he died in September 1987. Dressed in bridal finery and in front of four thousand spectators, Roop Kanwar was burnt to death along with the body of her deceased husband on a funeral platform that had been erected in the middle of the village. The uproar created by this incident, especially since sati had long been banned (under British rule in 1825) resulted in the government passing the Sati (Prevention of Glorification) Act. The former colonial government was in the vanguard of the movement against sati,[47] as were the many religious reformers, such as Raja Rammohan Roy, and reformation movements such as the Brahmmo Samaj. It came as a rude shock to the public that a widow is still glorified in such a death and is forced or at least encouraged to die rather than live. The controversy in regard to this incident pointed to the persistence of a high tolerance of sati culture in some Indian communities. Pro-sati factions, despite being heavily condemned, insist that the practice is religiously sanctioned. Moreover, although sati is legally outlawed, the state still appears to tolerate the many rituals and practices that glorify it in various parts of India.[48] The recent acquittal[49] of the male members of Roop Kanwar's family — responsible for her sati — has made many observers skeptical, and would seem to indicate that the criminal justice system has failed to actively enforce the Sati Prohibition Act.

The Devadasi System

Another ignominious system that still persists in certain pockets of the country is the system of *devadasi* (in which women are married off at a very young age to the temple deity and are forced to live a life of repeated gang rape by the head of the temple and other village leaders). The practice continues in several southern states including Andhra Pradesh and Karnataka.[1] Literally meaning "female servant of god," *devadasis* usually belong to the weaker sections of society. Once dedicated, the girl is unable to marry, is forced to become a prostitute for upper-caste community members, and is eventually auctioned into an urban brothel.[51] The age-old practice continues to exist and to legitimize the sexual violence and discrimination that have come to characterize the intersection between caste and gender. Although the custom is now illegal, girls who are dedicated to the deity when very young are often sold into prostitution.[52] According to research published in the Journal of the American Medical Association, the incidence of HIV infection has risen in female prostitutes from less than 10 percent in 1990 to between 40 percent and 50 percent in a 1996 survey of Mumbai (formerly Bombay) and other cities.[53]

Violent Treatment of Child Brides and Widows

Another disturbing practice in Hindu society that has survived, though with much less rigor, also involves the treatment of widows. The early part of the last century witnessed a large number of young girls married to older men, which eventually resulted in their becoming destitute widows without financial support. Child marriage for the sake of money was common practice and widow remarriage was almost unthinkable. Many reformers,[54] especially from Bengal, with the active support of the colonial government, fought against such religious practices, which involved the young widow leading a life of celibacy in a destitute home with hardly food enough to keep her alive. Many were forced into a life of prostitution in their homes. Though the Indian government made laws ensuring property rights for women[55] and strict punishment for child marriage, such homes can still be found in a few Indian states.[56] The recent census shows more than three thousand such widows eking out livings of a few rupees for prayers sung during the day.[57] This exists despite the creed of the religion favoring widow remarriage. This is what the Parasara Samhita had to say on this issue. That text, composed around 200–100 BCE and regarded as the authority on Hindu marriage, approved widow remarriage, and the remarriage of a woman whose husband is alive, under four situations: (1) the husband leaves his family without leaving a trace; (2) he becomes a recluse, renouncing the world for religious pursuits; (3) he is impotent and the marriage cannot be consummated; or (4) he is an outcast from society. The basic idea is that the wife should not suffer for the activities of her husband.[58] But in the holy city of Varanasi, on the banks of the Ganges, one could see a Hindu widow bent like a shrimp, her body wizened with age, white hair shaved close to her scalp, scampering on all fours, furiously looking for something she had lost on the steps of the Ganges. Her distress was visible as she searched amidst the early morning throng of pilgrims. She was paid scant attention, not even when she sat down to cry, unsuccessful in her attempt to find what she had lost. Though the law does empower women, we still have these examples. The traditions and institutionalized gender bias drastically restrict the human, physical, and financial resources available to these child widows, some of them as much as one hundred years old.[59]

CASTE-BASED VIOLENCE

India's caste system is perhaps the world's longest surviving social hierarchy. A defining feature of Hinduism, as was practiced for more than a millennium, caste encompasses a complex ordering of social groups on the basis of ritual purity. The word *caste*, however, is of Portuguese origin; its Indian variant was *varna*, or color. The *varna* system meant only a difference in complexion between the different communities, referring perhaps to the white Aryan invaders, who came to India from the Central Asian region, and the dark Dravidian native population. The *varna* system as has been found in many scriptures, is conspicuously absent in their philosophical sections. It is found mostly in the fables and legends that have been added to the scriptures to make them more relevant to all sections of the population. But with time, many practices developed within these communities and have been passed on to people as authentic interpretations of the Vedas. The Vedas themselves being only oral pronouncements, their actual textualization was largely influenced by the prevailing social arrangements. The authority of this indigenous version of the caste system rested partly on written laws, partly on legendary fables and narratives, partly on the injunctions of instructors and priests, partly on custom and usage, and partly on the caprice and convenience of its votaries,[60] which was common in the transition of society during the post-Vedic period. Thus we see an animated history of the system, which finds new explanations even today.

Originally, the caste system was seen as a way of defining the duty of a person in the community. It was never conceived of as a system of social stratification. A person is considered a member of the caste into which he or she is born and remains within that caste until death, although the particular ranking of that caste may vary between regions and over time. Differences in status are traditionally justified by the religious doctrine of karma, a belief that one's place in life is determined by one's deeds in previous lifetimes. Though the caste system in India has been attributed to the Bhagavad Gita and the Vedas, and its practice and rhetoric draw from those sources, neither the Vedas[61] nor the Bhagavad Gita ever conceived of a permanent caste system.

In the Gita, the barriers of caste, creed, and sex were all removed. Non-Brahmins were declared as much a part of the body politic of society and as important in their occupations as the Brahmins in their scholarly occupation. Krishna in the Bhagavad Gita said, "*Caathur varnam maya srustaam, guna karma vibhaagashaha, Thasya karthaaramapi maam, vidhyaakarthaara mavyayam.*" This verse, the thirteenth verse of the fourth chapter of the Gita, means "according to the division of *gunas* (behavioral traits) and actions, the fourfold division of castes was created by Me. Although I am the creator of this fourfold division, do know that I am the inexhaustible non-doer." Krishna says he created the above divisions to elevate man to the state of consciousness of the Supreme Self, to make him achieve the realization of the purpose for which his creation happened, to make him realize the distinction between him and animal society.[62]

But the very same verse has been interpreted differently by authors who indulge in condemning the Hindu religion. By a small grammatical change in the verse, they changed the meaning of the first two lines and said God created the caste system. This is but one example to show how a verse can be completely misinterpreted. The verse means that God created each and every division that is in existence, based upon the behavioral traits and attributes of each division. Such an act shall not be read, according to the Gita, as one of grading the divisions, because God himself (in Hinduism) is the illimitable non-doer. Now some modern writings have ignored the second part of the verse, finding a very emotional appeal in indulging in rhetoric against the Hindu religion.

The philosophies behind the *varna* system of the scriptures and the caste system of the present day are not the same. The varna system, as originally conceived of and previously existed, was not entirely translated into practice. It ordained different communities, engaged in different professions; it was connected with the way of earning a living. There was no harm in a person belonging to one varna acquiring the knowledge, science or art of persons belonging to others.[63] *Varna*, or caste, is a convenient arrangement for the conduct of worldly affairs; the stages of life are roots of supra-worldly joy. Each limb has to perform its task, for which it is specialized. You cannot walk on your head or think with your feet. Each is a cooperative commonwealth, the body as well as the body politic.[64] In the Mahabharata, it was explained that where the qualities of a Brahmin, (votary of truth and forbearance, cleanliness and kindness, penance and philanthropy, and equanimity with regard to pain, pleasure, prosperity, and poverty) are found in a Sudra (member of the lowest caste), he is to be regarded as a Brahmin. There have been practical examples of this line of thinking.[65]

The Gita gives a further explanation. The *Varnas* help man engage in acts that he finds congenial; they allow him to fulfill himself. Without it, man cannot earn happiness. Those who understand the *Brahmathathwam* (the Brahman or Supreme awareness principle) and foster spiritual, progressive living are the Brahmins. Those who stand by and guard a sound political system, law, and justice, and ensure the welfare of the country and traditional moral order are the Ksatriyas. Those who cater to the people by storing and supplying goods within proper limits are the Vaisyas. Those who lay the foundation of human welfare by service activities provide the strength and sinews of the social fabric and are the Sudras.[66]

The Purusa Sukta said, "*brahmanasya mukham aaseethah, baahoo rajanyah kruthah, ooroo thadasya yadhvysyah, padhbhyagum soodhro ajaayatah*" (Rig Veda). This means that the cosmic person (Brahman or the supreme selfless consciousness) created the entire universe and each group finds its position in the cosmic person; there is nothing beyond that cosmic person. So, according to the Rig-Vedic hymn of Purusa Sukta, the entire universe and every being, living and nonliving, came from that cosmic person and ultimately merges with him.

Most of the *Dalit* (untouchable) historians read this verse as Brahma created Brahmins from his mouth and the rest from each of his limbs. Such an interpretation is only a half-read opinion, because Brahma did not create anyone. It's the Brahman or cosmic person who created the universe. Brahma is only responsible for keeping the continuity of the universe, and is part of the trinity, which, according to the Hindu philosophy, continues, sustains, and ultimately merges with the Supreme Being. What this verse means is that every person was ordained with a specific duty on the basis of his behavioral traits. Most importantly, it means that every person has a role to play in the cosmic act.

A Sudra is no less than a Brahmin, because each has a specifically defined role in society. *Sudra* means a person who performed acts of welfare and lent strength to the societal harmony. The Rig Veda never actually classified members of the community as *Dalits*; that fifth category was unknown to the Rig-Vedic period. Seen in this light, there would perhaps be no difficulty accepting the concept of people with different aptitudes doing the tasks that they are best suited for. God has no favorite caste; he has not shown any partiality while organizing the *varnas*. He has no sense of inferior or superior. He is the source of all living beings. All the *varnas* are the same to him. This is not based on the Gita alone. Many of the commentaries on the Vedas, for example the Manisha Panchakam, by the sage Adi Sankaracharya, written in the eighth century CE, alluded to a similar thought. Many such writings described the creation of humankind without allusion to a separate production of the four castes. In the chapters where they discuss the distinct formations of the castes, the puranas (religious commentaries interspersed with fables) assign different natural dispositions to each. But they elsewhere represent all mankind at the creation distinguished by the quality of passion.[67]

While some modern-day writings on the caste system and social stratification find the roots of all the evils associated with the system in the texts of the ancient lawgiver, Manu, details about him are not known. While some authorities consider Manu the son of Vivasvat (the first person from whom most Hindus trace their ancestry), texts such as the Ramayana say the four castes were the offspring of a woman named Manu, the wife of Kasyapa, a son of Brahma. Theological and spiritual research classifies the Vedas into two major streams—the Brahmanas and the Aranyakas. While the Brahmanas catered to the ritual formalities that are attached to material living, the Aranyakas went a little further and explained the spiritual content of these rituals and traditions.

Toward the later period, the most immediate successor to the Vedic period (which, coincidentally, was also the time Buddhism took root on Indian soil), this essential difference between the Brahmanas and the Aranyakas nearly vanished, and the religion of the Vedas became more rigid and ritualistic, with the Brahmins as a class becoming more of a ritual-related class rather than one entrusted with espousing the Aranyakas and ensuring that men tread a path of spirituality. The post-Vedic period saw a near disappearance of this division between rituals and content of the rituals, which led to the line of thinking that Brahmins are representative of the supreme creator as they perform rituals in his name. This thinking found support with the rulers, who took the Brahmins under their wing and ensured a continuance of the system of hegemony over the people working under them. The Brahmins needed royal support for their sustenance and this equation ensured that the rituals' importance continued, thereby establishing a system of superiority in the society and laying the seeds for the later version of the caste system.

The Sudras are understood as outside the pale of the Aryan society. Historical research shows that they are to a large extent the indigenous tribal people who were living in India at the time of the Aryan invasion. That conquest subjugated the indigenous population and turned them into *dasa* — a servile population. From this came the understanding that Sudras are a servant class that live to serve the Aryans and are dependent upon the upper castes for their sustenance. But what was forgotten was the system of interdependence that existed in the first forms of this caste system.

Historical antecedents tell us that the Sudras had a most important place in the court administration during the later Vedic period. No decision could be finally taken without the Sudras' assent. They had a place in the royal court and seem to have played an important part in the political life of the period. In the formative stage of the Indo-Aryan polity, they enjoyed a considerable share in the functions of the state. It is striking that they found a place in the exalted body of about a dozen "high functionaries of the state" called *ratnins* (jewel-holders), which may be compared to the council of twelve, an institution of great antiquity among several Indo-European peoples such as Old Saxons, Frisians, and Celts.[68]

The Rig-Vedic society probably had a caste system that was flexible and allowed an individual to change his caste if he so desired. Already in the Rig Veda, division of labor existed. But although members of the same family worked as poet, physician, and grinder, this did not involve any social differentiation. The four distinct castes were these: Brahmins (priests), who had the exclusive right to perform Vedic rituals and studies; Kshatriyas (warriors), whose responsibility it was to protect the people, wage wars, and rule; Vaisyas (traders), who had the right to engage in commerce and own the agricultural lands; and Sudras (the working class) who had the burden of serving the other three communities in discharging their respective duties. As the son of a Sudra can attain the rank of a Brahmin, the son of a Brahmin can attain the rank of a Sudra — even so with him who is born of a Vaishya or a Kshatriya.[69]

THE POST-VEDIC PERIOD OF DETERIORATION

Toward the end of the Atharva Veda, differentiations of functions tended to develop into differentiations in rank. Tribes and clans gradually disintegrated into rigid homogenous groups, or strict social classes, with the earlier traditions attached to these groups now taking the shape of rigid community practices. The caste system fell into disrepute because of the injustices perpetrated in the name of the *varna* system, for which there was no scriptural translation or religious sanction.[70] The fault lies in the haphazard manner in which the caste system developed. The lateral infiltrations of superiority and inferiority complexes, partly associated with wealth, are the fundamental reason. Somehow, Brahmins came to regard themselves as superior, and treated the Sudras as inferior and untouchable. The onset of such an attitude represents an aberration and has nothing to do with the principle that was ordained in the scriptures. During post-Vedic Indian history, there was Brahminic dominance. The priesthood slipped from its divine vocation into a privileged class with an egoistic power over the rest.[71]

A person is considered a member of the caste into which he or she is born and remains so until death, although the particular ranking of that caste may vary among regions and over time. Differences in status are traditionally justified by the religious doctrine of karma, which says that one's place in life is determined by one's deeds in previous lifetimes. Traditional scholarship described this more than 2,000-year-old system within the context of the four principal *varnas*, or large caste categories. A fifth category falls outside the system and consists of those known as "untouchables" or *Dalits*; they are often assigned tasks too ritually polluting to merit inclusion within the traditional *varna* system.[72] Within the four principal castes, there are thousands of sub-castes, also called *jatis* (endogamous groups further divided along occupational, sectarian, regional, and linguistic lines). Collectively, all of them are sometimes referred to as "caste Hindus" or those falling within the caste system. The *Dalits* are described as *varna-sankara*. They are "outside the system"— so inferior to other castes that they are deemed polluting and therefore "untouchable." The word *Dalit* is in fact the modern and currently politically correct term for the traditional word *Harijan* — the children of God. This was the name given to the people who were considered to be members of the communities that engaged in menial tasks, like cobblers, scavengers, and so on.

Unfortunately, for economic reasons, these types of work came to have social stigma attached to them, and that is when the modern sociological history of India took a turn for the worse. The outcast communities came to be regarded as being on the periphery of social and economic relations. They themselves were divided into further sub-castes. A *chamar* (one who works with leather in a tannery) believes that he or she is pushed down the social ladder unjustly, but condemns other so-called untouchables to lower-caste status. Every caste or sub-caste practices its own methods of purification. Endogamy perpetuates this hierarchy in future generations. Although "untouchability" was abolished under Article 17 of the Indian constitution, it continues to determine the socio-economic and religious standing of those at the bottom of the caste system. Where the first four *varnas* are free to choose and change occupations, *Dalits* have generally been confined to occupations into which they were born.

Regarding the word *Dalit*, we cannot definitively trace its etymological development. Most writers find some kind of Indo-Aryan connection. Some of them borrowed its logic from the conflict between the Aryan migrants and the Dravidian indigenous population. While not much is written about this distinction, it has been cleverly put to use by successive invaders who were faced with the dilemma of governing a huge and diverse country. So history, rather than religion, has been the real cause behind the deprivation that is denoted by the word *Dalit*. In fact, the social connotation of the word is just about a few hundred years old. During the last century, it was used to refer to members of the communities under the category of the Sudras — the fourth in the original caste hierarchy. Untouchables came to be classified by Jyotirao Phule as *ati-sudras*, denoting the communities still languishing in economic and social deprivation.

The original understanding of the word *untouchable* was completely different. An untouchable was the person excommunicated from the village for violation of dharma by indulging in some kind of crime. In later times, it came to be interpreted as hereditary. According to the traditional meaning of the word, a person is reclaimed by the society once he has served his sentence decreed by the village judicial system. There was no stigma attached to his or her family, but rather the term was used as a kind of repentance for the violations he or she had indulged in. Over time and, to a lesser extent, through the policies of the British Raj, the term has acquired a social stratification connotation with groups of communities being branded as untouchables.

In southern India, the *Yadavs* formed part of the backward communities, but in Haryana, a province in northern India, they formed a majority community of landowners able to wield political pressure. So it is largely economic interests that dominate caste politics in the country. Each of these communities has now acquired a social insulation of its own, where the subcastes in these communities are stratified for economic reasons and inter-subcaste relations amongst these individual communities is to a very large extent discouraged in most parts of India, except perhaps in metropolitan cities where higher education has penetrated.

Caste differences and discrimination have found an immediate venting in violence, which to a very large extent is a method of retaining the established social hierarchy and reassuring the groups of their respective positions. While violence has been perpetrated on behalf of all the communities, it has largely been to the disadvantage of people belonging to the weakest sections (untouchables). This violence has acquired enormous proportions in certain parts of the country where the other communities have been more organized and the modern cosmopolitan society has not yet developed.

The weaker sections had their champions and intelligentsia. Examples of silent revolution within those communities include people like Jyotirao Phule in the early decades of the previous century, which resulted in legislative and special incentive measures for ameliorating the situation. These measures found a place in the constitution along with affirmative-action programs. But implementation problems ensured that those measures hardly reached the communities that are most affected, resulting in very little change where change is most needed.

The past few decades saw the caste differences taking the shape of organized resistance movements, through political as well as violent means. These movements also acquired the support of the intelligentsia. Some of this support resulted from the introduction of literature claiming that religious texts are the source of these discriminatory practices; intellectuals have called for either rewriting these texts or completely proscribing them.[73] While these claims are not completely untrue, certain secular writings have been mistakenly given the status of religious texts. The import of these texts largely remains unknown today and that has led to the misreading of certain social practices as having real religious sanction. Reading such notions into the religious texts and attributing the status of a religious text to a social commentary like the *Manusmriti* has immensely damaged the social fabric, alienating certain communities and giving the impression that the religion itself is a retrograde force.

The situation worsened further because of the differences within the so-called untouchable communities. To a certain extent, the aggravated situation also finds its causes in the information circulated by the newly organized *Dalit* movements and the writings of the intelligentsia. This happens at a time when affirmative action is not able to percolate down to the areas where its need is greatest. Unsuccessful economic policies compounded the situation, especially in rural areas where religion still holds sway as a cohesive force. Religion is often seen as an opiate, dulling the awareness of the evils perpetrated on these largely illiterate communities.

In India there also spring up examples of successes in these communities, but for each such example there are thousands who haven't had an opportunity even to enter a school. Such deprivation has been and continues to be a basis for violence. Because of the continuing prejudices and a failure on the part of the administration to protect the *Dalits*, they unfortunately suffer the most from the violence. Empowerment in the Constitution only continues to enrich those communities who have already benefited from such measures. The result is that large chunks of these communities continue their peripheral existence, living lives of deprivation, which finds approval because the social structure has come to be viewed as having religious sanction.

The *Dalit's* suffering is often attributed to practices founded on religious texts — texts that mean exactly the opposite. The Ramayana, or the story of Lord Ram, is said to have been written by a sage by the name of Valmiki, who belonged to the community of the nomads and the tribal archers, but it doesn't have its value reduced because of the caste rank of its author. In fact, it is venerated even more, and its sage is worshipped in most parts of the country as the fountain of knowledge.

Another text, the Mahabharata, which contains the immortal Bhagavad Gita, was written by the sage Vyas, who is said to have been borne to a fisherwoman. The Mahabharata is read today more than ever before. Krishna, who gave the Gita, was said to have been borne in a *Yadav* community but is venerated as a god by everyone, irrespective of caste. In fact, the *Dalit* movement found its religious sanction in the same structure to which they attributed the religious basis of the Hindu caste system. They trace their religious descent from the same Rig-Vedic person, the *Purusa*. They claim their descent from the lunar dynasty, its origin in the moon (the eyes of the cosmic person or *Purusa*). This legend, largely believed in Bihar, puts forward the claim of the *Kahar* (a *Dalit* community) to be over the Brahmin and the Kshatriya.

To a very large extent, caste discrimination is rooted in the hegemonic order perpetuated by men for their own superiority. It has been the bane of Hindu society for centuries, a clever invention of the later Vedic priests, who found it a convenient method for retaining their religious distinction, financial well-being, and social privileges. These privileged classes wrongfully ascribed qualities to people on a hereditary basis irrespective of individual distinctions and denied them the right to lead normal, decent, and dignified lives through self-effort.[74]

The caste system as practiced by these communities was also based on the ancient principle of purity and impurity.[75] Efforts to make men understand the real tenets of religion and eradicate caste discrimination are as old as the problem itself. A saint like Adi Shankara touched the feet of a *chandala*, an outcaste, and preached the unity of man before God. Such understanding continued even in the later periods, especially in the medieval period where religion was used as a tool to combat these discriminatory practices. The *Bhakti* Movement had achieved remarkable success in the society in this regard. Saints like Eknath, Narsi Mehta, and Chaitanya preached the unity of man and society as ordained by religion. But at some point in time, that movement lost much of its influence. The changed political structure in the country — Muslim rule and its administration — diverted people's attention from this social problem and shifted it to political unity in the name of religion. This did not improve much during British rule, despite isolated efforts by a few administrators against discriminatory practices.

Today, despite the Constitution declaring the caste system and untouchability crimes against the state, its vestiges remain quite visible, sharply dividing the population on various issues. The struggle against the caste system found a place in the freedom struggle, its votary no less a personality than Mahatma Gandhi. He declared the removal of "untouchability" a priority and declared that it was no less important than the struggle for independence itself. In 1923, Congress began taking steps toward the eradication of "untouchability" by educating and mobilizing support among caste Hindus. The campaign was perhaps most vibrant in the state of Kerala, where the problem was particularly acute and where social reform movements had been active since the end of the nineteenth century.

The passive resistance from 1924 to 1925 offered Gandhi his first opportunity to act on behalf of *Dalits* who were denied entry into temples and the use of roads outside the Vaikom temple in Kerala state. He negotiated with the trustees of the Vaikam temple and managed to convince them to open the roads to all. *Dalit* leader B. R. Ambedkar stated that, for *Dalits*, "the most important event in the country today is the satyagraha at Vaikam," but he also pointed out that, after a year of protest, there had been few results. *Dalits* remained unable to enter the temple until 1936.

The main weakness of the temple entry movement was that while arousing people against "untouchability," it lacked a strategy for ending the caste system itself.[76] Thus the caste system still prevails in the minds of many Hindus. The following points are worth noticing. Inter-caste marriages are not approved in many traditional and rural communities. Caste-based organizations and associations still exist in India and play a crucial role in perpetuating the idea and politics of caste. Caste conflicts often lead to violence and bloodshed in backward areas. Caste is an important factor during general elections and many politicians seek votes in the name of caste. Indian temples are still under the siege of caste chauvinism. The temple administrators, some of which are government officials, do not recruit people from other castes to act as temple priests. Despite the legal abolition of untouchability, the imposition of social disabilities on persons by reason of birth remains very much a part of rural India.

Representing over one-sixth of India's population, or some 160 million people, *Dalits* are nearly completely ostracized in a few communities. They may not cross the line dividing their part of the village from that occupied by higher castes, use the same wells, visit the same temples, or drink from the same cups in tea stalls. *Dalit* children are frequently made to sit at the back of classrooms. Entire villages in many Indian states remain segregated by caste. *Dalits* are routinely abused and even killed at the hands of upper castes. Laws are openly flouted while state complicity in attacks on *Dalit* communities continues to reflect a well-documented pattern.

Laws granting *Dalits* special consideration for government jobs and education reach only a small percentage of those they are meant to benefit. Laws designed to ensure that they enjoy equal rights and protections have seldom been enforced. Instead, police refuse to register complaints about violations of the law and rarely prosecute those responsible for abuses that range from murder and rape to exploitative labor practices and forced displacement from lands and home. *Dalits* are routinely abused at the hands of the police. National legislation and constitutional protections serve only to mask the realities of discrimination and violence faced by those living below the "pollution line."[77]

The caste system is an economic order. It prevents someone from owning land or receiving an education. It is a vicious cycle, a tool to perpetuate exploitative economic arrangements.[78] Owning land and being a high-caste member are coterminous. With little land of their own to cultivate, *Dalit* men, women, and children numbering in the tens of millions work as agricultural laborers for a few kilograms of rice or 38 to 88 cents per day. Most live on the brink of destitution, barely able to feed their families and unable to send their children to school or break away from cycles of debt bondage that are passed on from generation to generation.

At the end of a day they return to a hut in their *Dalit* colony with no electricity, kilometers away from the nearest water source, and segregated from all non-*Dalits*, known as caste Hindus. They are forbidden to wear shoes in the presence of caste Hindus. They are made to dig the village graves, dispose of dead animals, clean human waste with their bare hands, and to wash and use separate tea tumblers at neighborhood tea stalls because they are deemed polluting and therefore "untouchable." Any attempt to defy the social order is met with violence or economic retaliation.

Dalit women face the triple burden of caste, class, and gender. Some girls have been forced to become prostitutes for upper-caste patrons and village priests.[79] Sexual abuse and other forms of violence against women are used by landlords and the police to deliver political "lessons" and crush dissent within the community. Like other Indian women whose relatives are sought by the police, *Dalit* women have also been arrested and tortured in custody as a means of punishing their male relatives who are hiding from the authorities.[80]

In some states, notably Bihar, guerrilla organizations advocating the use of violence to achieve land redistribution have attracted *Dalit* support. Such groups, known as Naxalites, have carried out attacks on higher-caste groups, killing landlords and village officials and their families, and seizing property. They have also engaged in direct combat with police. Higher-caste landlords in Bihar have organized private militias to counter the Naxalite threat. These militias also target villagers believed to be sympathetic to Naxalites; the militias are believed to be responsible for the murders of hundreds of *Dalits* in Bihar since 1969.[81]

The potential of the law to bring about social change has been hampered by police corruption and caste bias, with the result that many allegations are not registered by authorities. Ignorance of procedures and a lack of knowledge of the law have also affected its implementation. Even when cases are registered, the absence of special courts to try them can delay prosecutions for three or four years. Some state governments dominated by higher castes have even attempted to repeal the legislation altogether. This official violence draws its justification from the language of religion and Vedic texts.

Unfortunately, for centuries the commentators on these texts have indulged in fanciful misinterpretation of them. The affirmative action schemes launched by the government have also not been completely successful and their manner of implementation has left a lot of distrust, both among its would-be beneficiaries and among the upper castes.[82] This distaste for one another has been one of the reasons for the violent disturbances in the society. Even the *Dalit* groups have been indulging in distasteful rhetoric, branding the Hindu religion as an evil dogmatic system. While much of it centered on demonstrating how Hindu religion is essentially the Brahmanic religion, it also attempted to provide a religious content to the *Dalit* movement by juxtaposing it against Hinduism.

While such attempts are most welcome, especially for the historical research into the *Dalit* religion and community, they have not been able to achieve much beyond chronicling the rituals of a few communities, largely because their efforts were tempered by anti-Hindu feelings. Dr. Kancha Iliah states that the *Dalit* religion is a very productive one, concerned with the give-and-take relationship between man and deity and nothing more than that. He finds this an improvement over the Brahmanic Hindu religion, which, according to him, loses its spiritual essence because of its emphasis on temporal activities and the discrimination perpetrated in its name.

What he loses sight of is that all religion has a content beyond the commercial relations that he has focused on. Religion is a tool in the hands of man to understand the essence of creation, to help him understand and live his life and to achieve realization of his mind. Dr. Iliah says Hinduism is a very violent, discriminatory religion that has justified and perpetrated violence. But the productive relationship in the *Dalit* religion, which Dr. Iliah so proudly discusses in his works and interviews, also has a distasteful kind of violence: sacrifice. He says that *Dalits* offer their deity animal sacrifice and in turn receive fulfillment of their wishes. He justifies violent practices like animal sacrifice as an important part of the man-deity transactional relationship.[83] He calls Hinduism a retrograde religion for not talking about equality of man and woman, which he claims is present in *Dalit* life (since widow remarriage among them is very common) and he thinks it is absent in Hinduism.[84]

Writings like these fail to understand that many religions are clouded by ritual practices that really have little or no religious sanction. The rituals change every few hundred miles in this vast country, and the customary law of marriage is different in different areas. The country also has matriarchal families in a few areas, which is not seen in most oriental religious practices. Attempts at chronicling *Dalit* history would be more credible if they understood the fundamental resilience that exists in the Hindu religion, and its history of tolerance with regard to thought.

The essential focus of Hinduism is on the individual and his salvation, not on his caste or its privileges. Scholars tend to quote the *Purusha-sukta*[85] as the basis for the emergence of the caste system. There are also references to a caste system in the Bhagavad Gita. Today we have examples of some communities that have been elevated into a neo-Kshatriya category, like the *Jats* in northern India, the *Gujjars* in Rajasthan, a federal unit in Northwestern India. We also see *Dalit* communities becoming a major political force. Examples of such organized activity include the *Ezhavas* in Tamil Nadu, in South India, and the *Mahars*, the community that paved the way for *Dalit* upliftment in Maharastra, in western India.[86]

Despite examples like these, there is a widely held and often discussed belief across India regarding religious texts being the source of caste discrimination and violence.[87] I call this an information explosion because this kind of literature is causing more than just a public debate. We have authors today calling for a rewriting of those texts. This only aggravates the differences rather than stimulating serious rethinking of existing beliefs. While the educated middle class in urban areas hasn't been persuaded by those who hold the religious texts responsible, the same cannot be said for people in the large rural areas.

Rural people often belong to homogenous groups, live in the same area, and have their disputes settled by their own elders. This is handled through a caste *panchayat* (a five-member group of elders of that particular geographical area). This group is the decision-making institution, and their decisions are largely binding because the people find affinity in the local group and don't take kindly to any violation in the social order or any interference from another group outside their community. Often, troubled relationships between individuals of different groups are viewed as activities against their respective communities and lead to violence. Such violence assumes the shape of caste conflict between these groups, and then we find the religion being blamed as the cause of the conflict.[88]

It is very difficult for an illiterate man to decide about a religious text; he would rather believe those he thinks are knowledgeable and well-read. Thus, he goes along with the opinions of the elders. For a serious student of history, however, it becomes obvious that these appear to be deliberate manipulations intended to justify an unjust system. What we often have for a reading of the Vedas is a commentary on them, albeit authoritative. But the beauty of the religion has been its resilience and the absence of any one single authoritative text. Hindus should be aware of the distinction between a sacred scripture and a book written by an individual such as Manusmriti. He was probably edited and reedited hundreds of times by scholars in different periods; each edition must have been colored by the opinion of the editor and his social milieu.[89]

INTER-COMMUNITY RELIGIOUS VIOLENCE

We now look at another angle of religious violence in India. This is even more dangerous given the meanings and proportions that it has assumed. What we are witnessing today are militant religious stands with regard to every aspect of community living. It is a well-known fact that, in the post-cold-war period, religion has come to play a dominant role. It is also a major factor in undermining the pluralistic basis of society.[90] Even a country like India, with its long-standing commitment to secularism and a strong tradition of liberal democratic institutions, is unable to escape the winds of intolerance. In fact, leaders of the religious majority in India have recently used the emotional appeal of religion to galvanize political power amongst the people. This has encouraged extremist religious forces in the country to create an environment of hostility, hatred, and fear vis-à-vis religious minorities. Religious violence in India is largely directed against minority communities — the followers of Islam and, more recently, followers of Christianity.

HINDU-MUSLIM ETHNIC CONFLICT

While the Hindu-Muslim rivalry has its roots in later-medieval history and the way those religious differences were handled by the colonial rulers, it is also true that, despite the secular program laid down in the Constitution[91] and protectionist measures adopted by successive governments toward minorities, the scars of partition of the country[92] have not completely healed. Today, the urban populations of both religions, especially those born after independence, largely overlook the history of partition. The main reason for this has been a successful working democracy that is bringing economic betterment. But the same is not equally true in small towns and rural areas where the people hold to religious differences much more passionately than their urban counterparts. Since India has a large rural population base and educational and social benefits have not gone to the grassroots level in the same measure as in urban areas, fanning religious resentments has been a common practice with political groups. Agricultural problems helped these groups ignite religious fervor among poor illiterate farmers and the agricultural working class. Sometimes money is used as an incentive to engage in religious militancy.

The middle class, till the 1980s, has largely kept away from this kind of religious violence. Thanks to a democratic political system that is able to provide practical benefits, inter-religion violence is largely unknown except in a few sporadic incidents and for reasons more political than religious. The 1980s, however, saw a virulent practice of religion in many communities. They indulged in militancy as a method of achieving separation or autonomy. What was basically a political movement for separation during the early period of colonial rule took on a religious flavor. Sikh groups in Punjab started using places of worship for preaching and planning attacks against other communities in their states and calling people to engage in a fight for independence. The administration's attempts to stop this kind of religious indoctrination were seen as interference and branded as attempts to suppress people of a particular religion.[93] The attacks and retaliations were branded by members of both religions as the fulfillment of their religious duty to defend their faith, and, for the first time, we witnessed organized religious violence.

The 1980s also saw the economically well-placed middle class, even in urban areas, looking toward religion as something more than an activity of personal preference. The Constitutional guarantees of minority rights and the legislative affirmative action for the minority groups since independence left a level of distaste among the majority community. This was an individual-based feeling rather than anything like group unrest. But the right-wing political players,[94] looking for a new agenda, lapped up this distaste in the majority community and projected it against minority appeasement activities. Those activities, just as the scars of the nation's partition and the religious violence that followed it were being forgotten, gave a new lease on life for these militant right-wing groups. Thankfully, Hindus do not have a system where a single head of a religious order gives sermons in a place of worship, exhorting the people to fight their fellow citizens of other communities. But politicians tried to fill in that gap largely with their cultural organs.

Religious groups that rallied under political influence have used religious figures to exhort people to violence. The trident in the hands of Lord Shiva is now seen by these fundamentalists as a weapon.[95] They distort the religious significance of the Hindu gods by saying they were a warrior community. Their most disturbing action is retelling the nation's partition in 1947 as a political mistake and a submission of the majority community. They feel they are being made to pay for being born into the majority community by having to appease the minorities. Such ideological distortion is branded as *Hindutva*[96] (a complete distortion of its original meaning regarding the essentials of Hindu philosophy — tolerance and compassion). Some *Hindutva* activists quote with approving bluster the dictum of Veer Savarkar (a freedom fighter and Hindu nationalist unfortunately remembered more for his views on Hinduism than his fight for independence) that for every Hindu woman dishonored by Muslims, a Muslim woman (if not a dozen) should be given the same treatment; and that would quickly teach the Muslims to behave. Another worrying trend has been the spreading of discontent among the majority community by reviving the historical facts and exhorting people to fight the minority community because of historical injustices. One such activity where both the communities have come very near civil war has been the Babri Masjid demolition.[97] A mosque where no prayers were offered for decades has become the bone of contention between the two communities. The Hindus say it is the birthplace of Lord Ram in Ayodhya (a town in Northern India) and that a Hindu place of worship was pulled down by the invading Muslim king Babur in the sixteenth century. It is a historical fact that the Muslim rulers attacked many temples and plundered them of their riches. The birthplaces of two of the most important members of the Hindu religious pantheon have been converted into Muslim shrines,[98] and the same is equally true of many other places of worship. But it is also a fact that, despite those activities, both communities lived in friendship and comradeship over the centuries and fought shoulder to shoulder against the colonial rulers. Now, when the people are adjusting to living together, these religious organizations in both communities use religion as a tool to incite the common man against his neighbor.

The events in Kashmir since independence in 1947 also had a major role in the changing mindset of the Hindu in the rest of the country. The Muslim fundamentalist parties, despite being citizens of India, owe their allegiance to leaders across the border and regularly engage in preaching against India as a Hindu country. Muslim religious leaders in the rest of the country have not worked toward integrating the community into secular India.[99] Whereas the Hindus have largely endorsed secularism, the same is not true of Muslims, especially those in the northern part of India, who are more insulated in their religion. And the minority support programs of the government, such as financial subsidies given to travel on hajj pilgrimage every year, only strengthened this feeling of insecurity among the majority, which was already disturbed by the role played by the religious heads of the Muslim groups. All this has enflamed passions in the majority community which was given more fuel by the Hindu militant groups which came to a head in December 1992 with the *Babri Masjid* dispute. The Hindu fundamentalists wanted the disputed structure pulled down and succeeded in razing it, but ignited the flames of communal tensions, which spread through the country, the embers of which still flare up at regular intervals.[100]

This brings us back to a lingering question. Can we call these militant groups Hindu fundamentalists? I find this an odd phrase, because *Hindu fundamentalism* is a contradiction in terms. Hinduism is a religion without fundamentals, no single sacred book, no Pope, no Hindu Sabbath, no uniform set of beliefs. The basic tenets of the religion are tolerance and compassion, as has been pointed out.[101] Why then is there such discontent in the majority community?

IDENTIFIABLE CAUSES OF HINDU DISCONTENT

Firstly, it has to do with a sense of identity. The quest for India's national identity through the route of Hindu religious nationalism began in the nine-teenth century and has continued ever since. In recent years, however, it has received an unprecedented boost from those communal forces that brought a virulent version of Hindu cultural chauvinism to the center stage of con-temporary politics and produced a warped perception of India's cultural past.[102] It is odd that Hindus should acquire a fundamentalist identity; for over 3,000 years, tolerance has been practiced here, and almost every faith has some place of worship in India. For this culture to suddenly be taken over by those with this notion of identity is a deeply worrying development. Unfortunately, recent political history has largely been tempered by an un-derstanding of the word *Hindu* as being against some other religious group.[103] This discontent is a vestige of colonial rule.

The British adopted a policy of divide and rule, which was not known before the East India Company came to this country. Though there were Muslim invasions, there were Hindus fighting in the Muslim armies. But the British changed that in a conscious effort to keep the two commu-nities separate and thereby rule the country. Even when they granted a min-imum franchise and self-government to the population, it was on communal lines. That is, Muslims voting for Muslim representatives, Hindus voting for Hindu representatives, to prevent mass mobilization that transcended religious grounds. When we analyze some of the elements of ethnic conflict, we also see human beings revealing their fundamental insecurities, irrespective of the geography they find themselves in. Basically, people want a life that answers their physical needs and allows them freedom to develop their minds. Ethnic conflicts arise when people in one group come to believe that they don't have those necessities while (and because) some other group does.[104]

ANTI-CHRISTIAN VIOLENCE

Another disturbing ethnic conflict in India involves violence directed against another minority, Christians. For centuries, the Christian community in India has engaged in community service and, to a lesser extent, proselytism. The religion has very strong roots, in the sense that we have our own indigenous branches like the Syrian Catholics, the born-again Christians, and so on. But throughout the more than five hundred years of its presence, Christianity has also engaged in conversion as a major activity. Today, most of the states in the Northeast witness the Christianizing of the community, and this even extends to tribal and indigenous people. The more enthusiastic and zealous among the preachers even preach condemnation of Hinduism because of the caste system and urge embracing Christianity because of its secular credentials.

We do not argue that the Christian community is not a part of mainstream Indian society.[105] In fact, the Christian community is known for its seminal work in the areas of education and healthcare among the masses. There isn't a town in India without an educational institution run by some Christian missionary group or another. A state like Kerala owes its high literacy rate, to a very large extent, to Christian missionary activities. Today we find the members of the various Christian groups engaging in healthcare services in remote areas of the country. But there have also been instances where these services have been offered in return for conversion to the faith.

Coupled with statements issued by religious leaders like Pope John Paul II asking for a new harvest in the faith in the new millennium, the funding of the Church from outside the country, and influencing the government to preserve the constitutional benefits of Hindus even after conversion to Christianity, the continuing efforts of the Catholic Church in the areas of healthcare and education were seen in a different light. Militant Hindus saw this as yet another attempt to rob them of their identity, feared the replication of the Northeast in the entire country, and saw this as a threat to the Hindu religion. The conversion laws passed by many State administrations only strengthened these beliefs, which even overlooked the likes of Mother Theresa and the charities initiated by her. The militant Hindu now thinks he has a mission to preserve his identity, and, as a result, we see violent attacks on the Church and its members.[106]

CONCLUSION

The original Hindu philosophy is a tolerant and relatively nonviolent one. Over the centuries, however, it evolved into a more rigid system of rituals, purity, and social hierarchy. Thankfully, the legal system for the last half-century has provided for the rights of members of every community regardless of its numerical strength, and the judiciary has upheld the secular credentials of this country. I began by saying Hinduism is more of a philosophy than a religion. For many of us today, religion is more spiritual than ritualistic. We perform the rituals because we believe them to be an act of internal discipline, which characterizes our way of life. Today, more than ever, we are also witnessing a very strong critique of the role of religion in our lives. Religion, however, has furthered spiritual understanding among us. For every instance like the communal riots in Gujarat, we have instances of the common man showing extreme courage in saving his neighbors, without considering the Islamic talisman he wears around his neck.

Even today, despite state funding for education, there is great demand for the education given in Church schools. It's also pertinent to look at why and how we have survived as a nation-state. The traditional explanations that have been offered for a successful nation-state have been geography, language, ethnicity, and religion. None of those exist in India, yet the country exists! The natural geography of the subcontinent with the Himalayas on the north and seas on the other sides has been breached by the partition of 1947. There are more than thirty officially recognized languages, more than one hundred dialects and languages without a recognized script, and, most importantly, the language changes every few miles. This land has every conceivable type of religion with complete freedom to practice and profess being guaranteed as a Constitutional right. We are an amalgamation of many ethnic groups. There are the Aryans, with different sub-groups, the Dravidians (our indigenous races), communities who came here as settlers, not to mention many other indigenous tribes. Ethnicity in India even cuts across national boundaries. A Kashmiri finds more in common with a fellow Kashmiri in Pakistan-occupied Kashmir than with a Delhiite. Yet we remain a unified nation!

But what does keep India flourishing if the traditional answers are faulty? It is a sense of belonging to a pluralistic society. Each Indian has more than one cultural identity of race, religion, and language, but there is also a single crosscurrent passing through them that is the ancient civilization that we trace ourselves back to. Both India and Pakistan have this shared history and remembering that helps us subscribe to the idea of pluralism. While the quest for identity remains a principal preoccupation, it involves multiple identities. While we disagree on certain things, we agree on others — including the right to disagree. What preserves us as a nation is the recognition of the freedom of the members of the community, the ideal of tolerance so seminal to the Hindu philosophy.[107]

Religion can be a force for peace, and we are working toward a revival of dialogue in relation to the politics of forgiveness and conflict transformation, even across cultural divides ridden with mistrust and violence.[108] As religious violence has a social aspect, if we solve social problems, perhaps we can mitigate the effects of violence and even stop the violence itself.[109]

Ahimsa literally means nonviolence, but it has a much broader meaning. It means that you may not offend anybody nor harbor uncharitable thoughts (even in connection with those you consider enemies). To one who follows this, there really are no enemies. A man who believes in the efficacy of this doctrine finds when he is about to reach the goal that the whole world is at his feet. If you express your love — ahimsa — in such a manner that it impresses itself indelibly upon your so-called enemy, he must return that love.[110] Thanks to Mahatma Gandhi, nonviolence hasn't lost any of its appeal. *Ahimsa Paramo Dharmah* (nonviolence is the greatest virtue) is the guiding spirit of this philosophy and way of life.

How do we strengthen this fundamental human value? We begin by looking into ourselves. Indian culture has lost the sense of community. If we begin by addressing this issue, we may see a more homogenous and cosmopolitan life, where caste and religion-based differentiations do not hold much weight. Second, this sense of community must transform itself into a social purpose. Somewhere in the period following independence, social purposes have given way to other priorities. If we prioritize the nation's development as our common goal and garner our energies for that purpose, we can put this fundamental human value into practice.[111] The third step is related to the second. Regarding this social purpose, society shall embark on this activity as a part of its dharma (duty). Whatever purpose the individual engages in shall be for the development of the nation, not for sectarian needs. Lastly, but most importantly, every individual should reject insularism, and specifically the feeling of superiority, which has been the bane of every culture. Indian religion and culture, though ever changing, have eternal values that provide answers to violence and sectarianism.

NOTES:

1. Verses from the Bhagavad Gita—Song of the God.

2. Haridas Bhattacharya, ed., *The Cultural Heritage of India*, Vol. 4 (Calcutta: RMIC, 1956).

3. M. Hiriyanna, *The Essentials of Indian Philosophy* (Bombay: Blackie & Sons, 1978).

4. T. K. Murthy, compiler, *Sai Digest* (a collection of sayings by Sathya Sai Baba) Vol. 3 (Magenta, Italy: European Foundation for the Dissemination of Human Values, 2000).

5. For more on this division, see R. C. Majumdar, ed., *The History and Culture of the Indian People* (Bombay: Bharatiya Vidya Bhawan, 1989).

6. Dwijendra Narayan Jha, "Looking for a Hindu Identity," Indian History Congress, 66th session.

7. M. Hiriyanna, *The Essentials of Indian Philosophy* (Bombay: Blackie & Sons, 1978).

8. A. L. Basham, *The Origins and Development of Classical Hinduism* (Boston: Beacon, 1989).

9. For further information, see R. C. Majumdar, ed., *The History and Culture of the Indian People* (see note 5 above).

10. S. Radhakrishnan, *The Hindu View of Life* (New York: Macmillan, 1962).

11. Swami Ranganathananda, *Eternal Values for a Changing Society* (Bombay: Bharatiya Vidya Bhavan, 1994).

12. Ibid., p. 32.

13. T. K. Murthy, compiler, *Sai Digest* (see note 4 above).

14. Ibid., pp. 142–44.

15. Understanding Hinduism and the cults in it: www.caic.org.au.

16. Swami Sivananda, *All about Hinduism* (Rishikesh, India: Divine Life Society, 1997), web edition 1999 at http://www.rsl.ukans.edu/~pkanagar/divine/.

17. S. Radhakrishnan, *Indian Philosophy* (2nd Edition) (New Delhi: Oxford, 1999).

18. T. K. Murthy, compiler, *Sai Digest* (see note 4 above).

19. R. K. Lahiri, *The Spirit of Indian Philosophy*, www.boloji.com/hinduism/ 113.htm.

20. Frank G. Morales, *Understanding Sanatana Dharma: The Philosophical Roots of Yoga* (introduction brochure of the International Sanatana Dharma Society); see also Frank G. Morales, *Radical Universalism: Does Hinduism Teach That All Religions Are the Same* (New Delhi: Voice of India, 2008).

21. P. V. Kane, *History of Dharmasastra* (Pune, India: Bhandarkar Oriental Research Institute, 1930).

22. Robert Lingat, *The Classical Law of India* (New Delhi: Oxford, 1998) p. 41.

23. Sudheer Birodkar, *Hindu History: Religious Tolerance and Secularism in India*: http://www.hindubooks.org/sudheer_birodkar/hindu_history/freegraphics.html.

24. Swami Sivananda, *All About Hinduism*, 6th Edition (Rishikesh, India: Divine Life Society, 1997); see especially the section on Hindu theology, referring to the various divisions and sects in the Hindu religion.

25. A. C. Bhaktivedanta Prabhupada, *Bhagavad-Gita As It Is* (Mumbai: Bhaktivedanta Book Trust, 1989). This has the original Sanskrit text, roman transliteration, English equivalence translation, and elaborate purports.

26. Swami Sivananda, *All About Hinduism* (see note 24 above).

27. Ibid., chap. 9.

28. Ibid.

29. For more information, refer to Haridas Bhattacharya, ed., *The Cultural Heritage of India* Vol. IV (see note 2 above).

30. Sri Aurobindo, *The Synthesis of Yoga* (Pondicherry, India: Sri Aurobindo Ashram, 1972); web edition available at www.surasa.net/aurobindo/synthesis.

31. John R. Hall, *Religion and Violence: Social Process in Comparative Perspective* (Cambridge: Cambridge University Press: 2001).

32. T. K. Murthy, compiler, *Sai Digest* (see note 4 above) p. 128.

33. Ibid.

34. "Confronting Violence: Bridging the Sacred–Secular Divide," at a workshop held in 2003: "Violence and Spirituality: Workshop on Ending Atrocities": www.hinduo nnet.com.

35. V. Jayaram, "Hinduism and Violence": http://www.hinduwebsite.com/hinduism /h_violence.asp.

36. Anantanand Rambachan, "The Co-Existence of Violence and Non-Violence in Hinduism": http://www.wcc-coe.org/wcc/what/interreligious/cd39-05.html.

37. Swami Chinmayananda, *The Holy Geeta: Commentary by Swami Chinmayananda* (Mumbai: Chinmaya Mission Trust, 1997).

38. Anantanand Rambachan, (see note 36 above).

39. For example, the Ramayana, another important scripture of the Hindu community, explains how Lord Rama, the central character of the scripture (and believed to be an incarnation of Lord Vishnu), explains the value of diplomacy and peaceful settlement of disputes in the Sundara Kanda (the fourth section of the epic). Essentially, these scriptures have attempted to cultivate a pacific attitude toward fellow citizens, looking at any act of violence as the last resort.

40. "Hindu-Muslim Tension: Its Cause and Cure," *Young India*, 29/5/1924; reproduced in M. K. Gandhi, *The Hindu-Muslim Unity*; this work is now part of *The Collected Works of Gandhi* (New Delhi: Publications Division, Ministry of Information and Broadcasting, Government of India, 1994).

41. Masakazu Tanaka, "Sacrifice Lost and Found: Colonial India and Post-colonial Lanka," *Zinbun* 34(I) (1999), pp. 127–46. For further information on these ritualistic practices and their history, see Vasandakumari Nair 1972, Tamils Reform Association, Singapore (1932–36), Academic Exercise (History), National University of Singapore.

42. Recently, governments of states where these practices are not only followed but publicized have enacted legislation against them and have initiated prosecution against perpetrators. State laws banning these practices are no longer seen as interference with religion, as in colonial India.

43. There have been reports of human sacrifices in the small town of Khurja in Uttar Pradesh, one of the largest Indian states, ostensibly for religious and family reasons, but

sometimes it is also to settle scores among the community members. These practices are usually advised by tantriks (called holy men, they are also known as sorcerers) to the poor and illiterate people, especially the lower-caste groups. For a report of one such occurrence, refer to www.observer.guardian.co.uk.

44. Henry Whitehead, *The Village Gods of South India* (London: Oxford University Press, 1921).

45. Instances of animal sacrifices are still witnessed, though very rarely, in temples devoted to worship of the female form in Northeast India: www.en/wikipedia.org/Shaktism.

46. For more on this subject, see Radhika Coomaraswamy, "Human Security and Gender Violence," *Economic and Political Weekly*, October 29, 2005.

47. Lord William Bentick, the Governor-General for the British East India Company in the early part of the nineteenth century, banned the practice of Sati, a rare instance when colonial government interfered with religious practices. Lord William Bentinck passed the Sati Regulation, XVII of 1827 on 4 December after assuming the governorship of Bengal. The regulation was clear, concise, and unequivocal in its condemnation of Sati, declaring it illegal and punishable by the criminal courts. C. A. Bayly, ed., *The Raj: India and the British 1600–1947* (London: National Portrait Gallery Publications, 1990. See also Nehaluddin Ahmad, "Sati Tradition: Widow Burning in India: A Socio-legal Examination": http://webjcli.ncl.ac.uk/2009/issue2/ahmad2.html.

48. Due to strict interpretation of the constitution regarding religious freedom, the state is wary of interfering with such events, except for condemning them and providing physical security at the site.

49. Susan Abraham, "The Deorala Judgment Glorifying Sati," *The Lawyers Collective* 12(6) (June, 1997): pp. 4–12.

50. Refer to human rights report on the caste dimension of the *devadasi* system at www.hrw.org. The study, "Sexual behaviour and vulnerability of highway sex workers to HIV/AIDS in Andhra Pradesh in the year 2004–2005 and reported in 2005," conducted by the Foundation for Rural and Social Development (FRSD), has found a high 30 per cent of them to be HIV positive and 40 per cent afflicted by other Sexually Transmitted Diseases.

51. *The Skeptics Dictionary*, (New Jersey: John Wiley & Sons, 2003).

52. www.eurosur.org.

53. www.un-instraw.org.

54. Ishwara Chandra Vidyasagar, Raja Ram Mohun Roy, and others used the Brahmmo Samaj as a platform to condemn these inhuman practices and traditions. With the support of the colonial government, they actively campaigned against them and even conducted widow remarriages.

55. The Hindu Succession Act of 1956 gives women equal share in the property of their husbands and parents. Women are now treated as equal heirs along with men in the succession laws. The Child Marriage Restraint Act makes it a punishable offense to marry off a girl under the age of eighteen.

56. BBC reports show the incidence of such homes in the holy city of Vrindavan, associated with the birthplace and childhood of Lord Krishna in Uttar Pradesh: www.news.bbc.co.uk/southasia. The situation is shown in the film *Water*, which describes the plight of these widows who have been suffering for decades.

57. The NCW study (1996, undertaken by Deepali Bhanot) stated that women are paid 2 rupees (about $.04) plus 250 grams of rice and 50 grams of dal (Indian millet) for singing *bhajans* (religious songs) eight hours a day. Some of the widows have been brought under the social security net, but the monthly payments due them remain unpaid because of bureaucratic hassles and lack of basic records relating to the number of widows. According to the NCW study, a sum of six million rupees lies unclaimed in banks because the account holders have died.

58. Further information on the Parasara Samhita, the Manu Samhita, and other religious texts can be found here: www.rcfm.org/positions/hindu. The Manu Samhita also ordains that widows shall have rights to *sthridhan* (property acquired by her at the time of marriage) and may remarry.

59. Preeti Gill and Uma Chakravarthi, Eds. *Shadow Lives: Writings on Widowhood* (Delhi: Kali for Women, 2001). See also Martha Allen Chen, ed., *Widows in India: Social Neglect and Public Action* (Delhi: Sage, 1998).

60. W. J. Wilkins, *Modern Hinduism: An Account of the Life and Religion of the Hindus in Northern India* (Delhi: BRPC, 2001), reprint, first edition in 1887.

61. See O. P. Gupta at www.hvk.org. According to him, Hindu scriptures prohibit "casteism." Concepts like castes by birth, untouchables, and so on, are prohibited by the Rig Veda, Ramayana, and Bhagavad Gita, and are drawn largely from later commentaries, which have largely been a reflection of the contemporary societal practices and did not have scriptural authority and support.

62. A. C. Bhaktivedanta Prabhupada, *Bhagavad-Gita As It Is* (see note 25 above).

63. *The Message of the Lord: A Practical Philosophy* (India: Sri Sathya Sai Books and Publications Trust, 2006). This work is based on the Bhagavad Gita and the teaching of Sri Satya Sai Baba Prashanthi Nilayam.

64. Charlene Leslie Chaden, *A Compendium of the Teachings of Sri Sathya Sai Baba*, (Bangalore, India: Sai Towers Publishing, 2005) pp. 68–69.

65. The Mahabharata, book 3, part 5, chapter 5. "The serpent said, 'O Yudhishthira, truth, charity, forgiveness, benevolence, benignity, kindness and the Veda which worketh the benefit of the four orders, which is the authority in matters of religion and which is true, are seen even in the Sudra. As regards the object to be known and which thou allegest is without both happiness and misery, I do not see any such that is devoid of these.' Yudhishthira said, 'Those characteristics that are present in a Sudra, do not exist in a Brahmana; nor do those that are in a Brahmana exist in a Sudra. And a Sudra is not a Sudra by birth alone — nor is a Brahmana a Brahmana by birth alone. He, it is said by the wise, in whom are seen those virtues is a Brahmana. And people term him a Sudra in whom those qualities do not exist, even though he be a Brahmana by birth.'" http://www.harekrsna.com/sun/editorials/mahabharata/vana/mahabharata179.htm.

66. A. C. Bhaktivedanta Prabhupada, *Bhagavad-Gita As It Is* (see note 25 above) part 4, chapter 4, p. 272.

67. W. J. Wilkins, *Modern Hinduism* (see note 60 above) p. 250.

68. R. S. Sharma, *Sudras in Ancient India* (Delhi: Motilal Banarsidas, 2002) p. 54.

69. Quotation from online version of Manusmriti. The textual reference is Manusmriti Vol. 10:65.

70. A. C. Bhaktivedanta Prabhupada, *Bhagavad-Gita As It Is* (see note 25 above) p. 273.

71. M. N. Rao, *Our God and Your Mind* (Bangalore: Sai Towers Publishers, 1992) p. 157.

72. www.hrw.org/reports/1999/india994-04.

73. For more on intelligentsia support for the *Dalit* movement and its literature, see Kancha Ilaiah, *Why I am Not a Hindu: A Sudra Critique of Hindutva Philosophy, Culture and Political Economy* (Calcutta: Samya, 1996).

74. Jayaraman V., "The Hindu Caste System": www.hinduwebsite.com/hinduism/h_caste.asp.

75. Mukul Sharma makes an extensive reference to the Dalit situation in India in his article, "Dalit Situation in India": http://www.boell-india.org/pics/asp/suche_en.asp?language=englisch&qu=mukul+sharma&ct=boell&Trefferquote=160&naechste.x=67&naechste.y=5&naechste=++%3E%3E++&SearchPage=8. For more on this topic, see Mukul Sharma, *Landscapes and Lives: Environmental Dispatches on Rural India* (New Delhi: O.U.P., 2001) and Dipankar Gupta, *Interrogating Caste: Understanding Hierarchy and Difference in Indian Society* (Delhi: Penguin, 2000).

76. Bipan Chandra, ed., *India's Struggle for Independence: 1857–1947* (New Delhi: Viking, 1988) pp. 230–34. While Ambedkar held that the caste system had all its roots in religion, Gandhi appealed to the spiritual content of the religion to oppose the system. He largely appealed to the Gita in support of his argument that the caste system was an economic and social division based on convenience rather than an institution with a religious sanction. Further readings include Eleanor Zelliot, "Gandhi and Ambedkar: A Study in Leadership," in E. Zelliot, *From Untouchable to Dalit: Essays on the Ambedkar Movement* (New Delhi: Manohar, 1992) pp.160–65; and Sandeep Pendse, ed., *At Crossroads: Dalit Movement Today* (Bombay: Vikas Adhyayan Kendra, 1994) pp. 69–82.

77. Human Rights Watch, *Broken People: Caste Violence against India's "Untouchables"*: www.hrw.org/legacy/reports/1999/india/.

78. .See note 72 above; Human Rights Watch interview with R. Balakrishnan, chairman of the Tamil Nadu Commission for Scheduled Castes and Scheduled Tribes, Madras, February 13, 1998. R. M. Pal, "The Caste System and Human Rights Violations," in *Human Rights from the Dalit Perspective* [no date] (Madras: Dalit Liberation Education Trust).

79. See note 72 above.

80. For more information, visit the website of the Tamil Nadu *Dalit* women's movement: www.ngosindia.com/a-z/nfdw.htm.

81. Refer to www.hrw.org/reports/1999/India.

82. The Government of India runs an affirmative-action program aimed at the welfare of the backward classes of the population. It is, in fact, a constitutionally sanctioned program.

83. Dr. Kancha Iliah's interview with Yoginder Sikand on the necessity for dalitisation is available at www.ambedkar.org/reformers/KanchaIlaiah.htm.

84. Dr. Iliah's interview is in *Christian Today*, November 12, 2005.

85. Scholars refer to this scripture as the herald and religious sanction of the caste system. In fact, it aimed exactly at the opposite, demonstrating the equality of the various

sections of the population by saying that every person is equally important in the grand cosmic plan.

86. Mukul Sharma, "Dalit Situation in India" (see note 75 above).

87. Mukul Sharma, in his article "Dalit Situation in India," says the Rig-Vedic quotation, discussed earlier in this text, is the source of caste discrimination and violence. He opines that the texts condemned the "lowly sudras" to occupy a subordinate position because they were born from the feet of the *Purusa* (cosmic person). While he read the first few lines of the Rig-Vedic hymn, he lacks a complete understanding of it. It states that the cosmic person has no beginning or end and no gradations at all; it doesn't refer to any work as high or low but as a duty to be performed.

88. An example of this is marriage. If a person finds his partner outside his community, the group of elders loses no time in excommunicating that person from the community, in which he and his family can no longer live. Instances abound of violent attacks on family members — family and community honor having been affected. There are instances when such marriages were annulled by community elders. The parties sometimes married again despite being validly married under the law. These instances are not just between upper and lower castes but also within those categories. None of them have fundamental religious sanction; marriage procedures followed by Hindus developed in customary law or were mentioned in fables associated with religious texts.

89. V. Raghavan, "Variety and Integration in the Pattern of Indian Culture" [Sanskritization], *Far Eastern Quarterly* 15 (1956): pp. 497–505.

90. For more on sociology of religion, see John R. Hall, "Religion and Violence: Social Processes in Comparative Perspective," Michele Dillon, ed., *Handbook for the Sociology of Religion* (Cambridge: Cambridge University Press, 2003) pp. 359–81.

91. The Constitution, with secularism as its main agenda, allows every person to practice and preach his religion freely. It allows individuals the freedom to be governed by personal laws of the community.

92. Colonial India was partitioned into two independent nations in August 1947 on a religious basis, an idea promoted by Mohammed Ali Jinnah. There was a massive transfer of people living on either side of the border who had to be uprooted from their ancestral homes because of their religions. Massive violence followed this division of the country.

93. The government had to send the army into the Golden Temple premises (the highest religious seat of Sikhism) to wipe out militants operating from inside the temple in the year 1984. This act, though necessitated by circumstances, increased tension between the communities.

94. Over the last two decades, India has witnessed the rise of right-wing groups to political power at both the federal and the state level. Their political elevation has largely been through appeal to the religion of the majority community. With strong organizational support of nonpolitical groups, like the RSS, and Hindu religious groups, like Vishwa Hindu Parishad, they reach out to the common man and appeal for support in their bid to seek power.

95. The Vishwa Hindu Parishad and Bajrang Dal are parts of the *sangh parivar* (a euphemism for Hindu family, but which came to be a common name for all the right-wing groups), represented on the political scene by the Bharatiya Janata Party. They use the trident, the foremost symbol associated with Lord Shiva and the denomination of Shaivism and all its mutated forms, as a weapon of protection.

96. Today *Hindutva* is explained by these groups as putting Hindu at the center of all activity, despite putting others in a disadvantaged position. These right-wing groups understand it to mean there isn't anything except the Hindu.

97. A mosque constructed on the site of a temple at the birthplace of Lord Ram (the most important god in the Hindu pantheon) was pulled down by right-wing Hindu religious groups, with active support from political groups, in December 1992.

98. We find mosques that were constructed on temples believed to be dedicated to the birthplaces of Lord Rama and Lord Krishna at Ayodhya and Mathura respectively, important and religiously sensitive towns in Uttar Pradesh. The mosques appear to be fifteenth- and sixteenth-century constructions.

99. Birodkar, *Hindu History* (see note 23 above).

100. For information on Hindu right-wing groups' involvement in the power structure, see Romain Maitra, *In Search of True Democracy: Hindu Power Politics*: http://mondediplo.com/1999/09/11india.

101. Shashi Tharoor makes an interesting analysis of the reasons for this ethnic conflict. Read more on this from his talk at the Carnegie Council: www.cceia.org/shashitharoor.

102. Dwijendra Narayan Jha, "Looking for a Hindu Identity" (see note 6 above).

103. M. V. R. Sastry's reply to Kancha Iliah's article "Why I am Not a Hindu": www.bharatvani.org.

104. Amartya Sen makes an interesting analysis of this identity search in his work on identity and violence, *Illusion of Destiny* (London: W. W. Norton, 2006).

105. Refer to the statement of Rev. James Massey, a Minister of the Church of North India, saying that caste insecurity is the root factor for anti-Christian violence in India: www.ncccusa.org.

106. There have been instances of violent physical attacks on members of the Catholic Church all over the country, largely directed at conversion efforts. States like Tamil Nadu in Southern India legislated support to conversion activities of the Church, funded by ministries from outside the country. Unfortunately, the attacks were also directed against the social activities undertaken by church groups, with Christians being attacked while in performance of their service-related work. Graham Staines, an Australian missionary, known for his work in leprosy eradication in one of the backward districts of the State of Orissa in Eastern India, was killed by Hindu fundamentalists.

107. Shashi Tharoor's interview on pluralism in *The Hindu*, November 13, 2005.

108. Muchkund Dubey, "Challenges of Pluralism: Reaching out to Minority Communities," *The Times of India*, February 25, 1999.

109. For more on this aspect, see Amartya Sen, *Illusion of Destiny* (see note 104 above).

110. Jayaram V., "Hinduism and Violence": http://hinduwebsite.com/hinduism /h_violence.asp.

111. A. P. J. Abdul Kalam, *Ignited Minds* (Delhi: Penguin, 2002).

COMMENTS ON SAI RAMANI GARIMELLA'S ESSAY

ANDREW L. GLUCK

I would like to thank Professor Ramani for enlightening us so much about Hinduism and its relationship to violence. Although I have been exposed to Hindu ideas for many years, this was a real learning experience for me. Therefore, my remarks should be viewed as those of a nonexpert and, indeed, one to whom Hinduism is quite foreign.

Having said that, however, we should admit that Hindu and Western thought are not entirely foreign from or incommensurable with one another. We in the West are acquainted with monism and polytheism as well as with rigid class systems. So my remarks will inevitably emerge out of a Western point of view in the hope that some analogies can indeed be drawn.

It is extremely interesting to me that Hinduism, whether as a philosophy or religion, encompasses so many diverse ways of thinking. It might be baffling for Hindus to attempt to comprehend the rigid distinctions we make in the West between Judaism, Christianity, and Islam. It is true, of course, that the caste system traditionally created rigid divisions within Hindu society, even though such rigidity is not to be found in the ancient sources. Yet all of the castes considered themselves to be part of one overarching system — social, philosophical, and religious. This cannot be said of the sectarian divisions that developed within the Abrahamic tradition. (In fact, Professor Ramani seems to indicate that even such sects as Jains and Sikhs are broadly considered to be Hindu. This indicates a great tolerance within Hinduism that we in the West could learn much from.)

I will attempt to ignore recent aberrations such as the kinds of fundamentalisms developed both by upper- and lower-caste Hindus in recent years since they obviously are not traditional. I will focus on the caste system itself, which almost everyone in the West associates with traditional Hinduism. For purposes of argument, I will agree with Professor Ramani that

125

such a rigid class system is not really demanded by the great Hindu scriptural sources, and that many devout Hindus, such as Professor Ramani herself, reject it. Nevertheless, I find it interesting that it became so crystallized and rigidified.

We in the West know quite a bit about class systems. Some of us view them as totally evil, while others, like myself, see some provisional value in distinct traditions carried forward by social classes and families. I think we all — Westerners and Hindus alike — see such class distinctions as ultimately evil or at least irrelevant to spiritual perfection. My question is why the class system in India was so much more rigid than in the West. Is it because Western culture and religion are more worldly and, therefore, we are bothered more by social injustice? Despite the evils of slavery in the West, we do (historically) find slaves there being freed — and even marrying into upper-class families. Apparently, such fluidity was not allowed by traditional Hindu society. With all the bad things that the British might have done in India, they should perhaps be given credit for abolishing the caste system — at least legally.

I find it extremely interesting that Hinduism, which in other respects is so tolerant and accepting, clung to the caste system for so long. I tend to view it as part and parcel of a very fundamental evil tendency that can be found in just about all human societies and religions.

Sai Ramani Garimella's Reply

Jains, Buddhists, and the Sikhs have their theological and philosophical bases in Hindu thought. The holy book of the Sikhs, for instance, has many references to the Hindu gods. Even the legislation, for that matter, treats these religions as offshoots of the Hindu religion.

I do not think that Hinduism was less worldly and more mystical and hence less concerned with social justice. But certain traditions that have been built into it make it seem more ritualistic and promote procedures that retard social progress. This conflict between the original ideas and the developed practices is quite evident today. Hence, those practices are coming under a great deal of scrutiny.

Hinduism as a philosophical/religious system has largely been left uncodified, even today. The absence of a codified authority in fact enriched the literature of the religion. But this did have pitfalls. One of them is that we very largely failed to expect a difference between the religion and the commentaries on religion, and so took it for granted that the commentaries were the perfect authorities on the textual ordinances. The development and practice of the caste system is an unfortunate result of this tendency.

Hinduism, according to most authors, is a collective noun given to practices such as this, and thus it came to be known that Hinduism practiced the caste system. But historically, most of these practices, which were given the name of caste system, were largely concerned with temporal activities, and only peripherally with the religious and spiritual life. Then, the religion itself ordained that the so-called *varna* should not be seen as discriminatory in nature.

The classification of society into four distinctive classes or castes was made not according to birth but according to *guna, karma, swabhav* — that is, qualities, actions, and nature or aptitude. The Shukraniti states, "*Na jatya brahmanashchatra kshatriyo vaishya eva na shudro na cha vai mlechao, bhedita gunakarmabhih* (By birth nobody is a Brahmin, Kshatriya, Vaishya, Shudra, or Mlecho; the distinction is due to qualities and actions or deeds)."

This brings me to ask why the religion as practiced in the society clung to the caste system for so long. The medieval period, which saw the caste system mean much more than the classification as seen in the Vedas, turned the system itself into some kind of social order, and the organized political society at that time found it very convenient to adopt this system to further its political and economic ends. The advent of Muslim rule only strengthened this practice. There was not much support for the saner voices of religious tolerance, as the political structure used these practices to garner support for their programs of conquest.

The caste system, contrary to the predominant idea of its being a religious offshoot, was not a major feature of the Vedic period. The early Vedic period was more concerned with the family identity of people than with castes — as is evident from the Rig-Vedic hymns. That the caste system took on a more rigid social form was a post-Vedic development. It is also wrong to assume that the Hindu ideas of karma and rebirth contributed to the caste system. Birth and caste do not figure in the content of the karmic philosophy. Karmic philosophy preached the necessity of action and or-dained people to act for the benefit of humankind.

There was originally no physical suppression of castes. Rather, it was a limitation of opportunities, imposed largely by traditions and beliefs drawn from religious practices. The system survived for a long time because the continuance of it proved to be advantageous to most classes in the society — the ruling classes, the members of the royal court, the invaders coming from the west, all of them found reasons to perpetuate the caste divisions. In support of their real motivations, they quoted religious verses, which were to a very large extent unwritten and passed on from generation to generation through oral renditions. The absence of the written word allowed these classes to add new verses into these religious texts, thus justifying their prac-tices. Thus survived one of the most unjust systems in human relations. Being preoccupied at most times with the political machinations in the royal court, the members of the so-called upper classes hardly spared time to hu-manize this system and work toward its eradication.

I would say with conviction, therefore, that the caste system survived in India largely because of the social structure that created it, rather than from any scriptural support. It did have religious support through later interpretations, but to quote the scriptures as supporting the caste system is far from the truth.

Jewish Fundamentalism and Violence

Andrew L. Gluck

Is there a significant causal or meaningful connection between traditional Judaism and violence? That is the question addressed by this essay.[1] A great deal of controversy currently surrounds historical research regarding Jewish violence (and contemplations of it) against Gentiles.[2] I rely upon historians for the facts, but I desire to analyze current underlying psychological and cultural trends. They should be distinguished from one another. Facts can be things of the past, freak incidents, and so forth, and underlying trends may not yet have expressed themselves clearly or fully. At times, historical patterns can belie the real underlying dynamics that await the proper circumstances for their fruition. Furthermore, both historical patterns and underlying psychic trends should never be confused with the kind of unvarying laws that we seek in the natural sciences.

We cannot deal here with the question of whether such psychological and cultural phenomena have real causal power, though I tend to think they do. Be that as it may, I would still think that those inner psychological trends, which I mean to unearth, are significant and especially so if we believe human beings can learn from them and adjust their behavior accordingly. In order to excavate them, we require something like a phenomenological investigation, though such understanding as can be derived from it will not be, strictly speaking, empirical. It should not be confused with sociological or historical generalizations that purport to be universal. It will merely elucidate the life of a particular religion and people just as the aforementioned phenomenological investigations shed light on particular individuals.

Nevertheless, the acquisition of such understanding involves the apprehension of actual human utterances in a manner somewhat analogous to how psychopathologists listen to subjective complaints or to the ravings of the severely mentally ill. What may occur in such investigations is the coming into prominent display of certain cultural motifs or ideal types (in a Weberian sense) that may not depict the actual life of the people. It is analogous to mental patients' suicide threats, which usually are not acted upon. Therefore, this investigation must begin with a disclaimer. If I got the facts wrong on occasion, I would still hope that I analyzed the psychological trends correctly. And if I erred regarding the latter, let us hope it is an error on the side of caution that might still be of heuristic value for decision making in the future.

I would also like to state my opinion that violence is not a major Jewish problem *at the present time.* That is not to say there has not been violence (against outsiders and within the community) or that there will be none. But, compared to many other religions, Jews are not profoundly guilty of violence. The situation in Israel is of great concern and is a problem with no easy answers. Without absolving Israelis of any culpability, I still think that most of the violence there is not the fault of Jews or Judaism, though some of it surely is. Nevertheless, one must not be fooled into thinking that violence cannot become a major Jewish problem. I am quite concerned about possible violent consequences of trends in Jewish thought in the Holy Land and the Diaspora — but mostly in the former.[2]

Those who read my introduction to this book will recall that Judaism generally forswears the use of coercive force against non-Jews (at least until the coming of the messiah). The one major historical and possibly theological exception to that, however, regards the Holy Land. The following example may be of some value. We often find the curious yet somewhat widespread phenomenon of liberal secular Jews who generally are reluctant to support the use of force in American foreign policy but are highly supportive of no less aggressive policies of Israeli governments. This may not be the best example of religiously inspired violence in Judaism since support for Israel can also be viewed in completely nonreligious terms as a just war to defend a small, outnumbered nation, or as a purely ethnic or tribal defensive instinct. I use this flawed example nevertheless because I don't want to restrict my consideration of Judaism to Orthodox Jews or even to traditional Jews. Liberal secular Jews are also influenced by Jewish tradition even though they may not be as aware of it as those who are more traditional or Orthodox.

In the past, a majority of Orthodox Jews were anti-Zionist, but today the majority are enthusiastic in their support of the Jewish state. At first they were bothered by traditions regarding the return to the Holy Land being dependent upon messianic redemption. But those traditions were put aside under the influence of even greater concerns. For them, defense of the State of Israel has become a proxy for their underlying concern for the Jewish people and the land of Israel. Religion and nationalism are not completely separate in Judaism (as I hope to elucidate) and the significance of Israel (both land and people) emerges out of the Hebrew Bible, the founding document of Judaism.

PEOPLEHOOD AND RELIGION

One of the most prominent and distinctive features of Judaism as a religion is that it is a secondary phenomenon (and irrevocably attached) to Jewish peoplehood. This may be denied by some, but the Bible itself speaks of God choosing the Jewish people (descendants of Abraham, Isaac, and Jacob) long before it speaks of anything remotely resembling a Jewish religion.[3] It was the rabbis who largely created Judaism as a religion, in terms of both practices and beliefs. Since Jewish belief is centered on divine commandments, a religion completely based upon rabbinic ordinances would be unacceptable. For that reason, the rabbis made an effort to deduce their ordinances and beliefs from the Bible. But this connection was often tenuous, because the biblical sources were more concerned with ethical precepts, peoplehood, and priestly rites than with the popular religious ceremonial performances (*mitzvot*) that the rabbis enacted and that still characterize Orthodox Judaism today.[4] In a sense, those ceremonies are a democratization of the priestly rites. Those actual priestly rites have not been in force for a long time (though many seem to yearn for their restoration), but the seminal concern for Jewish peoplehood remains very much alive along with the strong ethical orientation of the Bible.[5] But the latter is no longer the sole property of the Jews and sometimes gets downplayed as not specifically Jewish. In other words, the chosenness of the Jewish people seems to be the most fundamental aspect of the Jewish religion, with the exception of belief in the existence of one God and the ethical precepts.[6] And those latter concerns are now shared to one extent or another with other religions.

A contrast of Judaism with Christianity and Islam may be instructive. The significance of peoplehood is very different in the three religions. In both of the later religions, the founding ethnic group (Jews and Arabs, respectively) has some importance, but pales in significance with universal ideas and values.[7] In Judaism, peoplehood shares center stage with those more universal concerns.[8] Therefore, a major concern in Judaism (though perhaps secondary to ethical monotheism in its more enlightened versions) is the survival of the Jewish people. That concern has often been rationalized as being instrumental to more universal ones and/or as a direct inference from revealed Jewish law, but it exists as a basic datum nevertheless.

Something else that the rabbis added on top of that primary concern was a religion that could deal well with oppression by accepting it and not responding to it head-on. That was the price for Jewish survival and sometimes was even rationalized as an ethical virtue.[9] Yet the underpinnings of that quietist approach were always wobbly, especially since they included belief in the special status of the Jewish people. Once the restraints of an oppressive environment and rabbinic authority were lifted, the potential for violence against non-Jews increased.

I will attempt to argue that, as difficult as it may be to differentiate the two phenomena, traditional Judaism tends to restrain violence against non-Jews while Jewish fundamentalism encourages it to a certain extent. On the other hand, traditional Orthodoxy has a long history of violence against members of the Jewish community deemed sinners or heretics.[10] This was not substantially different from many other religious traditions prior to modernity and seems to be largely a thing of the past (although some communities, particularly in Israel, still practice it). We have not, however, distinguished Orthodoxy and fundamentalism in a satisfactory manner or discussed their relationship to one another. I would ask the reader's indulgence while we attempt to do just that. Perhaps we can begin by describing two fairly recent events.

RECENT CASES OF JEWISH RELIGIOUS VIOLENCE

On February 25, 1994, we were shocked by an apparently unprecedented act of violence. Baruch Goldstein, an Orthodox Jewish physician, originally from Brooklyn and a disciple of Rabbi Meir Kahane, murdered 29 Muslim worshippers in the Machpelah Cave in Hebron: a site sacred to Jews and

Muslims as the burial place of Abraham, Isaac, and Jacob. The date of that massacre was also sacred to both faiths in their respective calendars (Purim and Ramadan). There had been antecedents, of course, both in Israel and in the United States, but, in recent memory, nothing of that magnitude or perpetrated by a man of such intellectual and educational attainment.

Again, on November 4, 1995, an immense tragedy struck. Yigal Amir, a young right-wing religious and political fanatic, assassinated Israeli Prime Minister Yitzhak Rabin, who had been conducting peace negotiations and territorial compromise with the Palestinians. Both violent events occurred in the Holy Land — perhaps not a coincidence. Amir also had an interesting biography. His parents were Yemenite Jews (often thought of as gentle and nonviolent). His father was a rabbi and he was a law student at Bar Ilan University, the pride of Modern Orthodoxy in Israel. While there, he joined a radical right-wing movement that opposed the peace talks that Rabin was conducting. The fact that right-wing rabbis indoctrinated this bright young man is well documented, yet he stated unequivocally that he consulted no one prior to his terrible deed. This is quite significant.

The reason those events so shocked the Jewish world had little to do with their essential enormity or even their deadly consequences. Jews, and Israelis in particular, have become inured to violence and the reporting of violence in Israel. But violence inspired by Judaism is quite another matter. For many centuries, a naive belief persisted regarding such violence — that is, that it hardly existed at all. Compared with their Christian and Muslim neighbors — so the standard belief went, — observant Jews were a gentle, nonviolent people. Perhaps they were too nonviolent for their own good!

Since the establishment of the State of Israel, that belief was modified to insist that Jews now were quite adept at self-defense and that such defensive violence was indeed sanctioned by Judaism. The Israeli was viewed as a new and perhaps superior type of Jew — more masculine and assertive, far less accommodating. But violence of any sort was still considered somewhat alien to the traditional Jewish character and moral outlook. This was symbolized by Prime Minister Golda Meir's quip that she could forgive the Arabs for everything except forcing the Israelis to kill them. Another good example is the following excerpt from Rabbi Norman Lamm's eulogy for Prime Minister Rabin at Yeshiva University on November 6, 1995:

Let me begin these few ruminations by saying that in addition to shock and grief, I for one experienced a vital element of *teshuvah*,[11] and that is *bushah*, shame. I am chagrined that it was a Jew who murdered the prime Minister. I was always proud that Jews do not behave in this way…And I am deeply embarrassed that it was one of us — a religious university student, who did it — even if he is a mad man. . . . Yigal Amir and Baruch Goldstein were, otherwise, fine representatives of what we stand for. So we have a lot of thinking and pondering to do.

Since the two aforementioned murders occurred, there has indeed been some soul searching among Jews (mostly in Israel) and some unpleasant historical claims have been revived regarding previous, relatively unknown episodes of Jewish violence against both Gentiles and fellow Jews.[12] The veracity of those claims, and/or the extent to which they are valid, is a hotly contended issue. But this chapter does not purport to be a historical treatment or even a review of the historiography. It is an attempt to understand what is lurking in the psyches of some religious Jews today.[13] Therefore, I will focus only on those two well-documented cases of murder perpetrated by religious Jews in relatively recent times.[14]

One thing that both murderers had in common, in my view, was a Jewish fundamentalist outlook. This assertion may seem unwarranted to some, but I will present arguments for it. At any rate, both men were surely observant, Orthodox, educated, and extremely committed Jews. What is also interesting is the fact that both had been educated within what one might call mainstream Orthodox Jewish institutions.[15] So in some sense both could claim to be normative Orthodox Jews and not just Jews by an accident of birth or members of some marginal or extreme Jewish sect. The Orthodox community accepted them as good Jews.

It is true, however, that neither was a typical Orthodox Jew and we must keep this in mind. But I know of no evidence that either of them was a "mad man." This may indeed be significant because, at times, the effects of religion and insanity can be quite similar. We need to pay attention to this fact in order to make the proper distinctions between the kind of irrationality that is typical of normal human life (whether it be religious or secular) and truly abnormal manifestations of religious zeal. The fact that neither man consulted rabbis prior to his act is also significant. Yet both were surely under the influence of Orthodox rabbis. Therefore, the key to understanding fundamentalist Judaism may not be to see it as identical to or as antithetical to Orthodoxy — but as a curious subset of it.

FUNDAMENTALISM AND ORTHODOXY

One typical hallmark of Orthodox Judaism, based on my experience and that of many others, is the apparent inability or unwillingness to make personal decisions regarding ethical issues — referring such issues to rabbinic authorities instead.[16] Fundamentalists share that attitude but tend to internalize some even more "authoritative" views to a remarkable extent. Such an approach sets them somewhat apart from the other typically more cautious and nuanced Orthodox Jews. Hence, fundamentalists might have less need for contemporary rabbinic guidance.[17] Interestingly, however, Orthodox Jews themselves have not made a serious attempt to distinguish these two approaches to Judaism.

Most Orthodox Jews are nonviolent and follow the guidance of rabbinic authorities, who have been rather effective in restraining violence both within the community and against non-Jews. In part, however, this state of peace was enforced by words of hostility and domination. This is not my own insight but I learned it from David Hartman, whose views can be found in his books and on the Hartman Institute website. The idea of his that I consider quite important is that the rabbis, when faced with a hostile world, did not counsel a violent response but instead legislated rights and obligations of Gentiles that often reek of hostility and contempt. Legal decisions were used as psychological weapons of war. This state of affairs has generally prevailed for almost two thousand years. Although this method was quite effective in restraining violence at the time, it left an unfortunate legacy of contempt on the part of those who were not able to understand the causes and purposes of those rabbinic utterances.

In general, the Jew has inflicted most of his violent tendencies upon himself. Perhaps most historical cases of violence within Jewish communities, rather than being spontaneous or vigilante violence, were inflicted by Jewish courts as punishment. Recently, however, some Orthodox rabbis have shown more radical attitudes. They quote biblical, Talmudic, and later authorities to justify aggressive and even violent acts in a way that is somewhat untraditional.[18] Yet the religious ideas that they employ are not essentially different from those of more traditional Orthodox Jews. Perhaps these fundamentalists are less concerned with the minutiae of observance of the law and more concerned with romantic notions of land and people. But these are mere tendencies and the two are very much part of the same self-defined group.

In a period when most Jews have rejected Jewish law and Orthodoxy, mainstream Orthodox authorities may view such fundamentalist activists as important allies. This would explain the appearance at the funeral of Meir Kahane[19] of some important leaders of Orthodox Judaism in the United States. There has, therefore, been relatively little effort on the part of traditional Judaism to divorce itself from fundamentalist Judaism as it has from Reform, Reconstructionist, and Conservative Judaism.[20] Nor have fundamentalists divorced themselves from Orthodox Judaism.[21] In the minds of Amir and Goldstein, they were good Orthodox Jews and were accepted as such by that community. We must take that claim quite seriously and not whitewash it with the facile claim that what they did was contrary to Judaism.

No doubt, those actions were anathema to Judaism in its most widespread interpretation. Yet the suspicion remains that there is another strand of Judaism that accepts and even applauds such actions. A few months prior to Amir's crime, a prominent rabbi in Brooklyn (Abraham Hecht) justified the assassination of Prime Minister Rabin, invoking the authority of Moses Maimonides,[22] who had indeed allowed the killing of heretics without a trial[23] and who had also made light of the killing of certain non-Jews.[24]

As noted previously, violence against nonconformists was once common — and is still sometimes found in extreme right-wing Orthodox communities. But within mainstream traditional communities it has died out. Oftentimes, violence against fellow Jews is linked to a perceived threat from the detested non-Jewish world. The two murderers had in common an extreme nationalism bordering on racism. While one aimed his weapon at a fellow Jew and the other at Muslims, both were motivated by fear that part of the land of Israel would be turned over to non-Jews. That fear unifies many traditional Jews. Therefore, the act of Goldstein seems to me to be more paradigmatic and did indeed find more support among Jews.[25]

REACTIONS TO ACTS OF RELIGIOUSLY INSPIRED VIOLENCE

As perplexing and astounding as both those murders were, some of the reactions to Goldstein were even more so. A segment of Jewish nationalists took it upon themselves to glorify his deed and turn his grave into a shrine. I myself witnessed a well-meaning moderate rabbi attempt to come to grips with what Goldstein had done through what appeared to me to be hagiographic descriptions of his life.[26] A legend later emerged that Goldstein had been aware of impending terrorist attacks by the very individuals whom he had shot, and that he struck in order to forestall them.[27] A widely read newspaper in the Orthodox community called *The Jewish Press*, which had employed Meir Kahane as an editor in the 1960s, spearheaded such claims.

This conspiratorial theory is still touted by many Orthodox Jews. When the question arose as to why Goldstein had not told the authorities about his information, further justifications were concocted. He had indeed informed the authorities, but there was a conspiracy on the part of the government and the army to suppress such reports — so he was forced to act alone.[28] Perhaps the most disturbing justifications of Goldstein's actions, however, are to be found in a small book written partly by Rabbi Yitzhak Ginsburg[29] and entitled *Baruch Ha-Gever*.[30] Ginsburg combines traditional with quasi postmodern concepts that form both a justification for and an exaltation of murder.

We are not interested in analyzing the fascistic philosophy of Yitzhak Ginsburg; it has been done well by Don Seeman (see note 34). While Ginsburg's views don't represent Orthodox Judaism, past or present, we will be exploring whether they may have roots in traditional Jewish concepts and current Jewish thinking. Ginsburg was and still is loosely affiliated with the Lubavitcher movement, one of the Hassidic sects in Judaism. His followers portray him as a master of Jewish mysticism, mathematics, music, and philosophy. The movement of which he still considers himself a part has been spectacularly successful and is responsible for turning many secular Jews to Orthodox Judaism.[31] He continues to administer an outreach organization and is involved in other Jewish organizations that may be loosely affiliated with *Chabad* (the Lubavitcher movement).[32] He has been imprisoned in Israel under that country's rather stringent laws against racism and incitement to violence.

Ginsburg argues that the murders perpetrated by Goldstein constituted an act of expressing and achieving intimacy with God! Underlying this claim is a peculiar notion of "divine honor."[33]

> The crown that sits atop The Deed (*ha-ma'aseh*, i.e., the killings in Hebron) is, of course, the sanctification of the divine Name that it entails. The sanctification of the divine Name that was inherent to that Deed must be judged from several perspectives — from the perspective of The Deed itself and the manner of its perpetration, from the perspective of the impression that it made upon Jews, and from the perspective of the impression that it made upon the Gentiles. From the perspective of The Deed, someone who performs a commandment through personal sacrifice, and who diminishes his own honor (*kavod*) in order to magnify the honor of heaven (*kavod shamayim*), has certainly sanctified the divine Name through this.[34]

A number of questions arise from this. While I do not intend to do an in-depth analysis, I would like to point out certain motifs. Sanctification of the divine Name seems to be independent of any positive impression that such a deed makes on Gentiles but to be dependent upon (or at least related to) the impression it makes on Jews. He goes on to discuss the value of the deed in terms of restoring Jewish honor, and seems to extol violence as a means to that end. Thus, a curious connection is established between increasing God's glory/honor and increasing the honor of the Jewish people. This may have its roots in kabbalistic thinking, which allows for the efficacy of human (Jewish) actions for the restoration of divine unity or integrity.

There is also a complete disconnect between the way such a deed is perceived by Gentiles and the way it is perceived by God and the Jewish people. In my view, it is this very disparity between Israel and the other nations that can make such wickedness laudatory. But we have seen (see note 30) how, in Exodus, the obtaining of divine honor was connected with the Egyptians recognizing God as the Lord of the universe. In Ginsburg's thinking, on the other hand, it is as if Jews and Gentiles were separate species. And indeed, Ginsburg has opined elsewhere that in theory one can forcibly remove an organ from a Gentile in order to save the life of a Jew (analogous to how we treat animals). I believe it is that radical belief in Jewish exceptionalism that provides an underpinning for what I have termed paradigmatic Jewish violence. We will be seeking its roots in traditional Jewish thought but must always keep in mind that every generation is responsible for its own interpretation of such foundational material.

JEWISH FUNDAMENTALISM

The issue of quasi-racism (or at least inordinate pride in one's genetic background)[35] must be kept firmly in mind when we speak of Jewish fundamentalism. Unlike some other religions, Judaism has rather few dogmas. There is no Pope in Judaism who standardizes matters of faith or belief. Despite the perennial attempt to harmonize thousands of years of traditional, prophetic, and legalistic teachings, the variety and diversity of opinion to be found within the Hebrew Bible, the Talmud, and later philosophical and mystical writings is utterly astounding. It is, consequently, a very difficult task to determine which beliefs are essential to Judaism.

Prior to Maimonides, dogma actually played a very minor role in Jewish identity. In fact, one's status as a Jew has almost nothing to do with one's religious beliefs; as long as one was born of a Jewish mother, one is a Jew.[36] What Judaism does indeed have as a leitmotif is a peculiar and enduring concern with peoplehood, as we have seen. That is not necessarily a bad thing, but it does not take a great deal of imagination to visualize how that concern could spin off into quasi-racism and (under certain circumstances) violence. That possibility may be increased by possession of land considered sacred. We have seen similar phenomena in other places such as in the Serbian attachment to a land that is currently populated by other ethnicities. While Judaism is surely not more violent than Christianity and Islam, the burden of ethnicity may weigh more heavily upon it. How ironic it would be to discover that the religion and people that suffered so profoundly as a result of racism should also suffer from a variety of it as its own peculiar vice.[37]

Many argue, however, that the real foundation of Judaism is religious law. This is the fairly consistent claim of Orthodox Judaism. It must be taken seriously because it finds practically unanimous support in rabbinic thought. Traditional Judaism has often been described as *orthopraxis* — in contrast to the *orthodoxy* that more appropriately pertains to Christianity. That is because adherence to Jewish law is more of a traditional criterion for normativity in Judaism than is proper belief. No doubt, there is a great deal of truth to this, yet failure to follow Jewish law does not make a Jew into a Gentile. This leads to the suspicion that there may be things even more fundamental in Judaism than the law.

The question of the foundation of the law is not itself a legal question and therefore we must look not only at the views of the rabbis but also of historians, anthropologists, philosophers, and others. Neither Goldstein nor Amir consulted rabbinic authorities prior to their violent deeds, yet they were considered good Orthodox Jews. This leads me to argue that as important as law is in Orthodox Judaism, it has other concerns that may be greater.[38] Alongside adherence to Jewish law in traditional Judaism is a set of concerns for the land of Israel and the people of Israel, and those concerns seem to have become even more prominent since the majority of Jews abandoned rabbinic law.[39] Hence, a person who wants to convert to Judaism can not assert that he or she is willing to abide by Jewish law but will not share in the fate of non-observant Jews. That would-be convert most likely would not be accepted because of the centrality of peoplehood in Jewish thought. And a group like the Ethiopian Jews, long separated from the body of the Jewish people and unacquainted with Talmudic law (and therefore Judaism as we know it) is still considered by most authorities to be fully Jewish. Indeed, the religious law itself can be viewed as a means of keeping the Jewish people together and separate from the other nations.

Since we have already dealt with the term *fundamentalism* in the introduction and in many of the other essays of this book, we need not dwell on it now, but I would like to place it in the context of the Jewish tradition. When we speak of fundamentalism in Christianity we are dealing essentially with a belief system. Yet Judaism is not primarily a belief system, nor is it, generally speaking, literalistic in its interpretation of scripture. However, most traditional Jews do read the Talmud literally and place a great deal of trust in revered rabbis from the Talmudic period up to our own day. Therefore, if we are seeking to distinguish Jewish fundamentalism from ordinary Orthodox Judaism, we must look elsewhere.

Unlike many ultra-Orthodox Jews, fundamentalist Jews have abandoned quietism and have quite often been exposed to secular education. They are extremely passionate about their beliefs and may feel competent to act on their own advice. Unlike most Modern Orthodox Jews, they have little interest in achieving successful adaptation to Western civilization and/or modern ethical values. They often deride Western values as "Christian," "modern," "pop culture," and so on. There is also an overriding and aggressive concern for the Jewish people and the Land of Israel. One of the appeals of Jewish fundamentalism is that it speaks the language of postmodernity,[40] as do many radical countercultural movements, but also portrays itself as an authentic traditional defense of Jewish values and a rejection of unholy compromises with the Gentile world.

Traditional Judaism did, of course, reflect such compromises, as do all successful adaptations of religious belief. The fact that Judaism and the Jewish people have survived is in no small measure due to their adaptability to changing circumstances — which is fine, as long as core values were not compromised. This unwieldy mix of layers of disparate elements has often produced results that are less than harmonizable or comprehensible, but it has allowed for a fairly flexible and viable lifestyle that can adapt to changing circumstances yet retain the aura of adherence to religious tradition.

It would be a dogmatic leap of faith, however, to assert that only adaptive or normative points of view have achieved canonicity. It is possible that along with salubrious habits of thought, certain dangerous and atavistic notions have found their way into the tradition. Why some rabbinic interpretations have acquired that canonical status and others have not should constitute an important study, but we will leave such investigations for others. It is obvious to me, however, that certain traditional views that were rarely acted upon in the past have become the pragmatic bases of Jewish fundamentalism.

Take, for example, the biblical boundaries of the Land of Israel. This has achieved mythic significance among fundamentalist Jews even though the tradition had never really agreed upon the exact borders or upon the current obligations of Jews to retain or recapture that land. Similar problems were discussed in Talmudic literature for many hundreds of years. In general, Orthodox Jewish beliefs regarding the Bible are, as noted, anything but literalist. They derive from ancient interpretive legends (midrashim) or legalistic discussions by the rabbis of the Talmud. Hence, extreme disagreements always characterized traditional Judaism. But we don't find such large-scale disagreements among Jewish fundamentalists. They tend to cluster around a few key agreed upon issues while their opponents are divided on those and many other issues. This leaves the fundamentalists with an open field to successfully exploit their rather narrow agenda. Why is that?

It seems to me that every religion may at times appear to need a short, simple exposition of its basic tenets and that such simple expositions tend to become canonical, blocking out alternative understandings or explanations. This may be an almost inevitable aspect of the sociology of religion in an open society. When just a few popular expositions are taken extremely seriously and uncritically and begin to dominate the discussion, we can perhaps speak of such a phenomenon as fundamentalism. On the other hand, when a somewhat broader view of the tradition prevails, we might use different terms such as *orthodoxy* or *traditionalism*. Since the destruction of the Second Temple and their expulsion from the Holy Land, Jews were defined to a greater or lesser degree by their sociological condition and the problem of self-definition was not acutely felt. Though they differed on many issues and regarding local customs, there was never the felt need to splinter into official groups. That is not the case today, and many people ask themselves, "As a Jew, what should I (fundamentally) believe?"

But what seems even more interesting to me is the question regarding the basic nature of such fundamentalism. Are those popular expositions, which excite the interest of believers (or would-be believers) ephemeral, or do they represent something so foundational that they can never really be extirpated? And even when they go underground for hundreds of years, will they always recrudesce? This question really pertains to the nature of religious tradition. To what extent is it continuous, and when something seems to have disappeared, has it only been "minimized" (using a computer analogy) and not really "closed"? Conversely, once an ethical idea appears to be a tradition, can it ever really be eliminated?[41] Perhaps that is a relevant question regarding violence as something integral to Judaism.

For many years, violence was inconvenient and was consequently minimized, but lately it has returned to the screen. While we cannot answer the global question of religious tradition here, we can look at a specific feature within this particular tradition. Most Jews, of course, believe there are times when both Judaism and common sense require violence. We will not deal with such cases. We will focus on occasions where the vast majority of humankind would be horrified by violence yet a certain fundamentalist interpretation of religion seems to support it — and perhaps even demand it.

By looking at occasions in which violence or contempt was encouraged, commanded, or condoned, we may be able to comprehend how such attitudes can be carried forward into the conscious or unconscious attitudes of traditional Jews today.

THE BIBLICAL PERIOD

Such occasions are not difficult to find in the Hebrew Bible. They include the destruction of the Jebusites and other tribes and the conquering of the land of Canaan. God in the Hebrew Bible commands these acts — sometimes involving the wholesale destruction of entire peoples. It is possible to be a believer in the Bible and still think that such acts of genocide are no longer required or even permitted by God. It is also possible to believe in the Bible without taking everything in it literally. Admittedly, however, some passages are easier to view nonliterally than others. When the narrative is explicit and involves no hermeneutic problems, a nonliteral interpretation appears apologetic. Therefore, many of these passages are quite problematic from an ethical point of view — and if one wants to be consistent with the biblical ethos. The Bible begins with the firm acknowledgment that all humankind is related and created in the image of God. Violence (*chamas*) is the only sin mentioned in Genesis as serious enough to warrant the destruction of the world. The father of the Jewish people, Abraham, bargains with God and risks incurring His wrath in order to save the righteous (and perhaps the sinful) people of Sodom and Gomorrah. Indeed, the Hebrew Bible on numerous occasions commands the Jews to love the stranger[42] in their midst, remembering that they themselves had been strangers in Egypt. Regarding moral offenses such as murder, the Law of Moses knows no distinction between Jew and Gentile (Leviticus 24:21–22), just as the explicit prohibition of murder to the sons of Noah affirms that all humankind is created in the image of God (Genesis 9:6).[43] On five separate occasions in Genesis, God informs Abraham, Isaac, and Jacob that they and their descendents will be a blessing to *all* the nations of the world. One of the commandments of the Hebrew Bible is to love your neighbor as one like yourself.[44] The great prophet whose writings are included in the later chapters of the book of Isaiah refers to his role of saving his fellow Jews as a light (not heavy) thing and therefore God commands him to be a "light to the nations."[45]

The violent passages are difficult to reconcile with those alternate ones — or with a loving, all-powerful, and all-knowing God. Therefore, the wholesale destruction of the Canaanites does demand an explanation. Generally, it is argued that they were a snare to the nascent Jewish commonwealth that was to be a vehicle of salvation for the world, and that they practiced various abominable practices such as child sacrifice. There are ancient Talmudic legends that attempt to mitigate those events by explaining that the affected peoples had been given the chance to escape destruction. Some of those legends are hard to reconcile with the actual biblical text, however. We will also be looking at how Moses Maimonides interprets those passages.

Nevertheless, we will not dwell exceedingly on those problematic biblical passages for the following reasons. Rabbinic Judaism is rooted in the Hebrew Bible. But so are Christianity, the Samaritan religion, the Karaites, and other groups that have splintered off from Judaism. We could also argue that Islam is based upon the Hebrew Bible and on a modified biblical view of God, man, creation, and so on, even though Muslims do not accept the Bible as their sacred text.

In the Second Temple period there were a number of Jewish groups, all rooted in the Bible. Among them were Jewish Christians, Sadducees, and Essenes. But all of those groups, as closely related as they may have been, are historically distinct from what we now call Judaism. They were Jews, no doubt, and practiced forms of Judaism in their time. But if we are interested in Orthodox Jewish fundamentalism and its relationship to violence, we would be better off investigating texts that are clearly part of Rabbinic Judaism, which is the form of religion that we now call Judaism.

We will also not deal specifically with Jewish propensities or inhibitions regarding violence. They might be a part of a folk heritage that, strictly speaking, is separate from Judaism as a religion (though related to it) and separate from Jewish fundamentalism as a religious phenomenon. We will be looking at Talmudic philosophical and mystical texts within the ambit of Rabbinic Judaism to find evidence of thinking that supports violence not justifiable as punishment for crimes and/or as self-defense.

LATE SECOND TEMPLE JUDAISM

It is noteworthy that none of the Jewish military victories of the

Bible were ever memorialized as Jewish festivals. This is a hopeful sign that exaltation of violence may not really be foundational in Judaism. The Second Temple period was one in which the Jews had returned from exile in Babylonia, were threatened by powerful, oppressive empires, and faced a great deal of internal ideological strife. This period may be the key to future attitudes. First, the quasi-racist views of the Book of Ezra, with its notion of the "holy seed" may have been a response to the near dissolution of the Jewish people.[46] Some incidents of destruction and oppression by enemies became the occasion for fast days that are still observed.[47]

There were also two events (historical or fanciful) of Jewish violence that might have occurred during the Second Temple period and which did become occasions for celebration. One was purported to have occurred in Persia and was memorialized as the festival of Purim. (It was the anniversary of that feast which also became the occasion for arguably the worst act of violence by a religious Jew against innocent civilians in modern times.) Despite the carnage tucked away at the end of the Book of Esther, that is not its focus; Purim really celebrates the deliverance of the Jews from a tyrant. Another festival, Chanukah, seems to celebrate the military accomplishments of the Hasmoneans (Maccabees) against the Syrian Greeks — which appears to have been an actual historical event. In this case also, the rabbis made sure that the holiday would not celebrate a military victory or destruction, but a miracle regarding oil. Almost all later developments of Rabbinic Judaism have their origins in Second Temple Judaism.

Unfortunately, we do not have a great deal of unbiased historical writings from that period and often must rely upon more or less polemical ones that have obvious agendas. Nevertheless, such writings as The New Testament, the Talmud, and those of Josephus and Philo can be of great value when examined critically (factoring out their agendas) and compared to one another. As an introduction to the range of attitudes towards the non-Jew, we first look at two quotations from what might seem at first blush to be an unlikely source. They will be well-known to Christians and may reveal at least one Jewish attitude towards Gentiles in the late Second Temple period.

> Go not into the way of the Gentiles, and into any city of the Samaritans enter ye not. But go rather to the lost sheep of the house of Israel.[48]

> And, behold, a woman of Canaan came out of the same coasts, and cried unto him, saying, Have mercy on me, O Lord, thou son of David; my daughter is grievously vexed with a devil. But he answered her not a word. . . . Then came she and worshiped him, saying Lord, help me. But he answered and said, "It is not meet to take the children's bread and to cast it to dogs." And she said, "Truth, Lord; yet the dogs eat of the crumbs which fall from their master's table."[49]

It ought to be added that in the case of the Canaanite woman, Jesus of Nazareth did ultimately choose to help the Gentile in need.[50] Interestingly, these are not among the acts that seem to have incurred the ire of the Pharisees in the New Testament. Nevertheless, we can perhaps conclude, not only from those aforementioned quotations, but from others that we will examine as well, that the attitude of late Second Temple Jews towards Gentiles may not have been altogether favorable.

Gentiles were generally viewed as inhabiting a different world-space from the Jew. They worshipped false gods, practiced strange rites, and did not adhere to elemental moral standards. Oftentimes they seemed cruel and lacking in compassion. In many cases, they were to be shunned. While we do not know exactly when Gentiles came to be viewed as ritually unclean, this appears to be a part of the Levitical purity rites associated with the Temple in Jerusalem. When the zealots were preparing the people for violent revolt against the Romans in the first century CE, this attitude intensified. Yet we know that even during that period there was a great deal of commerce between Jews and Gentiles and that many of the latter turned to at least a modified form of Judaism.

The figure has often been bandied about that ten percent of the Roman Empire was Jewish. Whether or not we can trust that statistic, it does reveal something quite different from a kind of Judaism that completely shuns its neighbors and isolates itself from them. It has also been noted that, even though Jewish proselytism practically died out in the period after the rise of Christianity, negative rabbinic utterances regarding converts are few and far between and always Amoraic (after 200 CE).[51] This indicates that whatever animosity existed between Jew and Gentile, from the Jewish perspective it was not primarily racial. While it would take us rather far afield to detail the relationships between Jews and Gentiles in the Second Temple period, we can say that, despite the condemnations by some, there was a great deal of assimilation, conversion (both ways), intermarriage, and intermingling. Yet we also read about violent ethnic battles, refusal to eat with alien groups, and even reluctance to do business with them. Perhaps this apparent contradiction between fairly overt contempt and actual helpful and cooperative relationships in the Second Temple period can help us to understand the conflicting Talmudic opinions as well as the opinions still heard today.

It would be overly ambitious to attempt an exhaustive review of the Talmudic literature. It records rabbinic proceedings from the late Second Temple period till at least the fourth century of the Common Era. What is possible, however, is to show the diversity of that literature as it reflects the relationships between Jews and their fellow human beings. We will not be focusing primarily on relationships within the Jewish community but on what I consider the main problem (or at least the problem that I will focus on). In my view, that problem is the contempt for non-Jews.[52] I have termed its violent consequences *paradigmatic Jewish violence* not because it is particularly prevalent or characteristic but because, in my judgment, it is deeply rooted psychically and poses the greatest threat in the future.

We will also not attempt a survey of later exegetical, philosophical, and mystical literature and readily admit the diversity of views contained therein. Mention will be made of the views of Rashi because of his great influence, especially among Ashkenazic Jews. We will focus on two types of medieval texts: the Zohar and the writings of Moses Maimonides. Both have become canonical and influential within large branches of Judaism. Both betray bias with respect to the treatment of non-Jews. Our purpose is never to judge ancient or medieval thinkers by modern sensibilities, but to ferret out attitudes that, if left unacknowledged, might constitute fundamental problems in the future.

THE TALMUDIC PERIOD

In the intervening period between the reception of the biblical message and the destruction of the Jewish Temple in 70 CE, Gentiles gave the Jews many reasons to fear and dislike them. Those historical events would be too numerous to mention, but may help explain some of the more negative opinions in the Talmud regarding non-Jews. And they will present a challenge for us in understanding the more positive statements as well.

The Roman period is one in which anti-Gentile animus reached its pinnacle, only to be rivaled in the medieval period, when once again the Jews suffered severe discrimination. One saying from the Talmud that has received a great deal of attention (especially from anti-Semites) is attributed to Rabbi Simeon bar Yohai: "The best among the Gentiles — kill; the best among serpents — thwack its brains"[53] One must keep in mind here not only Roman oppression but Rabbinic hyperbole as well — as in the parallel Talmudic statement that the best of doctors are murderers. Another extreme statement is that of Rabbi Helbo: "Proselytes are as hard on Israel as leprosy."[54] Here one can question whether the reference is to proselytes themselves or the baneful effects of accepting them, in terms of persecution by the Romans.

Not all Jews of that period were anti-Gentile or even anti-Roman, however. The famous saying of Hillel — to the would-be convert who asked to be taught the entire Torah while standing on one foot — is instructive. Shammai, the rival of Hillel, chased him away, perhaps finding his attitude impudent. Hillel, replied with the negative golden rule ("Do not do to your fellow what is hateful to you.") stating that it is the essence of the Torah, all the rest being commentary.[55] That Gentile seemed to think that the two great rabbis would be eager for him to convert. In one case he was clearly mistaken, but Hillel answered in a universalistic manner that he could readily understand.[56] We also have the view of Rabbi Meir that a Gentile who occupies himself with the Torah is like a high priest.[57] We should also note references to righteous Gentiles having a place in the world to come.[58]

Rashi

I will briefly discuss Rashi, for he is perhaps the most influential thinker among Ashkenazic Jews (those descended from early German communities) through his commentaries on the Torah and the Talmud; his worldview came to dominate traditional Ashkenazic Judaism. We do not ordinarily think of him as expressing anti-Gentile animus since his writings are mostly from the period prior to the First Crusade. Nevertheless, facts have emerged that indicate some rather strong negative feelings towards Gentiles already existed prior to that watershed event. This explains the somewhat rabid response to the pogroms of the First Crusade by the Jews themselves despite the fact that high Church officials often made sincere attempts to save them from the marauding mobs.[59] Those facts lead us to believe that at least some anti-Gentile sentiments that can be found in Rashi are a reflection of his cultural environment and are not peculiar to him alone.

Rashi did not like to see charity given to Gentiles even though the Talmud clearly recommends doing so, if only for the sake of peace.[60] This is a further indication that negative Jewish attitudes towards the Gentile had hardened during the medieval period. It should be pointed out that the small and relatively backward Ashkenazic community in the Middle Ages is usually credited with the more accentuated xenophobia. Nevertheless, anti-Gentile sentiment can be discerned in prominent Sephardic writings as well, especially those dating from the thirteenth century on.[61] An earlier, more harmonious relationship with the Gentile world was on the wane.

MAIMONIDES

Moses Maimonides is widely esteemed as the greatest medieval Jewish thinker. The reputation rests on his halachic (legal) opinions, his extraordinary mastery and distillation of his incredible familiarity and retention of the vast sea of Talmudic literature/law, and his encyclopedic grasp of medicine, science, philosophy, and logic. There is no other figure in the history of Jewish thought that possesses his singular authority. He was a pivotal figure not only in the development of Jewish thought, but also in the evolution of Jewish law.

Before him, the Talmud and later legal traditions were impenetrable webs that no one seemed capable of fathoming. It was he who attempted to make sense of it all and to apply normative standards to Jewish law as well as to Jewish thought. This feat of systematization came at the price of some rigidity (yet despite that price, the unity that he sought to impose upon the Jewish religion never really was achieved). And the more closely one investigates his thought, the more perplexing it becomes. Many of his views (such as his disdain for music and effusive, repetitive praises of God) could never have become normative in Judaism. Like most medieval thinkers, he strikes us as far too ascetic and severe. In addition to that, controversies have swarmed about him. Especially since the work of Leo Strauss and Shlomo Pines, many have come to doubt whether everything that he wrote represented his true positions. How much of it did he really believe? Was much of it a subterfuge? Indeed, there are few thinkers in human history regarding whom there is more controversy. Our task here, however, is not to dissect the writings of Maimonides or resolve vexing hermeneutical issues. Instead, we would attempt to show how his vast prestige might have helped to lend respectability to a rather nasty fundamentalist streak in Jewish thought. We do not relish this task since, in many respects, Maimonides rescued Judaism from a great deal of obscurantism and confusion.

Maimonides was demonstrably not as universalistic as the stubborn and perplexing insistence of many would make him out to be — nor was he egregiously particularistic either. Regarding the taking of an innocent non-Jewish life, Maimonides rules that it is forbidden. Unlike the taking of an innocent Jewish life, however, it is not punishable by Jewish courts but must be left to Heaven[62] On the other hand, three times his *Mishneh Torah* codifies the Talmudic teaching that righteous Gentiles have a share in the world to come.[63]

When codifying the Israelite treatment of the seven Canaanite nations, Maimonides defies understanding as being either lenient or severe. He comes down hard on idolatry and considers certain ways of thinking to be idolatrous that most traditional Jews would not. It should come as no surprise, therefore, that he rationalizes the harsh scriptural decree for those seven nations by alluding to their vile idolatry. But then he immediately mitigates the decrees by asserting that, if they were to renounce idolatry, peace should be made with them and all strictures should be removed. Even so, he insists that, barring their renunciation of idolatry, it is the duty of every Israelite to kill any member of those tribes that he finds.[64]

This abhorrence of idolatry (and heresy, for that matter) is no less pronounced in Maimonides' philosophical work: *The Guide for the Perplexed*.[65] In 3:51 of that work, he discusses those who "have adopted incorrect opinions." He declares that "necessity at certain times impels killing them and blotting out the traces of their opinions lest they should lead astray the way of others."[66] This refers not to Gentiles or even apostates but most likely to heretics who remain within the Jewish fold. Perhaps even more shocking and perplexing is his opinion regarding primitive non-Jewish peoples, whom he compares to apes: "They have the external shape and lineaments of a man and a faculty of discernment that is superior to that of the apes."[67] These may be similar to or the same as those he describes in *The Guide*, 3:18 as "ignorant and disobedient" and who are "like the beasts who speak not." He concludes that "it is a light thing to kill them."[68] I suspect that the key to their deserving death is their disobedience.

Another area where Maimonides might appear to be particularistic to an extreme — but really is not — is on the subject of non-Jewish slaves. Exodus 2 and Deuteronomy 14 demand that Jewish (*Ivri*) slaves be freed every six years (or the tenth day of the seventh month of the Jubilee year according to Leviticus 25) but says nothing about the freeing of non-Jewish slaves. In contrast to Jewish slaves, non-Jewish slaves are to serve in perpetuity (according to Leviticus 25). Does this mean that it is a commandment to keep them enslaved — or merely a license?

During the Talmudic era, non-Jewish slaves were indeed manumitted and the rabbis prescribed the formulation of the bill of manumission. It is true that an opinion of one rabbi (Yehudah) is recorded as having been opposed to the manumission of non-Jewish slaves. On the other hand, an earlier rabbi (Eliezer) was reported to have freed a non-Jewish slave in order to make up a quorum of Jews requisite for certain prayers.[69] The anonymous editor (*Stam*) of the Talmud latched upon this apparent discrepancy by implying that the freeing of non-Jewish slaves is a violation of a biblical law unless it serves a Jewish religious purpose such as Rabbi Eliezer's prayer quorum. Maimonides also prohibits the emancipation of non-Jewish slaves as an impoverishment of the Jewish people, but he implies that it is not a biblical commandment at all but a rabbinic one.[70]

This perhaps is key to many of the legal positions of Maimonides. When the opinion of the Talmud is clear, he almost never goes against it, but he makes great efforts to ascertain whether it is a rabbinic ordinance or one that the rabbis of the Talmud inferred from the Bible. When he finds a clear legal ruling in the Talmud and not simply homiletic advice or a confusing difference of opinion, he feels constrained to note what the law is. The net result often appears quite stringent as in this particular case. Nevertheless, this approach also leaves greater leeway to the possibility of changing the law than if he had agreed with the then widespread view that those laws were derived from the Bible itself.

In general, he is harsher with heretics than with non-Jews. Some people are puzzled that Maimonides, who seemed to harbor some rather radical opinions himself, was so strict regarding heresy. Perhaps it was a sop to the traditionalists. More likely, he had very strong and confident views regarding which beliefs were absolutely essential to Judaism as a viable way of life. At any rate, he goes so far as to advocate the killing of heretics (if possible) without the benefit of a trial and certainly forbids saving their lives.[71] We saw how that opinion was used in modern times to justify the assassination of an Israeli Prime Minister (though Rabin was classified by the fundamentalists as a *rodef* — pursuer — rather than as a heretic per se).

The conclusion that I draw is that, when he has a choice, Maimonides does not instigate new inter-group warfare. He generally counsels meekness and discourages anger and revenge, unless mandated by the Bible or the rabbis. In one area, however, that may not be the case. When it comes to heretics, he goes above and beyond rabbinic parameters when he allows for vigilante actions. Nevertheless, his codification reveals a frightening particularistic strand in some of the Talmudic sources themselves (perhaps exaggerated by his own cultural milieu and/or his own personality) that coexists uneasily with gentler, more universalistic ones.

THE ZOHAR

Before discussing the Zohar's role, it may be useful to briefly describe its place in Jewish kabbalah, often referred to as mysticism. The two words have become roughly equivalent despite the fact that much of kabbalah is not mystical in the ordinary sense of the word. Some of it is, however, and quite often the word is used to denote ancient mystical movements as well as much more recent ones. On the other hand, the word *kabbalah* is also used to denote a school of thought that originated in the Middle Ages whose classical and most representative example is the Zohar. I will be using the word in this more restricted sense. Kabbalah betrays vestiges of Gnosticism, Neo-Platonism, and even Manichean thought (in a broad sense). One of its cardinal features regards a peculiar kind of pantheism in which divine elements are divided and dispersed in the physical world. They can be unified and restored to their original pure state by the actions of humans (namely Jews), through their adherence to religious commandments. Hence, religion is viewed as a way of not only improving human life here below and in the afterlife but of impacting the upper realms.

The Zohar appeared in Spain in the thirteenth century but portrays itself as an ancient writing of Simeon bar Yohai who lived some twelve centuries earlier in the Holy Land.[72] It may be no coincidence that it was attributed to bar Yohai. We saw his name associated with the most hateful anti-Gentile pronouncement of the Talmud. From the time it first appeared, it caught the Jewish imagination. At times prohibited as dangerous, sometimes only allowed for older men, its appeal has shown itself to be extremely resilient. It probably holds more sway than all of Jewish philosophy. We will examine some specific Zoharic doctrines that may be related to fundamentalism and violence. The book is in the form of a commentary on the Five Books of Moses, but its nexus to the biblical text is loose. Quotations here are from the Soncino Press edition (London, 1984). These excerpts are by no means exhaustive.

VOLUME I

Quasi-racist thinking is evident in a number of passages in the Zohar.

> The *eighth precept* is to love the proselyte who comes to be circumcised and to be brought under the wings of the "Divine Presence" (*Shekinah*), which takes under its wings those who separate themselves from the impure "unholy region." . . . Think not that the same "living soul" which is found in Israel is assigned to all mankind. The expression "after its kind" denotes that there are many compartments and enclosures one within the other in that region which is called "living" beneath its wings. The right wing has two compartments, which branch out from it for two other nations who approach Israel in monotheistic belief, and therefore have entrances into these compartments.[73] Underneath the left wing there are two other compartments which are divided between two other nations, namely Ammon and Moab. All these are included in the term "soul of the living." There are besides under each wing other concealed enclosures and divisions from whence there emanate souls which are assigned to all the prose-

lytes who enter the fold — these are indeed termed "living soul," but "according to its kind": they all enter under the wings of the Shekinah, and no farther. The soul of Israel, on the other hand, emanates from the very bowels of that earth.[74]

"And the Lord God formed man. 'Man' here refers to Israel, whom God shaped at that time both for this world and for the future world."[75] The Bible, which clearly declares all human beings created in the image of God, is thus re-interpreted to refer to Jews only. This extreme freedom with the text points out another typical feature of kabbalistic literature. It is not interested in worldly matters but rather in a deeper, more "spiritual" meaning that must perforce inhere in religious texts. But that "spirituality" imputes demonic features to other humans. There is also a presupposition that processes in the spiritual world mirror those that occur on earth. As we will see, evil thoughts and deeds on earth imply a whole spiritual hierarchy of evil (demonism). Hence the domination of Jews by the Gentiles implies a temporary spiritual power structure in the universe that will be obliterated in the messianic age.

"E. Abba said that 'living soul' designates Israel because they are children to the Almighty, and their souls, which are holy, come from Him. From whence, then, come the souls of other peoples? R. Eleazar said: 'They obtain souls from those sides of the left which convey impurity, and therefore they are all impure and defile those who have contact with them.'"[76] Notions of impurity and defilement are common in kabbalistic literature, as they are to a far lesser extent in the Bible and other ancient Jewish religious writings. Some scholars view them as a continuation of prior pagan motifs. But the biblical texts confusingly use the same words to denote moral and ritual defilement. It was the prophets who most forcefully attempted to distinguish the two types of purity and impurity. Kabbalistic literature, however, makes explicit reference to cosmic *realms* of impurity, something the Bible and the other writings shy away from. Here the souls of non-Jews are viewed as having origins in an impure realm; therefore they are essentially demonic. This is akin to the prior claim that only Jews are created in the image of God and is a repudiation of one of the most revolutionary teachings of the Bible: that all human beings are kindred spirits and descended from Adam.

On the Feast of Tabernacles, according to the Talmud, the Jews offered sacrifices for all seventy nations. There were, of course, many more than seventy nations or peoples at the time, but the number may be all of the peoples that the ancient Jews were acquainted with or may represent a general notion of universality. This is often regarded as an example of Jewish universalism and benevolence on what was perhaps the major biblical festival. The Zohar, however, reinterprets it very differently: "Afterwards, when Israel celebrates the Feast of Tabernacles, the 'right side' is awakened on high, so that the moon may attach herself to it and her face may become completely bright. She then shares out blessings to all those presiding chiefs of the lower world, so that they may be fully occupied with their own portions, and not attempt to draw sustenance from the side from which Israel obtained their portion."[77] The purpose here in sacrificing on behalf of the nations is to prevent them from desiring the blessings that the Jews have! A benevolent act is degraded into something defensive, stingy, and even malevolent.[78]

VOLUME II

"Said R. Jose: 'You rightly said that when the serpent had carnal intercourse with Eve he injected into her defilement. We have, however, been taught that when Israel stood at Mount Sinai that defilement left them . . . whereas all the other nations, the idolaters remained infected with it.'"[79]

> Said R. Abba: "Happy is the portion of Israel, who are exalted above the idolatrous nations, in virtue of their grade being above on high, whereas the grade of the idolatrous nations is down below. The former are of the side of holiness, the latter of the side of uncleanness; they are on the right, the others on the left. . . . But when the Temple was destroyed . . . the left side has since been gathering force and uncleanness, and will continue to do so until God shall rebuild the Temple and establish the world on its right foundations . . . the unclean host being then extirpated from the world. . . . There will thus be one and only one King on high and below, and one and only one people to worship Him.'[80]

While the precise meaning of the excerpt can be debated, it certainly seems to look forward to a day when the other peoples will no longer exist.

VOLUME III

"As the eagle watches lovingly over its own young, but is cruel towards others, so does the Holy One manifest His loving mercy to Israel and His severe judgment to the heathen nations."[81]

The next quotation predicts an apocalyptic war involving Edom (Christendom), Ishmael (the Arab world), and another earthly power. The Zohar is quite aware of the then prevailing oppression of the Jews by both Christianity (Edom) and Islam (Ishmael). It justifies it by pointing to a higher metaphysical realm in which only Jews have a place and a future that will reflect that ultimate reality and only Israel (the Jews) will prevail.

> What did the Holy One do? He banished the children of Ishmael from the heavenly communion and gave them instead a portion here below in the Holy Land, because of their circumcision. And they are destined to rule over the land a long time, so long as it is empty, just as their form of circumcision is empty and imperfect; and they will prevent Israel from returning to their own land until the merit of the children of Ishmael shall have become exhausted. And the sons of Ishmael will fight mighty battles in the world, and the sons of Edom will gather against them, and make war against them, some on land, others on sea, and some close to Jerusalem, and one shall prevail over the other, but the Holy Land will not be delivered to the sons of Edom. Then a nation from the furthest ends of the earth will rise against a wicked Rome and fight against her for three months, and many nations will gather there and fall into the hands of that people, until all the sons of Edom will congregate against her from all the ends of the earth. Then the Holy One will rise against them, as it says: "A slaughter of the Lord in Bazrah and a great slaughter in the land of Edom" (Isaiah 34:6). He will "take hold of the ends of the earth that the wicked might be shaken out of it" (Job 38:13). He will wipe out the children of Ishmael from the Holy Land, and crush all the powers and principalities of the nations in the supramundane world, and only one power will remain above to rule over the nations of the world, namely the power representing Israel, as it is written: "The Lord is thy shadow at thy right hand" (Psalm 121:5).[82]

R. Simeon taught: "Blessed are the Israelites, for that the Holy One calls them 'Men' (Adam), as it is written, 'Ye are my sheep; the sheep of my flock; ye are men' (Ezekiel 34:31). Why are they called 'men', in contradistinction to the heathen nations? Because they 'cleave to the Lord their God' (Deuteronomy 4:2). . . . Contrariwise, Ishmael was a 'wild man' (Genesis 16:12); he was only partly a 'man.' . . . But the seed of Israel, who were perfected in all things, they are 'men' in the full sense."[83]

VOLUME IV

"The truth is that the holy spirits cannot approach their Lord until the spirit of impurity has been banished from their midst, for holiness cannot be mixed with impurity any more than the Israelites can be mingled with the heathen nations."[84]

VOLUME V

In Genesis 24, Abraham's steward is viewed in a favorable light, even though he was obviously not genetically related to the Jewish family.[85] When he enters the house of Rebekah, in order to find Isaac a wife, he is greeted, "Come in, thou blessed of the Lord." This is not altogether acceptable to the Zohar, which resolves the problem by inventing a type of caste system whereby the lower impure caste serves the higher pure one: "So, too, Eleazar, the servant of Abraham, was accursed in virtue of being a Canaanite, but because he was a faithful messenger he escaped from his curse and was blessed in the name of the Lord (Genesis 24:31).[86]

LATER WRITINGS

We do not have the space for an exhaustive list of writings in which quasi-racist sentiments exist and which continue to influence religious Jews. It may, however, be useful to single out the Tanya, which is the definitional text of the Lubavitch movement. We have already seen how a self-proclaimed Lubavitcher, Yitzhak Ginsburg, promulgates racist doctrines. The Tanya, as previously noted and cited, asserts that Gentiles only have an animal soul, in contrast to Jews who also have a spiritual soul. But perhaps the reason some are so amazed at this is that it is their first exposure to this genre. That is because Lubavitch is a missionary-style movement, whose mission is to bring secular Jews to Orthodox Judaism.

Those who were born into religious families have often been exposed to similar pronouncements and might not find this shocking at all, even if they disagreed with it. In the nineteenth century and even earlier, it became common for traditional religious Jews to reject the more atavistic elements of Jewish tradition under the influence of rationalism and higher education. The more right-wing elements, however, refused to admit that anything wrong or unworthy could be found in traditional Jewish belief. This is analogous to other kinds of fundamentalism described in this book. With the breaking up of Judaism into competing movements (Reform, Conservative, and Orthodox) and the destruction of whole communities in the Holocaust, the right-wing elements have gained far greater influence in traditional Judaism than they had in the past.

CONCLUSION

If in fact there are so many Orthodox Jews who disagree with the previously described quasi-racism, why are they not more vehement in denouncing it? Given the extremely broad range of opinions contained in the Talmud and later authorities, and the long history of accommodation between Jews and Gentiles, how did it come about that the bias of the writer or writers of the Zohar has come to play such a dominant role in Jewish thought? Why do thinkers like Yitzhak Ginsburg, whose views are condemned (albeit quietly) by most Orthodox Jews, still command such a devoted following?

One fears that the more sensible authorities are too often dismissed as inauthentic and pandering to world opinion rather than reflecting authentic Jewish tradition. This view is not completely unfounded, but stems from something quite real in Jewish tradition — the radical division of humankind into Jew and non-Jew. It engenders distrust of the Gentile and a disinclination to condemn one's fellow Jew for being quasi-racist. It marginalizes those Jewish thinkers who stress the essential kinship of all human beings.

In the Talmudic period, there existed vibrant debates regarding the Gentile. It was never doubted, however, that all human beings were created in the image of God. On the other hand, there was obviously something radically wrong with humankind, which Judaism had come to ameliorate. This might indicate to us moderns the importance of the non-Jew in justifying Judaism as instrumental to human salvation. In the modern world, we tend to think that good people will help others to be good, but that was not the typical way in which pre-modern Jews (or anyone else) saw things.[87] Demonization of the other was a standard motif, as it remains in certain circles today.

The distinction between Jew and Gentile can in theory be healthily maintained, but only with critical philosophical analysis. Happily, such freedom of thought was never entirely extirpated from Judaism, but it is not a celebrated virtue in contemporary Orthodox or fundamentalist discourse today. Perhaps the most urgent (or pressing) challenge for Jewish thought today is the reconciliation of the doctrine of the chosen people with a belief in the essential equality and dignity of all human beings.

We looked at Maimonides and the Zohar as possible sources of intolerance. A critical and/or generous reading of Maimonides can overcome many of his own prejudices. That is because of the subtlety of his analyses and the obviously changed times in which we live. As a jurist, he could hardly be more tolerant than the rabbis of the Talmud, but he is sometimes oddly less so. He never, however, refers to Gentiles as inherently evil and even defers to them in philosophical matters, considering many of them more advanced than his own co-religionists. The Zohar, on the other hand, adopts a clear demonological stance towards non-Jews. This is not a matter of a sentence here or there in some manuscript; it is a systemic bias. It is morally perilous to confront its quasi-racist thinking with anything less than a clear denunciation.

We must be willing to seek out the roots of religiously inspired hatred, contempt, and violence both in the sources and in later interpretations. We consider the idiosyncratic source of Rabbinic Judaism to be the Talmud. We have indeed found some sources of contempt for outsiders (as well as non-conforming believers) in those sources, but they pale in comparison with later medieval misinterpretations. Nevertheless, just as enlightened Christians understand the polemical nature of some New Testament writings and their baneful effects on Christian-Jewish relationships, Jews should understand the historical factors underlying many Talmudic discussions.

Those who deny themselves freedom of thought may end up oppressing others, at least in words and thought if not in action. This is a well-documented psychological mechanism that releases the discomfort of one's own doubts when under pressure to conform. Such conformity is a hallmark of Orthodox Judaism even if not necessarily a defining characteristic.

I would like to repeat two sentences from Rabbi Lamm's fine eulogy for Yizhak Rabin: "Yigal Amir and Baruch Goldstein were, otherwise, fine representatives of what we stand for. So we have a lot of thinking and pondering to do." Norman Lamm is as upstanding and responsible a person as one can find, but this quotation may point out something quite significant that needs to be addressed. Amir and Goldstein were *not* "fine representatives" of what Rabbi Lamm stands for. I am not even sure that they would have *appeared* to be, if one had taken the time to talk to them. They may have been fiercely devoted to the Jewish people and may have fervently kept the ritual commandments and even some of the moral ones; but they were filled with hatred and/or contempt for humankind. As Charles Taylor stated it so beautifully, "Being good involves *loving* something and not just *doing* something."[88] Motives are important, and there is indeed "a lot of thinking and pondering to do"!

While the vast majority of Orthodox Jews are not violent, we conclude that at least one strand runs through the tradition — and the Talmudic sources as well — that shifts Israel's chosenness from a mark of grace to a cause for self-congratulatory arrogance that has the potential for ugly and violent manifestations. That strand expresses itself in the suppression of people both within and outside the community who appear to pose a threat. Hence, there seems to be at least a meaningful connection between feelings of weakness/vulnerability and the mistreatment of heretics and aliens.[89] In the past, Jews were powerless to oppress other peoples and could only take out their frustrations on nonconformists in their midst, themselves, and their loved ones. Or they indulged in character assassination against their oppressors as a means of getting back at them and restoring their psychic equilibrium. Such "letting off of steam" may not appear to be violence. But when such attitudes are carried forward to an era when Jews have power, these attitudes may, unless they are restrained or modified, result in death and destruction.

There is also a wider problem that may run even deeper. It involves the inability to decide regarding what is right or wrong and the need to defer to authorities. Our analysis finds deep continuity and similarity between fundamentalist and Orthodox brands of Judaism in that regard. We propose that fundamentalists are more individualistic and activist, even though they utilize the same source materials and may interpret them in similar ways. In their self-satisfaction and self-righteousness, they latch on to radical authoritative sources. They and the more cautiously Orthodox Jews are natural allies, however, against the freedom to question and think critically about the tradition. Like many other Orthodox Jews, fundamentalists have a penchant for kabbalah yet are also at times thoroughly involved in politics.[90] They seem relatively incapable of communal self-criticism as they defer to the group for their own values and morality.

Nevertheless, even most fundamentalist Jews remain nonviolent today just as Jews have traditionally been and this may actually be attributable in part to their Orthodox beliefs, values, upbringing, and rabbinic authority. It is certainly not a particularly violent tradition, even if it may tolerate violence under certain conditions. There is a great deal of value in their traditions and much to learn from them. But that should not blind us to whatever dangerous countervailing tendencies may exist — and might manifest in the future, even more than they have in the past. In prior periods, traditional Jewish authorities, while deferential to tradition, were willing to disagree vehemently with one another. Today's authorities feel threatened by secularism and see a need to coalesce and harmonize their disagreements. But since 9/11, some of us feel that everything has changed. We now must speak out against contempt and intolerance wherever it raises its head, whether it is from current spokespersons or from traditional authoritative sources.

ACKNOWLEDGMENT

I especially thank Isaac Sassoon for his help. Most of the Talmudic references and interpretations and some interpretations of medieval thinkers are the result of his guidance. He read the chapter and suggested revisions. We discussed when one should be silent and when one should speak out. Both are valued in Jewish tradition, and I hope I made an adequate judgment. I also thank Charles Manekin for his on-the-ground assessment of the situation in Israel and for recommending the work of Elliot Horowitz. Louis Kessler was also helpful in researching sources. Despite their help, only I am responsible for the final product and the opinions expressed within it.

NOTES:

1. have been criticized for my understanding of peoplehood and chosenness and would like to make a disclaimer. I am not discussing what should be or what God intends but what is and has been understood by large segments of Jews. If someone wants to argue that such widespread views are misunderstandings of the Bible, Talmud, and other sources, that is fine with me.

2. Though this chapter is not specifically about the Arab-Israeli conflict, I feel constrained to comment on it. Many (perhaps most) Israelis are concerned about violence against Arabs. A fairly substantial group, however, is not so concerned; they even encourage it. Few would deny the existence of a tough almost thuggish mentality in certain quarters, but it may be fostered by the preexisting violence in the region. Many of the more strident Israeli spokespersons for more aggressive actions against Arabs are former Americans or Russians. Educated Israelis are quite often kindhearted yet realistic regarding Arab-Israeli relations. There is even an Israeli organization (B'Tselem) that chronicles Israeli violence against Arabs in the occupied territories. But no parallel Arab organizations exist, either in Arab countries or in those disputed territories. Therefore, though human rights violations and unnecessary violence do indeed characterize the occupation, they may be a universal and inevitable result of armed conflict and occupation. We are concerned about the interaction between those external factors and underlying religious ones.

3. The concern for the people of Israel becomes prominent in Exodus, though it is prefigured in Genesis where there are promises regarding peoplehood, but the descendents of Abraham are an extended family or at most a clan and the focus is primarily on individuals. The tribes are first described as an actual people in Exodus. This abrupt shift from family to people is signified dramatically by the use of four Hebrew verbs in one sentence to describe the population explosion (Exodus 1:7). One comes from a root rarely used in the Bible to describe human reproduction (*sharatz*) but used to describe swarming, creeping, crawling creatures. It was used after the flood as part of the commandment to be fruitful and multiply. This should be kept in mind by those who interpret peoplehood or covenant in an entirely spiritual sense.

4. Many religious commandments are explicit in biblical texts, but the vast majority are either enactments of the rabbis or their extrapolations from those texts. This does not invalidate them, but I am attempting to excavate levels of Judaism in order to understand why peoplehood is such a fundamental concern.

5. One could venture the opinion that liberal Jews are strongly influenced by the ethical teachings of the Bible while Orthodox and traditional Jews are influenced more by its concern for the Jewish people. Some are also peculiarly attached to the sacrificial rites. It is the professed hope of most Orthodox Jews that the Temple will be restored and those rites resumed. Presumably, it occurs in the messianic age when all humankind will recognize God and His chosen people. This should be an era of peace, kindness, and ethical behavior, and the fascination with bloody sacrifices seems inconsistent with that messianic dream.

6. There are many scholars who disagree with this assessment completely or, as in the following example, the extent to which it is true. In his most recent book, Menachem Kellner states, "Traditionalist Judaism today is often understood by its practitioners . . . as if the crucial element in Judaism is ethnic, determined by descent from Abraham, Isaac, and Jacob. . . . Maimonides sees the crucial event in Jewish religious history as the revelation at Sinai, when the descendents of Abraham, Isaac and Jacob converted to Judaism." Kellner agrees with my interpretation of what traditionalists usually (or often) believe but places Maimonides in opposition to those beliefs. There are three points that I would like to make. Firstly, descent from Abraham, Isaac, and Jacob need not entail "ethnicity" in the cultural sense. All Jews don't speak Yiddish or eat bagels. Nor does it necessarily involve genetics. One's genes can be 99 percent or even 100 percent Gentile and one can still be a Jew. It also need not entail "some essential characteristic which made them ontologically distinct and superior" (in the words of Kellner). It need only involve a kind of broad tribal identity. Secondly, as Kellner seems to agree, while Maimonides created a kind of "orthodoxy" in Judaism, it did not completely stick, and Judaism reverted to what he calls "proto-kabbalistic" thinking. In the past, Kellner has argued that pre-Maimonidean Judaism was less dogmatic — a situation he thought somewhat preferable. I agree, but also insist that beneath all those disparate intellectual trends (rabbinic, kabbalistic, Maimonidean) is a deeply rooted concern for Jewish peoplehood, which unites the various factions. See *Maimonides' Confrontation with Mysticism* (Oxford: Littman Library of Jewish Civilization, 2006), p. xi.

7. In the case of Christianity, obsession with the Jewish people took on a negative tinge, and in Islam, descent from Arabs became a mark of honor. But those religions are universalistic and not tied to peoplehood in the way that Judaism is. That did not make them less violent than Judaism but affected why violence was expressed. In Christianity and Islam, universalistic concerns sometimes lead to violence. This has hardly ever been the case in Judaism. If Judaism becomes a proselytizing religion again, this might change.

8. That is not to say that nationalism or peoplehood lack universalistic significance. Even ancient civilizations such as Greece and Rome saw themselves as significant for the well-being of the rest of the world to a certain extent. Modern nationalism takes its cue from ancient Israel and has viewed itself as a political entity evolving under divine guidance. Even the aberration of modern imperialism can be viewed in that light. Nevertheless, one can still distinguish between national interest and the interest of humankind.

9. Judaism over its long history has included views that run the entire spectrum from nonviolence to holy war. It has never been exclusively associated with either pole, as have Christianity and Islam, though those latter two religions have also experienced that whole range of attitudes in their actual existences.

10. See Simha Asaf, *The Punishments after the Talmud Was Finalized: Materials for the History of Hebrew Law* (Jerusalem: Sifriyah Mishpatit, 1922).

11. A Hebrew term literally meaning "return" or "response," but generally equivalent to repentance (despite the insistence of some that it is a completely distinct concept).

12. Some of the most important research regarding violence against non-Jews has been done by Elliot Horowitz. Regarding the deaths of large numbers of Christians in Jerusalem after the Persian conquest of 614, see "The Vengeance of the Jews Was Stronger than Their Avarice," *Jewish Social Studies*, Volume 4, number 2 (available on the Internet). Also of great interest is *Reckless Rites: Purim and the Legacy of Jewish Violence* (Princeton, NJ: Princeton University Press, 2006). Horowitz has been criticized for digging up unusual events, but such a judgment in my opinion is premature because the job of a historian is often to merely chronicle events as long as those chronicles do not suggest trends or generalizations that are unwarranted. A work of more dubious value in that regard is *Jewish Fundamentalism in Israel*, by Israel Shahak and Norton Mezvinsky (London: Pluto, 1999) in particular Chapter Seven, entitled "The Religious Background of Rabin's Assassination." It is overstated and biased and suggests false generalizations regarding religious Jews. Nevertheless, it contains valuable material. For example, it references an important article in *Haaretz*, November 15, 1996, by Rami Rosen entitled "History of a Denial." The "denial" referred to regards Jewish violence. I quote one of the sources for the article, Yisrael Bartal, a Jewish historian at Hebrew University.

> Zionism has described the diaspora Jew as weak people . . . Orthodox Jews are also providing similar descriptions. They describe past Jewish society as one not interested in anything other than the Halacha and the fulfillment of the commandments. The entire Jewish literature produced in Eastern Europe, however, teaches us that the reverse is true. Even in the nineteenth century the descriptions of how Jews lived are filled with violent battles that often took place in the synagogues, of Jews beating other Jews in the streets or spitting on them . . . and of numbers of murders.

I suspect that Bartal was guilty of hyperbole, but no more so than the generations of apologists from whom we have received the more canonical version of Jewish history. These historical events may help us understand recent manifestations of violence in Israel. Following are excerpts from an article by Amiram Barkat about events occurring in the week of 10/11/04 and posted on Haaretz.com on Jan. 28, 2007.

A few weeks ago, a senior Greek Orthodox clergyman in Israel attended a meeting at a government office in Jerusalem's Givat Shaul quarter. When he returned to his car, an elderly man wearing a skullcap came and knocked on the window. When the clergyman let the window down, the passerby spat in his face. . . . Many Jerusalem clergy have been subjected to abuse of this kind. . . . On Sunday, a fracas developed when a yeshiva student spat at the cross being carried by the Armenian Archbishop during a procession near the Holy Sepulcher in the Old City. . . . According to Daniel Rossing, former advisor to the religious Affairs Ministry on Christian affairs and director of a Jerusalem center for Christian-Jewish dialogue, there has been an increase in the number of such incidents recently. . . . Former advisor to the mayor on Christian affairs, Shmuel Evyatar, describes the situation as "a huge disgrace." He says most of the instigators are yeshiva students studying in the Old City who view the Christian religion with disdain. "I'm sure the phenomenon would end as soon as rabbis and well-known educators denounce it. In practice, rabbis of yeshivas ignore or even encourage it," he says. Evyatar says he himself was spat at while walking with a Serbian bishop in the Jewish quarter, near his home. "A group of yeshiva students spat at us and their teacher just stood by and watched."

13. It is not difficult to get this information on the Internet. A Google search will reveal blogs, articles, and such, by right-wing religious elements, which justify violence against Gentiles and heretics. One repository of these teachings is an anti-religious organization in Israel called *Daat Emet*. They purvey writings of right-wing rabbis in order to discredit them. One rather voluminous tome is entitled "Gentiles in Halacha" written by Rabbi David bar Chaim of Yeshivat Mercaz HaRav. What is interesting is the sheer number of traditional sources cited as justification for quasi-racist doctrines. It also quotes (attempting to discredit them) modern sources within the Orthodox community who argue for equal treatment and respect for all human beings. This actually shows the wide variety of opinions within the traditional Jewish community much better than the more apologetic "liberal" expositions of Judaism, which ignore offensive or inconvenient material. Another notorious episode involved Rabbi Sadya Grama, who wrote a book asserting that Gentiles are totally evil and Jews are totally good.

14. There have been other documented cases of Jewish violence in Israel but these are the best known.

15. Yeshiva of Flatbush and Yeshiva University in the case of Goldstein, Bar Ilan University for Amir.

16. Of course, no individual can have the moral right to decide to do what is not ethical. I am referring to the means of ascertaining what is right and wrong. Clearly, there are cloudy

areas where we need guidance from others. But the reflexive need to go to a rabbi to decide regarding clear and fundamental ethical issues seems to retard the moral faculty. And since it is literally impossible to consult an authority for all of the necessary decisions of everyday life, such retardation can have quite negative effects. I do not claim that this difficulty is essential to Orthodox Judaism but merely typical of it. There are self-described "Orthodox" thinkers who have struggled with and continue to struggle with this and other moral problems.

17. Goldstein, while on the verge of court martial in the Israeli army, said he only accepted Kahane and Maimonides as rabbinic authorities. This was reported by *Yediot Acharanot* (3/1/94). Maimonides was long dead and Kahane was considered completely atypical of contemporary rabbinic opinion.

18. I say "somewhat untraditional" because it is not unprecedented, and examples can be found of similar pronouncements and vigilante-type incidents involving Jews as perpetrators. Nevertheless, for much of Jewish history, Jews did not antagonize their stronger and more numerous hosts; Jewish courts monopolized the use of force within their communities. Recently, the ancient laws of the pursuer (*rodef*) and informer (*moser*) have been invoked to justify violent actions against Jews. In ancient times, extraordinary means were employed to prevent someone from killing other Jews or informing on them to hostile foreign authorities. Individuals have also been incited to revolt against secular authorities in Israel, mostly regarding the uprooting of settlements. What is new is that these activist rabbis are no longer acting simply as heads of their respective communities but as instigators of violence within a larger Jewish community. Jews today also feel newly emboldened to make public statements that disturb the sensitivities of their non-Jewish neighbors. This may be in consonance with a much more general trend towards exhibitionism and lack of restraint in modern society. Counterexamples do not necessarily invalidate this generalization. Public events in the Middle Ages, such as executions and torture, would surely offend current sensibilities. Nevertheless, modern societies are characterized by a lessening of both traditional authority within groups and less use of power between religious groups of varying strengths. Hence, today there is relative freedom to make offensive public statements that might not have existed in the past.

19. Meir Kahane was a radical rabbi who jarred Israeli politics by advocating forceful relocation of Arabs and coercion against Jews who had intermarried, and by arguing that democracy and Judaism may be irreconcilable. He and his party were *persona non grata* among mainstream Israeli politicians and were considered racist under a law passed in 1988. But earlier on, he was involved in support of Soviet Jewry and Jewish self-defense activities in the United States, for which he garnered a good deal of support among some American Jews. Later on, his group was accused of terrorism, including bombings and intimidation. He was assassinated in the United States on November 5, 1990 by an Arab terrorist.

20. Some Orthodox Jewish leaders divorced themselves from Kahane while others have

been reluctant to do so. I recall after his assassination being in the presence of a leader of Modern Orthodoxy and an uneducated man who extolled the virtues of Kahane. The leader said nothing critical of Kahane. This could perhaps be attributed to the traditional Jewish reluctance to say anything bad about the dead. Some of the faculty of Yeshiva University attended Kahane's funeral. Rabbi Lamm (the president of the university), to his credit, attempted to deal with Jewish violence after the assassination of Rabin. Unlike in the past, when Jewish communities enforced internal conformity (often violently), present-day fundamentalists seem not to be particularly concerned with that. Usually their ire is confined to Jews who convert to other religions or marry outside the faith, both forbidden contacts with non-Jews. Hence I am not convinced that the main danger from Jewish fundamentalists is the establishment of a Khoumeni-style regime in Israel as it is not politically feasible. Even in ultra-Orthodox communities, conformity is generally achieved through social pressure. Exceptions to this are the rock throwing and other violent acts that are mostly confined to Orthodox enclaves in Israel. While such deviant behavior may be tolerated by Israeli governments for political reasons, there is no reason to think that it poses a mortal threat to Israeli democracy. The greater danger, it seems to me, is violence against non-Jews (and Jews who consort with them) in Israel and the occupied territories. This might be a politically feasible expression of solidarity between religious and secular elements in Israel.

21. On the other hand, ultra-Orthodox Jews have separated themselves somewhat from Modern Orthodoxy.

22. See *New York Times*, November 18, 1995, p.24.

23. See *Mishneh Torah*, Laws of Murderers, 4:10–11, also Hilkholt Mamreem, 3:3.

24. See *The Guide of the Perplexed*, III: 18.

25. Perhaps the most outrageous statement made at the funeral was by Rabbi Jacob Perrin: "One million Arabs are not worth a Jewish fingernail." Fingernails are significant in kabbalistic thought. See *Halacha-Yomi* by Rabbi Ari Lobel and *Project Genesis*, Chapter 72:14 (available on the internet). "According to the *Zohar*, fingernails are associated with evil and impurity, and were often used in the performance of black magic." In Talmudic times, it was believed that fingernails should not be left lying on the ground lest a pregnant woman might walk over them and miscarriage (*Moed Katan* 18a).

26. The main point seemed to be that he was a good, religious person who flipped-out. Much has been made of the claim that Goldstein refused to treat non-Jews while in the army. Others like the rabbi, whose sermon I heard, denied it. Perhaps both claims are true regarding different periods of his life.

27. Not only is it permissible and perhaps mandatory under Jewish law to preemptively attack one who is about to attack you, it is sometimes an obligation to attack one who is violently pursuing others.

28. While it would be wrong to glorify such conspiracy theories, they can easily be found on the Internet by performing a Google search for Baruch Goldstein.

29. Sometimes the name is spelled "Ginsburgh" on the Internet.

30. The title is a pun. It comes from the Bible: "Blessed is the man who trusts in the Lord." *Baruch* means blessed and is the name of the murderer. *Ha-Gever* in Modern Hebrew means the man or the hero.

31. The Lubavitcher movement has been criticized by some Orthodox Jews. Most of the criticism has focused on its messianic ideology, which many view as similar to Christianity. The other aspect of its ideology that some find disturbing is its quasi-racism. The book that is canonical to the movement, the *Tanya*, asserts that non-Jews only have animal souls (See chapters 1 and 2). Yet this aspect of its ideology has received less attention.

32. For example, Jews for Judaism and The Inner Dimension.

33. The Hebrew word for honor, *kavod*, has two distinct (though perhaps related) meanings. Firstly, it refers to a mystical or ethical quality of God (often translated as "glory") and secondly to the honor bestowed upon persons. Sometimes the latter meaning is also applied to God, as in Exodus 14:4, where it is stated, "And I will harden Pharaoh's heart, and he shall follow after them; and I will get Me honour (*kavod*) upon Pharaoh . . . and the Egyptians shall know that I am the Lord." I would suggest that there is a confusion of these two meanings in Ginsburg's analysis. He seems to be implying that Jews can increase God's glory and/or honor, while in the Bible both are normally dependent upon God and His actions. Jews are to be a blessing to the other nations of the world by teaching them ethical virtues and God's will. For Ginsburg, this beneficent role is reversed to that of holy executioner.

34. This quotation can be found in the original Hebrew text of *Baruch Ha-Gever*, p. 4. The book was distributed by a group in Israel but some US libraries, such as the New York Public library, possess copies. The translation is by Don Seeman and can be found in his article, "Violence, Ethics, and Divine Honor," Journal of the American Academy of Religion, December, 2005, Volume 73, No. 4.

35. It is important to distinguish what I call quasi-racism from racism of the Nazi or white supremacist variety. If some Jews are racists in the latter sense, it has little or nothing to do with the phenomenon that I am describing here. Despite existing prejudices between Jewish ethnicities, fundamentalists insist on a strong kinship between all Jews. This does not depend on beliefs, ethnicity, or racial characteristics but on a perceived commonality of ancestry and a mythic notion of spirituality adhering to that ancestry.

36. Some would also stipulate that one must not be a practitioner of another religion.

37. I hope my analysis is not confused with the infamous equation of Zionism with racism by the United Nations or the extremely ill-advised use of the term *apartheid* in Jimmy Carter's recent book. But we must not shrink from speaking the truth out of fear that it will be misinterpreted, misused, or confused with other views. An overriding concern with shared ancestry, while not the same as racism in a strict sense, shares many properties with it and therefore justifies the term *quasi-racism*. This is especially the case when it is used to justify the mistreatment of the outsider. I generally use the term *peoplehood* to describe the healthier manifestation of this concern. The term "nationalism" is not adequate, because it is not clearly negative in connotation and also because the existence of (or even the desire for) a nation-state is not crucial to what I have called quasi-racism. The term *ethnocentrism* is also not adequate since Jews belong to a number of ethnicities: Sephardic, Ashkenazic, Yemenite, and others. Nor is *xenophobia* the right word. The psychic phenomenon I am describing need not involve fear of strangers or even lack of acquaintance with them.

38. I am speaking from a historical, sociological, and anthropological perspective. Someone could still argue that adherence to Jewish law normatively trumps those other concerns.

39. Orthodox thinkers often argue that concern for the land and people of Israel are deducible from Jewish law. I tend to discount the importance of this (though it is technically correct) since those concerns pre-dated the revelation of the law on Mt. Sinai. Though incorporated into Jewish law, they retain an extraordinary significance, evidenced by their importance to Jews who have abandoned Jewish law.

40. Many Jewish fundamentalists are acquainted with the postmodernist critiques of the Enlightenment and reason, and the problem of founding an ethical standard upon them. Perhaps their vehemence is a result of their lack of a reasoned justification for their faith and the resulting need to reject all "reasonable" compromises in favor of a romanticized "purity" of belief and practice.

41. I specify "ethical idea." According to many Jewish authorities, one can ignore scientific or factual notions that were part of the tradition (such as the belief in spontaneous generation) if they are proven false.

42. The same Biblical Hebrew word (*ger*) is used for alien resident and for convert, and this created a great deal of confusion. Often the rabbis interpreted the word as convert even though resident alien seems to be the more likely meaning. This may reveal a post-biblical negative attitude towards Gentiles.

43. Some have asserted that the Bible does indeed distinguish between the unjustified killing of Jews and non-Jews. Their assertion, however, rests upon Talmudic exegesis, not the biblical text.

44. The Hebrew word for neighbor (re'a) is interpreted by some to include only fellow Jews. This may even be a traditional rabbinic interpretation. But clearly the word is sometimes used in the Bible to refer to non-Jews as when the Jews are told to request jewelry from their "neighbors" in Egypt upon leaving.

45. This sentence has sometimes been interpreted by Christians to refer to Jesus and by Jews to refer to the Jewish people. Most modern critical scholars, however, view it the way I have described.

46. See James A. Sanders, *Torah and Canon* (Eugene, OR: Cascade, 2005) p.51. "It is not at all stretching the evidence to suggest that until Ezra worked his wonder, fragmentation and disintegration had reached advance stages in the several Jewish settlements throughout the world."

47. Aside from *Yom Kippur*, these are the only institutionalized fasts in Judaism. One fast day, *Tisha b'Ab*, is traditionally considered to be the anniversary of the destruction of both the first and second temples, but its connection with the former is more tenuous.

48. Matthew 10:5–6.

49. Matthew 15:22–27.

50. The longer story is also recorded in Mark 7:24–30 where the woman is described as a Greek. The fact that it is recorded in two gospels lends it greater credence; it surely reflects a segment of popular opinion.

51. Bernard Bamberger only found four such statements in the Talmud. See his *Proselytism in the Talmudic Period* (Cincinnati: Hebrew Union College Press, 1939).

52. Animosity towards heretics and non-Jews may partially stem from a heightened sense of vulnerability nurtured by persecution, often aided and abetted by renegades from within the Jewish community.

53. Mekhilta Beshala, *Masekhta de-Vayhi*, I, Isaac Sassoon's translation. See his *Destination Torah*, (Hoboken, NJ: KTAV, 2001) p. 263.

54. Sappahat, Leviticus 13:2.

55. Shabbat, 51a.

56. "One's fellow" might perhaps be interpreted to refer only to a fellow Jew in which case the reply is not as universalistic as it first appears. The would-be convert could still reason that if he becomes a Jew he will be treated well by his "fellows." The rabbis later prohibited conversions based on such utilitarian motives.

57. Sanhedrin, 59a. Meir expounded doctrines that the other rabbis of his generation were not able to accept and the law most often does not follow his opinion. A more accepted position was that Gentiles were not allowed to study the entire Bible but only certain sections. Given his nonconformity, it is odd that some have gone to such great lengths to reinterpret his saying to apply only to the study of the seven Noachide commandments, which all agreed could be studied by Gentiles. Such extreme exclusivity is not biblical in spirit and cannot even be found among the *Tannaim* (early rabbis) some of whom even described Moses as having inscribed the Torah into the seventy languages of the Gentiles. Psalm 112 bids the nations to glorify God for the miracles that He performed for Israel. Gentiles generally must read the Bible to know about those miracles and the sacred history of Israel. Deuteronomy 4:6 specifically states that the nations of the world will praise Israel when they hear about the laws ("all these statutes") that were given to them.

58. There has been a great deal of discussion and controversy regarding the rabbis of the *Talmud* and their views regarding Gentiles and the afterlife. We cannot offer an exhaustive treatment here but it is fair to say that there was no consistent tradition. The view that righteous Gentiles will survive death is found in Sanhedrin 13.2. An even more inclusive assumption that most human beings will survive death (with the exception of those who like Balaam "forgot God") is found in the Mishnah (Sanhedrin 105a). The early rabbinic view of punishment after death generally was for a temporary period of time or involved extinction but not eternal damnation except for an opinion that the extremely wicked receive the latter.

59. See Robert Chazan, *European Jewry and the First Crusade* (Berkeley: University of California Press, 1987).

60. It is of even greater interest that the narrative takes place on Purim, when it is a custom in many places for Jews to give charity to Jew and non-Jew alike and even involved the servants or slaves of Jews as recipients. See *Mahzor Vitry* (Nuremberg, 1923) p. 211.

61. This was obviously a result of the Christian *Reconquista* of the Iberian Peninsula but a similar hardening of attitudes may have occurred much earlier with the invasions of the *Almohades* and *Almorivides* (fanatical Berber sects who persecuted the Jews and helped destroy the *Umayyad* caliphate in Cordoba.

62. Mishneh Torah, Laws of Murderers (*Rotseach*) and the Saving of Lives, 2:11. Over the years, most versions were edited to remove offensive statements and one must often go to very old versions such as the Rome edition, medieval manuscripts, or modern critical editions such as Frankel. For example, the very first sentence in the section defines murder as the unmitigated killing of a human being in most versions, but, in those specifically mentioned, it refers only to an Israelite victim.

63. See Mishneh Torah, Laws of Kings, 8:10–11; Laws of Repentance, 3:4; Laws of Testimony, 11:10.

64. See Book of Commandments, positive commandment # 187 and Mishneh Torah, Book of Judges, Laws Concerning Kings and Wars, 6:1. Also see Mishneh Torah, Laws Concerning Forbidden Intercourse, 12:17 for his rationale for allowing all of the seven nations to convert to Judaism.

65. Some have argued that the attitudes of Maimonides towards idolatry as well as certain other subjects can best be understood in relationship to his Muslim/Arab environment.

66. See *The Guide of the Perplexed* (Pines translation) p. 619.

67. Ibid., pp. 618–19.

68. Ibid., p. 475. Though this appears to conflict with the Mishneh Torah passage previously cited, these Gentiles are guilty of disobedience and therefore are not innocent.

69. See *Berachot*, 47b. This shows how close to conversion non-Jewish slaves really were. The males were circumcised, they all renounced idolatry and agreed to observe the Noachide commandments. All that was required for full Jewish status was possibly immersion in a ritual bath and manumission, since Jewish slaves did not have the responsibilities of free male Jews and could not be counted for the quorum (*minyan*).

70. See Mishneh Torah, Slaves, 9:6. This would explain Rabbi Eliezer's freeing of his non-Jewish slave as described above. On the other hand, if the Bible actually forbade the freeing of such slaves, the prohibition could not be waived to facilitate a rabbinic ordinance such as communal prayer. I thank Rabbi Sassoon for pointing this out.

71. See Mishneh Torah, Laws of Murderers, 4:10–11.

72. Most scholars consider Moses de Leon, the supposed discoverer of the book, to be its real author or at least compiler. Some, such as Yehudah Liebes, have noted similarities between Zoharic and Christian doctrines such as the Trinity. While the Zohar, and kabbalah in general, is overtly anti-Christian, influences from Christianity were quite probably absorbed imperceptibly along with Gnostic and philosophical elements.

73. While the nations are not specified, Christianity and Islam naturally come to mind. This statement is therefore a somewhat puzzling departure from a generally xenophobic literary genre.

74. The Zohar (London: Soncino Press, 1984) Volume I, p.55.

75. Ibid., p.101. Some commentators believe that this was not in the original text but was added later.

76. Ibid., Volume I, p. 147.

77. Ibid., Volume I, p. 209. Note the familiar reference to the two sides (left and right, good and bad). This preoccupation with forces of evil and impurity increases potentiality for violence and its justification.

78. There is a tendency in rabbinic literature towards stinginess regarding the good deeds or good qualities of Gentiles. This is in marked contrast with the Bible itself, which often portrays them in a very positive light. But as we have seen, the Talmud is essentially an argumentative tradition in which many divergent views are to be found. The kabbalistic literature, such as the Zohar, portrays itself as a recipient of secret esoteric traditions going back to Moses and therefore as capable of definitively resolving those prior controversies.

79. Ibid., Volume II, p. 12. This legend comes from the Talmud and is not an invention of the Zohar.

80. Ibid., Volume II, pp. 126–27.

81. Ibid., Volume III, p. 241.

82. Ibid., Volume III, p. 103.

83. Ibid., Volume III, p. 261.

84. Ibid., Volume IV, p. 99.

85. While not specifically called Eliezer in this passage, Jewish tradition has equated him with the servant by that name in a previous narrative. What is puzzling is the Talmudic *aggadah* that insists that he was a Canaanite even though the text in Genesis 15:2 states that he was from Damascus or Aram and should therefore be descended from Shem rather than from Ham.

86. Ibid., Volume V, p. 224. The Zohar's insistence that Eliezer was a Canaanite must be attributable to the aforementioned midrash (generally called *aggadah* if it appears in the Talmud itself).

87. The notion of Jews being a light to the nations is an old one and the Bible mentions many times the blessing that Gentiles receive from the Jewish people, but we suspect this was not uppermost in the minds of most traditional Jews. In the nineteenth century, when cosmopolitan Jews sought a rationale for remaining Jewish, it did become a powerful motif. It could be argued that in the twentieth century it was partially eclipsed by the Zionist ideal, though there is no inherent contradiction between nationalism and universalism.

88. See Charles Taylor, *Sources of the Self* (Cambridge: Harvard University Press, 1989) p. 534. He argues that even consequentialist ethical systems involve *concern* for those consequences rather than for internal purity or some other good.

89. There is an obvious tendency for groups with power to oppress others. It is often argued that weakness and persecution lead to Jewish intolerance. This view should be approached critically and skeptically. It is true that those who informed to the Gentiles and/or became apostates were traditionally considered worthy of persecution. This can be illustrated by the addition to the *Amidah* prayer of a benediction asking for the destruction of *minim* (heretics). It has traditionally been *justified* as a reaction to those who vilified their fellow Jews in the eyes of Gentile oppressors and may have achieved its present form under Christian persecution. Those who converted to other religions (even if they later desired to return) were often treated harshly. It is possible and even probable, however, that the same kind of intolerance would have manifested itself even if Jews had been in a relative position of security and power.

90. This is an anomaly and perhaps a dangerous one. We might expect the rational religious types to be involved in politics and the more mystical types to eschew it. See Max Weber, *Economy and Society*, Volume I (Berkeley: University of California Press, 1978) 590–602. In the nineteenth century, rational yet traditional Jewish thinkers could openly criticize Kabbalah. This has become much more difficult and may signal an increasing degree of power wielded by its partisans.

COMMENTS ON ANDREW GLUCK'S ESSAY

CAROL DELANEY

Dr. Gluck's essay* has a lot of information, almost too much to absorb, and could easily be expanded into a book. Thus, my major problem with the essay is its structure and focus. Although he says he will leave the historical facts to historians and instead "analyze current psychological and cultural trends" using two cases for illustrative purposes, that is not exactly what he does. We do not get to the cases until after many pages of parenthetical and qualifying material; that is confusing. For example, he wonders whether psychological and cultural phenomena have real causal power. My response as an anthropologist is that culture is not epiphenomenal but forms the conceptual worlds that we live in, including the psychological issues we deal with, and that a person's behavior is always relative to a specific culture, even when there is considerable overlap between some cultures.

A second general critique is the use of the words *Holy Land* and *Gentile* which come already loaded with religious meanings; *Israel* and *non-Jew* would be much better in this context. I think the essay would have had much more coherence and greater impact if he had *begun* with the two cases of religious violence — those of Baruch Goldstein and Yigal Amir. I would like to have learned more about their religious backgrounds and the religious beliefs they used to justify their acts.

Dr. Gluck's own critique, not revealed until the conclusion, of a comment by Rabbi Lamm would have been a good place to begin to explore

---

* It is somewhat intimidating to be asked to comment on the essay of the valiant person who organized this important and timely project. So, before I begin that task, let me say a special thank you to Dr. Gluck and commend him for initiating the project and for his persistence in pursuing the various contributors to get their essays to him. That is not an easy task.

the connections between Judaism and violence. Rabbi Lamm — commenting on Goldstein's massacre of Muslims at prayer at the Tomb of the Patriarchs in Hebron and Amir's assassination of Yitzhak Rabin — said that, except for those acts, both of the men were "otherwise, fine representatives of what we stand for." As is well known, many Jews made heroes out of these murderers; that is what should be investigated with much more depth.

I do not agree with Dr. Gluck that "violence is not a major Jewish problem at the *present time.*" There is violence in the way Jewish settlers illegally take land and property that belong to the Arab people living there and justify it with reference to the Bible: "The land is ours. It was given to us by God." There is violence in unprovoked strikes against the Palestinians in Israel or Lebanon whether in the air or on the ground. Nor does Dr. Gluck mention the several plots by some radical, ultra-Orthodox Jews to blow up the Dome of the Rock so that a new temple can be built. If it ever came to pass, this act would ignite a huge — maybe worldwide — conflagration. The fact that religious Jews are even plotting such a thing is a violent act.

As I have stated in my article in this volume and reiterated in my comments, I personally think any religion that claims to have the one true interpretation of God's will, whose adherents claim they are the "chosen," the "saved," or the "elect" is, *ipso facto*, violent, for it divides the world into "us" and "them" and too easily becomes "If you are not with us, you are against us." The barrier wall being constructed to keep the Palestinians and Israelis separate is literally a concrete example of this. Have they learned nothing from Berlin?

The claim that one is "chosen" is arrogant. Such arrogance can provoke violence from nonadherents against their dehumanization, but it can also call forth violence among believers against those who do not believe as they do or who cannot join the "chosen" because of certain restrictions based on blood or birth.

Finally, many depictions of God are also violent. Consider the story of Abraham who is revered because of his faith — which he showed by being willing to kill his son at God's command. One might ask, "What kind of God would require such a thing?" Nor did that God restrain himself when he "smote all the first-born of the Egyptians."

Dr. Gluck has done a service in turning our attention to violent strains in the thought of well-respected Jewish thinkers from history, but these aspects need much more exposition than is possible in an essay. And more importantly, they may not be directly linked to the violence that is going on at the *present time*. I do not think that Goldstein and Amir are aberrations but are expressions of something more fundamental.

ANDREW GLUCK'S REPLY

I would like to thank Professor Delaney for her frank assessment of my chapter. Regarding the format and style of my writing I will have nothing to say except that I will go over it again to make it more readable. I also have little to say about the terms Holy Land and Gentile. I think that in our culture they do not require any explanation and I feel it is futile to attempt to eliminate all religious-cultural connotations from my writing. In fact, my intention of providing a kind of phenomenological flavor practically requires such connotations.

I agree with her regarding the causal efficacy of psychological and cultural phenomena. However, there are those who will argue that the real underlying causes of human behavior are climate, natural resources, genetics, and so on. As a philosopher, I feel the need to at least admit the legitimacy of such a point of view, even if I don't agree with it.

Now let us get to the crux of our disagreements. My honest attempt to criticize contemporary Jewish thought and institutions as failing to come to grips with fundamental problems of violence was not sufficient for Professor Delaney. My statement that violence is not a major Jewish problem was contested. Perhaps I should have defined what I meant. Here we need to put things in perspective. Jews are generally less violent than the people amongst whom they live. They are not perfect, however. I will leave it up to the readers to do the research or not, depending upon their desires. Admittedly, when I said violence was not a major Jewish problem I was not referring specifically to the minority of Jews who are usually referred to as "religious" or "orthodox" although the generalization does apply to them also. Nevertheless, we can't blame a religion for everything that its nominal adherents do. Hence, what Israelis, most of whom are nonreligious, do is somewhat but not totally irrelevant.

An even more fundamental disagreement has to do with the Jewish religion, which maintains that the Jews were chosen. This could indeed be interpreted as a scandalous dogma. She finds it both arrogant and tantamount to violence; and that charge I believe is essentially anti-Judaism. Judaism is not a violent religion! It would have been better if she had stated that it is a silly superstition. I could not argue with such a characterization even if I believed it to be false, since this is a matter of faith. But to call it a violent belief must be responded to.

As I stated in my essay, accommodating the belief in chosenness to tolerance and goodwill is a challenge, but that is not because the belief itself is violent. It does, however, carry within itself the possibility of violence if not understood correctly. Perhaps there is indeed a violent strand in Judaism. I tried my best to expose it. But to call Judaism a violent religion is wrong. For thousands of years, Jews have maintained their belief in chosenness and still were less violent than their neighbors. Even when they were in positions of power, they did not generally become hyper-violent—though, as we all know, power corrupts.

In Israel today, most Jews are quite concerned about not becoming violent or oppressive, despite the obvious existence of fringe groups that do not share that concern. If one were to impartially compare all the problems that Professor Delaney cites in Israel and the Middle East with contemporaneous ones in Africa and Asia or previous ones in Europe, the Arab-Israeli conflict would appear minor. It is only because that part of the world and the Jewish people is so central to our civilization that it appears to be so immense. Our dependence upon Middle East oil is also a practical factor in making that conflict a crucially significant one.

Of course, as I stated previously, Jews are human, and, in times of war, atrocities do occur—as does oppression generally, by the strong against the weak. As for arrogance, that is a moral flaw which many Jews and non-Jews share. But the belief in chosenness is not necessarily arrogant. I would recommend the reading of the prophets who believed that the Jews were chosen yet also believed that they were guilty of many sins including arrogance. Being chosen is essentially an example of undeserved grace and is therefore antithetical to arrogance.

The case of Abraham is critical since Professor Delaney uses it as a central motif in her writings. I believe that Abraham's willingness to sacrifice his son has often been misunderstood by Jews and non-Jews alike. At that time, human sacrifice was normal and not at all extraordinary. The meaning of the story to me is that God does not desire human sacrifice and Abraham originally misunderstood God's demand.

Regarding the killing of all the first-born in Egypt, this was an unusual event meant to impress upon the Jewish people and the Egyptians the power of the one true God. It was the culmination of a number of plagues that showed God to be compassionate and just (for example, bidding the Egyptians to come in from the fields to avoid the hail) as well as all-powerful. Admittedly, it was a shock, but the message of the Bible is that human beings occasionally need to be shocked. It eventually led to the establishment of monotheism in the West and the Islamic world, which I believe are vast improvements over what came before.

The extreme brutality of those ancient civilizations is difficult for us to fathom, and I would wager that a cultural critic such as Professor Delaney could not have survived in them. We have also been influenced by a prior episode regarding Abraham, when he dared to argue and negotiate with God to save a few innocent people in Sodom and Gomorrah. I believe that, without knowing it, Professor Delaney with her obviously well-meaning agenda is heir to that daring compassion of Abraham, even as she rejects his God.

THE PSYCHOLOGY OF ISLAMIC FUNDAMENTALISM

Seyyed Nassir Ghaemi

A Friday in Kufa

On a hot sunny Friday in the year AD 661, some thirty years after the passing of the Prophet Muhammad, the fourth Caliph, Ali ibn Abi Taleb, walked toward the mosque of Kufa in present-day Iraq. He was the Prince of the Believers, the political and religious successor to the Prophet, and it was Ali's duty to lead the prayers each week. This he had done for four years of his Caliphate, but in the face of much conflict and strife.[1] A group of Muslims, generally wealthy and recent converts who had not been among the Prophet's early followers, had risen up against him in Damascus. They were fated to defeat him, and led by Muawiyah (who became the next Caliph), they were to found the Umayyad Caliphate that would rule Islam for two centuries, spreading the religion across three continents and laying down the basic structure of Islamic society that remains to this day.

But that was in the future. This day, Ali was walking to prayers possibly thinking about what sermon he would deliver. He had delivered many attacking Muawiyah and his camp, of course, but he had also made a habit of criticizing his own people, the followers of his caliphate in present-day Iraq, even the people of Kufa, who had been the most loyal of all parts of Iraq to him. When one reads those sermons today, collected in a classic book, *Peak of Eloquence (Nahj-ul-Balagha)*[2] one gets the sense of a man who was trying to prod a recalcitrant horse to move forward. Ali cajoled, he threatened, he pleaded, he taught, he lectured, he harangued.

185

I am faced with men who do not obey when I order and do not respond when I call them. May you have no father! What are you waiting for to rise for the cause of Allah? (p. 174)

Woe to you. I am tired of rebuking you. Do you accept this worldly life in place of the next life? Or disgrace in place of dignity? When I invite you to fight your enemy your eyes revolve as though you are in the clutches of death, and in the senselessness of last moments. My pleadings are not understood by you and you remain stunned. (p. 167)

O people! We have been born in such a wrongful and thankless period wherein the virtuous is deemed vicious and the oppressor goes on advancing in excess. We do not make use of what we know and do not discover what we do not know. We do not fear calamity till it befalls. (p. 164)

He tried quiet and calm, he tried fire and brimstone. It was all to no avail; his people did not understand his mission.

Much discord had arisen about the fact that Muawiyah and his followers, though the last to convert to Islam, now tried to hide behind their status as Muslims. When Ali reproached them for their corruption, the Umayyads replied that Ali sought to kill other Muslims. Ali had to convince his reluctant Iraqis to take up arms against a complex—no longer simply pagan—enemy:

We have been with the Prophet in battles wherein those killed were fathers, sons, brothers, and relations of one another. . . . We now had to fight our brethren in Islam because of entry into Islam of misguidance, crookedness, doubts, and false interpretation. However, if we find any way by which Allah may collect us together in our disorder and by which we may come near each other in whatever common remains between us, we would accept it and would give up everything else. (p. 270)

Ali was especially burdened by a third group, besides his avowed enemies among the Umayyads, and his presumed friends in Iraq. These people he called Outsiders (*Kharijis*). Like Ali, they rejected the Umayyads, viewing them as irreligious pretenders; but they also rejected Ali, viewing him as insufficiently assertive in putting down the Umayyad crowd. Ali had fought them, but he also had spared them; he was slow to shed Muslim blood, even if he thought it was hypocritical blood. He spent much effort trying to convince them that their complacent sense of authenticity was misplaced; he saw them not as cleverly vile, like the Umayyads, but rather as dangerously confused: "You are holding your swords on your shoulders and using them right and wrong. You are confusing those who have committed sins with those who have not" (p. 279). He feared these confused extremists more than his calculating Umayyad foe. "Certainly you are the most evil of all persons and are those whom Satan has put on his lines and thrown out into his wayless land" (p. 280).

So Ali was trying to walk a middle line: between the laxity of the Umayyads (who drank alcohol publicly and reveled in wealth and palaces and splendor) and the narrowness of the Kharijis, all the while trying to mobilize a confused and slovenly middle-of-the-road populace.

He leaned over, on the walk into the mosque, and tapped a sleeping man on the shoulder. "Wake up," said the Leader of the Faithful, "you have important work to do today." The young man had arrived from elsewhere the night before, and had slept that evening outside the mosque; he wanted to be sure he was there for the prayers.

He followed Ali into the mosque; the faithful cleared a path, as the Call to Prayer flowed smoothly: "Hurry to prayer! Hurry to prayer! Hurry to your duty! Hurry to the best deed!" Ali stood in front; the young man behind. Ali lifted his head to the dome above, he raised his hands by his ears: "Allahu akbar!" he intoned. "Allahu akbar!" the congregation bellowed. Ali bent forward, Ali kneeled down, Ali prostrated his head on the floor.

A sword, curved and clean, a broad stroke at Ali's neck, blood and screaming, the young man dragged away (a Khariji, it turned out), a Leader lying motionless and dying. He held on for a few days, forgave his murderer, and died. Ali, the Lion of God, the first human being to proclaim Muhammad as the Prophet of Allah, the husband of the Prophet's beloved only daughter, was dead. Muawiyah became Caliph, the Umayyads destroyed the Kharijis, and the path for the future of Islamic history was set.

We are still walking along that path.

ISLAM IS ITS HISTORY

In the Shiite Muslim world, this is the kind of story that is told over and over again. On religious holidays, which occur more than twenty days out of the year, the faithful gather in their houses to hear the story of Ali, the story of his life, and—most importantly—the story of his death, a moment-by-moment account, one that transports the listener to that day in Kufa. One finds oneself right there behind Ali, one sees the fatal blow, smells the sweat, feels the squirting blood. For Shiite Muslims, the suffering of Ali, and the martyrdom his son Hussain and of ten more Imams (Shiite leaders, each the son of another going back to Ali himself) is as real as the meal one had last night, as real as the birth of one's child and the death of one's parent. For Shiites, all history is the history of these tragedies;[3] nothing much else matters.

For Sunnis, the same history haunts their lives in two ways: one is a sense that the Shiites are holding a grudge too extensively; another that they need to be defensive about the history of Islam, to defend the idea that their Islam of today is the true religion, the same religion as the Islam of Muhammad and the righteous first four Caliphs who succeeded him before Muawiyah.[4]

Any understanding of Islam as a religion is inseparable from an understanding of the history of Islam. For the religion was a historical fact: it happened in a certain place with certain people, and its growth was an equally historical fact, happening in certain ways and not others. The psychology of Islamic fundamentalism too is inseparable from this history: it grows out of it.

THREE APPROACHES TO ISLAM

The example of the Kharijis shows how fundamentalism dates back to the very beginning of Islam; it is not simply a modern phenomenon. Even in the period of the Righteous Caliphs, there were fundamentalists who saw the very Companions of the Prophet himself as insufficiently pure.

To some extent, one might view the history of Islam as a long struggle between fundamentalist and mainstream Islam. The problem is that mainstream Muslims also accept the idea that, historically, Islamic leaders deviated from the right path after the first four Righteous Caliphs, a mere century after the Prophet's death. Thus, supporters of mainstream Islam cannot simply point to a historical continuity of acceptable Islam as practiced in the real world from the time of the Prophet until now. All Muslims, in some way, reject the way Islam was appropriated by some of the rulers of the Islamic world in the past. Thus, there has always been a tension in the Islamic culture between rulers who were viewed as usurpers by Muslims (Sunnis as well as Shiites, though the latter emphasize this matter more). This back and forth between mainstream Islam (with faults) and revolts against the mainstream (both fundamentalist and not) represents the history of the Islamic world.[5] In the nineteenth century, this see-saw was complicated by the need to also react to the modern West. There are perhaps three basic reactions which happened then: one is fundamentalism, a return to an earlier better time, either through Wahhabi austerity,[6] or through millennial sects that directly recreated the Prophet's era through the arrival of a new Messiah— such as the Bahai sect in Iran,[7] and the Ahmaddiyah sect in India.[8] Instead of harkening back to the Golden Age of the prophet, these latter groups created a new "Golden Age."

A second approach is the modernist approach, such as those of Jamaluddin Afghani,[9] Muhammad Abduh,[10] and Muhammad Igbal.[11] Here the idea was not to return to the Golden Age of the Prophet's lifetime, but rather to the Golden Age of Islamic culture, centered around the rule of the Abbasid Caliphs, when philosophy and science and theology all seemed to reach their peak in Islamic history.[12] The paradox here is that this period of cultural refulgence grew—not out of Islam, but—from the interaction with other cultures (in particular, Greek culture). This is why Islamic philosophers were viewed with suspicion and seen as heretics ultimately by Islamic theologians and the mainstream of Islamic society. In a way, Afghani's wish to return to that aspect of Islamic culture was bound to conflict with the fundamentalist response.

The third approach is the mainstream view, Islam viewed as a tradition, a series of customs and habits. This is the Islam of the common people, not a wish to return to the era of the Prophet, or to create a new cultural Golden Age, but a wish to continue the customs and traditions of daily life. This view is not particularly charismatic and has a hard time competing intellectually, and in times of conflict, with the other two perspectives.

Seyyed Qutb, a student of Abduh, tried to combine the other two perspectives when he saw that the desire for the Golden Age of Islamic culture ultimately conflicted with a return to original Islamic notions.[13] His goal is to modernize, yes, but to do so while at the same time trying to revive original Islamic values. This is perhaps what underpinned the Islamic revolution in Iran. There, Ali Shariati[14] tried to respond to the challenge of Western ideas by picking up those ideas (especially existentialism) and translating them into Islamic terms—not to learn Western theories, but rather to understand Islam better ("We still do not know our religion"). For him, the suffering of the Shiite Imams became stories of existential angst, which each and every one of us lives out in our lives today. ("The form of solitude, exile, defeat, despair, and pain was to be seen, in that desert covered with blood; it raised its head above the red wash of martyrdom, and stood silent and alone."[15] The approach to life that the Imams represented was a kind of redemptive suffering in a world where otherwise no meaning could exist: Shariati's response to the perils of existence was not all too different from that of Kierkegaard and other Christian existentialists—a personal refuge in divinity as understood within his own tradition: "The ideal man is the theomorphic man in whom the spirit of God has overcome the half of his being that relates to Iblis [Satan], to clay and to sediment. . . . Like Spartacus, he is a rebel against slaveowners, and like Abu Dharr, he scatters the seed for the revolution of the hungry. Like Jesus, he bears a message of love and reconciliation, and like Moses, he is the messenger of jihad and deliverance."[16]

Yet, just like Kierkegaard, Shariati was viewed with suspicion by traditionalist religious leaders (even by the revolutionary Shiite leadership in Shariati's case). Nonetheless, Shariati also had a fundamentalist aspect to him—like Qutb, by focusing on life in the Prophet's era and highlighting figures from that time (often unheralded ones, like the Companions Abu Dharr and Salman Farsi) as exemplars for modern souls.

VIOLENCE AND FUNDAMENTALISM

The Saudi, Sunni-based fundamentalism of al-Qaeda harkens back to the Wahhabi wish to return to the Prophet's era, a more purely cultural fundamentalism,[17] with few of the modernist trappings of people like Qutb or Shariati. Their use of terrorism as a tool is perhaps what separates them the most from the other groups. The Iranian fundamentalists were quite willing to have a revolution, though it was mostly peaceful. They were quite willing once in power to use arrest and execution to suppress dissent, though usually with some level of legal process. But they generally did not engage in terroristic activity. The approach by Al-Qaeda thus adds to fundamentalism the willingness to use violence against civilians.

This strategy is not to be found, certainly as a prime method of activity, among other modern Islamic groups, including other fundamentalist groups. The historical precedent for this approach is mainly to be found in the Khariji movement during the Prophet's era,[18] and a few centuries later in the Ismaili movement centered in Iran under the leadership of Hassan al-Sabbah.[19]

Al-Sabbah lived in the mountains of what is today the Alburz region outside of Tehran. The Shiite movement in the tenth century had divided into two main factions. One was the mainstream group—called Jaafari after the sixth Shiite Imam Jaafar al-Sadiq. It had coalesced around a specific written theology, much as the Sunni world had codified four theological schools. (In fact, those who wish to emphasize the similarities between Sunnism and Shiism sometimes argue that Jaafari Shiism is simply a fifth school of Islamic theology, on a par with the four accepted Sunni schools of Maliki, Hanbali, Hanafi, and Shafiite theology). The Jaafari mainstream school of Shiism, while continuing to reject the legitimacy of the Abbasid Caliphs and their successors, had forsaken direct revolt against them in favor of a patient waiting for the return of the Mahdi, the Shiite Messiah, who was the twelfth Imam in hiding.[20] The Ismaili school, named after one of Jaafar's sons, had broken off from the mainstream in two ways: it rejected a written theological code of religion, instead viewing Islam as subject to the revision and interpretation of the living Imam[21] (Ismail and his successors—currently these leaders are the Aga Khans); second, the Ismailis of the tenth century did not view the Mahdi as their deliverer and thus continued to support direct revolt against the Caliphs.[22] Since this was the Golden Age of Islamic culture, and Abbasid power was at its zenith, the Ismaili rebels chose guerrilla tactics over direct attack, and they began to use the method of political assassination as a means of weakening the Abbasid regime. (They most famously succeeded in killing the powerful chief vizier of the Caliph, Nizam-ul-Mulk, in 1092).

For about a century or more, the mere name of Hassan al-Sabbah and his Ismaili guerrillas in the mountains of Persia sowed fear in the cities of the Islamic empire. Scholars such as al-Ghazali were merciless in their critique of the Ismailis.[23] Rumors grew rife about the doings of these militants; they were said to abuse hashish (from which comes the word *assassin*, derived from *hashishiyoun*, meaning those who use hashish); they were said to literally promise a paradise of virgins and honey to their zealots on martyrdom missions; they were seen as a cult, whose activities behind their closed villages and hamlets were viewed with suspicion.[24] George Orwell prefigured the danger that we may never know the truth of history. Where original documents can be destroyed—and history written only by the victorious—the truth underneath the bodies of the vanquished may never by uncovered.[25] Thus, it is not known historically whether some or all of these accusations are justified. What is the case is that al-Sabbah and his followers set a precedent for terrorist activity in the Islamic world on a larger scale, and with a more defined doctrine, than had the Kharijis. Compared to current fundamentalists, however, the Ismailis were not at all conservative. Rather, they were freethinkers, rationalists in a way, who supported the value of philosophy and rational thinking as opposed to simply following the dictates of theological schools.[26]

Thus, fundamentalism has always been with Islam, but organized terrorism has been uncommon, and, in the past, has focused on political assassination rather than general attacks on civilians.

WILLIAM JAMES AND THE PSYCHOLOGY OF RELIGION

The psychology of fundamentalism is perhaps best approached by thinking first about the psychology of religious belief in general. William James examined this matter in his *Varieties of Religious Experience*,[27] in which he pointed out that the psychology of religious belief, though important, is different from the truth value of religious belief. What mattered from his perspective was not whether a certain religious belief was true or not, but rather what characterized the believer. Before him—and still to this day in discussions of "natural theology" and the like—intellectuals tended to get into discussions about reasons for believing or not believing in God. These purely rational discussions (with the famous logical arguments, such as the Argument from Design and so on) were shown to be philosophically empty (by Kant) and biologically wrong (by Darwin).

This left James with a new approach, an attempt to provide an emotional, rather than rational, justification for religious belief. In doing so, James at first had to dispense with religion as we know it. In other words, if religion is to be justified psychologically on emotional grounds, rather than rationally on philosophical grounds, we would have to give up any specific system of religion or religious organization, since such systems are cultural rather than psychological entities.

In a letter to a correspondent, James laid out the two main goals he had in his *Varieties*: "first, to defend experience against philosophy as being the real backbone of the world's religious life . . . second, although all the special manifestations of religion have been absurd (I mean its creeds and theories), yet the life of it as a whole is mankind's most important function."[28]

For James, divinity has to have some relation to individual experience, since, in his view, individual experience forms the basis for all human knowledge and all facts. He states that, for his purposes, he will ignore institutional religion and focus on personal religion: "Religion . . . shall mean for us the feelings, acts, and experiences of individual men in their solitude, so far as they apprehend themselves to stand in relation to whatever they may consider the divine."[29] He distinguished "refined" from "piecemeal supernaturalism"—refined being "the theism where God is above and does not intrude on existence," while "piecemeal admits the here and now workings of God in people's lives."[30] Hence James redefined religion as a personal matter, as reflecting an individual person's belief. He then identified two types of such persons: the "healthy-minded" and the "sick soul." These terms imply value judgments, although it is important to note that James was not devaluing the sick soul; he placed himself in that group and he clearly critiqued the healthy-minded approach.

Most humans, and thus most religious individuals, James believed, are healthy-minded souls. These persons have not suffered from great depression or anxiety, and thus they have simply inherited their religion as a "dull habit." While accepting the reality of the religion of the masses, and the organized traditions of institutional religion, James calls this "second-hand religion," and he emphasizes that the origin of all these religions is in the personal experiences of prophets and saints, all of whom were sick souls, people who suffered with intense inner distress, and for whom their religious experience was a personal divine salvation. For them, religion was an "acute fever" rather than a dull habit, and it is in the experiences of sick souls that we can find the secrets of the origin and significance of religious belief.

In some ways, James emphasized the emotional source of religion and the role of sick souls to counteract the highly rationalistic evolution of Christianity. For centuries, Christian theology had been highly connected to rationalist philosophy (derived especially from Aristotle). Even the liberal Protestant reformation of Christianity (especially in its Deist, Unitarian, and Emersonian varieties) had remained highly rationalistic. These views of religion ignored the emotions of man, and did not connect to the personal emotional experiences of individuals.

Perhaps we should use less value-laden terms such as a *traditionalist* approach for the healthy-minded and a more *personalist* approach for the sick soul. The healthy-minded traditionalist temperament is positive and optimistic; for them, religion is just one more mechanism for success in life. Church joins the country club and the office as places where relationships can be made, socializing can occur, and goals can be achieved. The personalist sick soul reflects the existentialist approach to religion. These persons realize that life is a problem; they simply showed up in ways they cannot understand, and they are destined to leave. They realize that there is a great deal of unhappiness in life, and religion is a mechanism for coping with that unhappiness. Religion is not a set of rules, customs, traditions, or a way to get ahead in life (such as Benjamin Franklin's puritan rationalist version). Rather, religion meets a deep emotional need, it provides grounding in a world without grounding; it provides a rationale and meaning for life, a hope for the future, especially after death. Religion, in its deepest sense, is a response to these deep psychological needs. Karl Jaspers expressed it this way: "I must die, I must suffer, I must struggle, I am subject to chance, I involve myself inexorably in guilt. . . . To ultimate situations we react either by obfuscation or . . . by despair and rebirth."[31] Jaspers viewed that we all need to respond to these needs, and a personal attitude toward God or a larger spirituality is how we do that.

This was James's view: true spirituality and religion was about this deep personal connection to a belief in a larger, unseen world. While this belief was deeply personal at root, James did not reject formal religion; he believed it could be consistent with true religious belief if combined with a personal approach to faith.

THE PSYCHOLOGY OF FUNDAMENTALISM

Religious fundamentalism, as opposed to mainstream religious tradition, often reflects this personal approach. The concept of being "born again" in Christian evangelism is derived from James's notion of the "twice-born" sick souls who are reborn after discovering the religious meaning of their lives (usually through mystical experiences). In some sense, James would view fundamentalism as meaning religious faith; nonfundamentalist mainstream religion was viewed by him as less authentic, perhaps not even meeting his definition of faith at all.

The fundamentalist approach to religion, thus, may have more psychological value than the mainstream approach. It may have more psychological impact and truth-value, one might conclude, and thus James might view it as more truly reflective of religious belief than mainstream traditionalist religion.

If that is the case, what do we make of fundamentalism when it shades over into violence or even terrorism? James's perspective was that this subjective personal basis for religious faith needs to occur in the context of an awareness that this is what is happening, that one's religion is relevant to oneself and not necessarily an external truth that would apply to other people. What happens when a personal commitment to faith is connected to an organized religion interpreted in a violent or repressive manner? The example of the Kharijis shows that this can happen, and has happened in the past in Islam. They were quick to label as heretics—and thus, punishable by death—those whom they viewed as insufficiently Muslim. This was their rationale for killing Imam Ali. Here is the problematic combination: a deeply personal commitment to religious faith (which is not in itself objectionable) combined with an organized religious system that is exclusionary and violently judgmental.

THE PERSONALITY OF THE BELIEVER

When James speaks of temperaments, he implies that these are biologically given. One might distinguish, however, as do some current psychologists, between temperament and character, viewing the overall personality as the combination of the two. C. Robert Cloninger, a prominent personality researcher, suggests that temperament is biologically based and inborn, is notable in small children, and changes little over time.[32] (Although it is biological, it is not purely genetic; it is also influenced by habits and learning early in the first few years of life). The basic axes of temperament, in his view, are harm avoidance (how anxious one is), persistence (how focused one is), reward dependence (how sociable and approval-seeking one is), and novelty seeking (how curious one is).[33] (It is notable that novelty seeking is also characterized by proneness to anger and violence.)

All of us are somewhere—high, low, or middle—on each of these axes of temperament. Studies of normal individuals and of persons with mental illnesses (especially what are called personality disorders) suggest that there are more than just these four axes to personality. As Cloninger put it, based on temperament alone, he could not distinguish his friends from his patients—everybody has temperament traits in similar patterns. To be able to explain more extremes of personality, he had to look for other features, which he calls character. While temperament does not change much with age, character does develop as we learn to adapt our goals and values rationally. (Thus, both are partly genetic and partly environmental, but character is more malleable with later experiences in life). The dimensions of character, according to his research, are self-directedness (which is like the executive branch of government: the ability to do things), cooperativeness (the legislative branch: the ability to join with others), and self-transcendence (the judicial branch: the ability to see beyond one's own individual needs or wishes).[34]

The personality of an individual is a composite, therefore, in this view at least, of temperament and character. Hence, James's insight that religious belief is conditioned by the personality of the believer does not condemn us to viewing this matter as purely biological and fixed. Rather, the personality of the believer is, in part at least, amenable to the influences of the environment. Perhaps the most important influences come from the immediate family—one's parents, grandparents, and siblings. Other influences come from the overall culture, one's schoolmates and teachers, what one sees on television, and whether or not one's neighbors and friends participate in organized religion.

THE RELIGION MEME

Twin studies have always been the main scientific mechanism to tease out such matters. Since identical twins share 100 percent of their genes, and fraternal twins or non-twin siblings share 50 percent, one can compare those groups on psychological features, and, with mathematical models, demonstrate what percentage of those features are attributable to genetics versus environment. Further, the environmental component can be mathematically distinguished between shared environment (family and culture) and unshared environment between siblings (random experiences for an individual and peer relationships).[35] Many twin studies have been conducted on psychiatric disorders but also on psychological aspects of behavior including religious belief and political affiliations. Most psychiatric illnesses can be shown to involve a combination of genetic risk and unshared environmental influences (we cannot blame the mother for schizophrenia). Religious belief and political affiliation, on the other hand, have repeatedly and clearly been shown to have no genetic source (whew!), and are entirely (in scientific confirmation of George Orwell's *1984*)[36] conditioned by one's environment.[37] Further, the environmental component is entirely *shared*; it is family and parents and neighbors and the larger culture.

Another phrase for the environmental component of things is to call them *memes*, as suggested by the biologist Richard Dawkins:[38] The sources of all our behaviors then consist of genes and memes, genes being packets of DNA and memes being "information packets with attitude" (the philosopher Daniel Dennett's phrase).[39] Where genes are replicating nucleotides, memes are replicating ideas. It turns out that the personality component of religious belief appears to be entirely produced by memes, not by genes, it is produced by us—by families and the larger society.[40] What we create we can change; memes are created by our minds and represent our ideas. Here is a lever that parents and teachers and societies can use to influence the psychological approach of young persons to religion (and to politics, for that matter). If a dogmatic fundamentalism is to be averted, then it needs to be explicitly critiqued in the public forum, from the days of toddlerhood onwards.

RELIGIOUS PLURALISM

In contemporary Iran, there is an approach to religion from former fundamentalists who advocate another variation on fundamentalism, clearly influenced by James, which Abdol-Karim Soroush has called "Islamic pluralism."[41] These thinkers are highly committed to the personal commitment to religious faith, but they disconnect it from formal religious systems that argue for one approach as better than others. Soroush, for instance, argues that Islam has always been interpreted, even since the Prophet's era, and thus it is not a simple matter to say that there is one way of interpreting Islam in preference to others, or that certain Islamic beliefs need to be accepted by all. "[Religious] knowledge is, like other forms of knowledge . . . human, fallible, evolving, and most important of all it is constantly in the process of exchange with other forms of knowledge. . . . Ideologization of religion binds it to a single interpretation and generates a class of 'official' interpreters."[42] Even matters on which there is wide accord in Islam are often matters of consensus. Many aspects of Shariah law, for instance, rather than growing directly from clear revelation in the Prophet's era, reflect the consensus of Islamic scholars who devised the four major schools of theology. This perspective is not too unusual in the Shiite world, since Shiite jurisprudence had always retained a role for contemporary interpretation by living Shiite leaders in Islamic theology, whereas Sunni theology has strictly forbidden any new interpretations of Shariah beyond those established by the four major schools in the tenth century. It is perhaps not surprising then that reformist thinking in Islam should be more prevalent in the Shiite than in the Sunni world, and, conversely, that a foundational fundamentalism should hold the strongest attraction in the most purely Sunni regions of the Islamic world (such as Wahhabi Saudi Arabia). It is also notable that Soroush's perspective grows out of his training in philosophy of science, which currently is seen as involving a pluralistic openness to ideas and hypotheses, rather than a simple positivistic notion of proof of absolute truth.[43] Thus, Soroush's view is that Islamic modernism, to become consistent with modern science, needs to be pluralistic ("I believe that truths everywhere are compatible; no truth clashes with any other truth.")[44]

Similarly, Karl Jaspers had argued that one could be committed, at a very personal level, to religious belief while not being committed to the notion of possessing absolute truth. The idea is this—as Jaspers always put it: "Truth is on the way."[45] It is a matter of communication between sincere parties, an end result of the historical process of honest discussion, not a past reality that we simply need to accept or reject. "What matters is not our knowledge of God but our attitude towards God."[46] The same idea is reflected in the thinking of the Spanish philosopher Miguel de Unamuno, a contemporary of James, who said he wanted to be, not a "freethinker" (*librepensador*), but a "free believer" (*librecreyente*).[47] Like James, he viewed faith as a personal attitude towards divinity, one whereby one could believe that there is a truth without believing that one knew that truth with certainty. (Martin Nozick put it this way: "Truth is possible but certitude is impossible.")[48] Unamuno saw faith as "the happy uncertainty which allows us to live."[49] These thinkers tried to lay out a personal, subjectively strong attitude toward religion—one which can hold its own against the challenges of secularism—which is at the same time tolerant and pluralistic, and thus immune to violent fundamentalism.

George Santayana, a student and later faculty colleague of James in the Harvard Department of Philosophy, had a skeptical take on this kind of religious pluralism. Of James, he wrote, "Faiths, not their objects, were the hard facts we must respect. There was accordingly no sense of security, no joy, in James's apology for personal religion. He did not really believe; he merely believed in the right of believing that you might be right if you believed."[50] (33) A believing Catholic, Santayana was unimpressed by this attempt at pluralism in religion, as likely will be those who are committed to a specific religious dogma.

Yet James and his followers have at least asked the right questions and they have done so clearly. Religion has to be personal and emotional to have any meaning, yet if it is dogmatic it carries many risks. Can the two be combined so that religion is personal, emotional, and undogmatic? Or does the rejection of dogma entail secularism and the rejection of any religious belief?

POVERTY AND TYRANNY

Besides this discussion of the historical and psychological aspects of modern Islamic fundamentalism, one should mention the importance of economic and political factors. It is no coincidence that fundamentalism tends to take root in the context of poverty and repression. In Iran, for instance, before the Islamic revolution, all secularized opposition to the Shah had been repressed and religion was the only mechanism of expressing such opposition. Islam itself first was a revolutionary movement; the early followers of Muhammad were the dregs of Arabian life—the foreigners, the destitute, women and children. Most rich Meccans opposed him fiercely, until finally becoming late converts after his army had defeated them.[51]

The fundamentalist fervor of Islam takes root most deeply in a soil previously nourished by poverty and tyranny. One might say the same about Christian evangelism in the United States, which is strongest in the Southern states, the poorest and least educated region of the country. Perhaps Marx was right when he said religion is the opiate of the masses, but not in the sense of drugging them into passivism. Rather, (as apparently was his intended meaning) it is because, like opium in its medical usage, religion numbs the pain of life for those who suffer this world's hardships harshly and acutely.

If William James is right, and religion is, in a way, inseparable from many psychological features (of the believer) that we see in religious fundamentalism, then the problem of fundamentalism overlaps—or reduces to— the problem of religion itself. In the case of Islamic fundamentalism, it seems to be that the turbulent mixture that matters so much today is a combination of a subjective, emotional, and personalist attitude to faith (James's psychological temperament of the fundamentalist believer) tied to a dogmatic religious doctrine, a history that consists of an often corrupt mainstream, the intellectual and economic challenge of Western secularism, and current conditions of poverty and tyranny.

If any one of these factors were not present, then the phenomenon of Islamic fundamentalism today would change, at least—perhaps markedly so. History cannot be changed, nor is Western secularism going to go away. The most pliable factors seem to be the other two: the psychological approach of the believer (which is highly influenced by family and culture), and economic/political conditions.[52] As parents and neighbors, we are responsible for the first factor, and as citizens for the second.

WHAT IF . . . ?

One day, the eighth Shiite Imam, Ali Reza, was conversing with some of his disciples when a man arrived with a message from the Abbasid Caliph Mamun: "Become my successor. You deserve to be the Prince of the Believers after me." Mamun was a progressive Caliph, a sponsor of a rationalist approach to theology and sympathetic to the Greek-oriented philosophers. Imam Ali Reza was skeptical, though. He went to the court and asked,

"Why me?" The Caliph answered, "Because you are the most worthy among us." After much hesitation, especially on Ali Reza's part, the idea fell away, and ultimately, the Shiite Imam, like his successors and followers, was imprisoned and killed by Mamun's successor.

There is a school of history now that asks "What if?" questions—a school of counterfactual history that examines what might have happened if things had turned out differently in the past.[53] What if Napoleon had not invaded Russia? What if any one of the European powers had taken a less belligerent stance before World War I?

Well, here is a counterfactual question for Islamic history: What if Ali Reza and Mamun had worked it out so that the Shiite Imam became the new Caliph? What if his successors were both Caliphs and Imams who brought religious legitimacy back to the mainstream of Islamic culture? What if they fostered, instead of murdered, the flowering of Greek-inspired philosophy and science? What if the Golden Age of Islam had not died out in the eleventh century but lived a few more centuries to be renewed by the European Renaissance? What if authentic (even fundamentalist) religious belief and political rule and cultural progress worked hand in hand in the Islamic world, instead of competing with each other?

Asking these questions reminds us that, while the past cannot be changed, the future is always a work in progress.

ACKNOWLEDGMENT

The author thanks C. Robert Cloninger and Daniel C. Dennett for commenting on the manuscript.

NOTES

1. M. A. Shaban, *Islamic History: A New Interpretation* (2 volumes) (Cambridge: Cambridge University Press, 1971).

2. Ali ibn Abi Taleb, *Peak of Eloquence* (*Nahjul Balagha*): Sermons, Letters, and Sayings of Imam Ali ibn Abu Talib (New York: Tahrike Tarsile Quran, 1984).

3. Allamah Tabatabai, *Shi'ite Islam* (Albany: State University of New York Press, 1975).

4. Ibid.

5. Ali, *Peak of Eloquence* (see note 2 above).

6. Hamid Algar, *Wahhabism: A Critical Essay* (Oneonta, NY: Islamic Publications International, 2002).

7. William Sears, *Release the Sun: An Early History of the Baha'i Faith* (Wilmette, IL: Baha'i Publications, 2003).

8. B. M. Ahmad, *Invitation to Ahmadiyyat* (London: Routledge & Kegan Paul, 1980).

9. Nikki R. Keddie, *An Islamic Response to Imperialism: The Religious and Political Writings of Sayyid Jamal Ad-din "Al-Afghani"* (Los Angeles: University of California Press, 1983).

10. Muhammad Abduh, *The Theology of Unity* (Selangor, Malaysia: Islamic Book Trust, 2004).

11. M. Iqbal: *The Reconstruction of Religious Thought in Islam* (Chicago: Kazi, 1999).

12. In the same era in Spain, descendants of the Umayyads ushered in a Golden Era in al-Andalus also, but their rule was largely a cultural extension of the reigning Abbasid culture. William Montgomery Watt and Pierre Cachia: *A History of Islamic Spain* (Edinburgh: Edinburgh University Press, 1965).

13. Sayyid Qutb, *Basic Principles of Islamic Worldview* (North Haledon, NJ: Islamic Publications International, 2005).

14. Ali Shariati, *On the Sociology of Islam* (Berkeley, CA: Mizan, 1979).

15. Ibid., p. 14.

16. See the existentialist poem on which Shariati ends one of his lectures:

Man this rebel against God
Who has given one hand to the devil—intellect
And the other hand to Eve—love
Who bears on his back the heavy burden of the Trust

Descended from the paradise of painless enjoyment
Alone and a stranger in this world.
He is a rebel, but constantly yearning to return
And now he has learned through worship how to attain the path of salvation.
And through submission to the constraints of the beloved
After escaping blind constraint through his rebellion
He is now delivered too from the torment of the escape of desperation.
He who fled from God
Was tested and purged in the furnaces of this world—
Awareness, solitude, decision—
And now knows
The path of return toward God
That great Friend Who is awaiting him
The path that leads to Him by becoming Him. (Ibid., pp. 124–25)

17. Algar, *Wahhabism* (see note 6 above).

18. Ibid.

19. Bernard W. Lewis, *The Assassins: A Radical Sect in Islam* (New York: Basic Books, 2002); Samuel M. Stern, *Studies in Early Ismailism* (Leiden, The Netherlands: E. J. Brill, 1983).

20. Tabatabai, *Shi'ite Islam* (see note 3 above).

21. Ibid.

22. Stern, *Studies in Early Ismailism* (see note 19 above).

23. Iman Abu Hamid al-Ghazali, *Al-Ghazali's Path to Sufism: His Deliverance from Error* (Louisville, KY: Fons Vitae, 2000); Majid Fakhry, *A History of Islamic Philosophy*, 2nd edition (New York: Columbia University Press, 1983).

24. Lewis, *The Assassins* (see note 19 above).

25. Christopher Hitchens, *Orwell's Victory* (London: Penguin, 2002).

26. Seyyed Hossein Nasr, *Islamic Life and Thought* (Chicago: Kazi, 2001).

27. William James, *The Varieties of Religious Experience* (New York: Mentor Books, 1901, 1958).

28. Quoted in Reinhold Niebuhr, "William James on Religious Experience," in *The Cambridge Companion to William James*, edited by Ruth Anna Putnam (Cambridge: Cambridge University Press, 1997) pp. 214–36.

29. James, *The Varieties* (see note 27 above).

30. Robert J. Vanden Burgt, *The Religious Philosophy of William James* (Chicago: Nelson-Hall, 1981).

31. Karl Jaspers, *Way to Wisdom: An Introduction to Philosophy*, trans. R. Manheim (New Haven, CT: Yale University Press, 1951).

32. C. Robert Cloninger, *Feeling Good: The Science of Well-Being* (Oxford: Oxford University Press, 2005).

33. Ibid.

34. Ibid.

35. L. J. Eaves, H. J. Eysenck, and N.G. Martin, *Genes, Culture, and Personality: An Empirical Approach* (London, Academic Press, 1989).

36. George Orwell, *1984* (New York: Plume, 2003).

37. Eaves et al., *Genes, Culture, and Personality* (see note 35 above).

38. Richard Dawkins, *The Selfish Gene* (Oxford: Oxford University Press, 2006); Daniel Dennett, *Breaking the Spell: Religion as a Natural Phenomenon* (New York: Penguin, 2007).

39. Dennett, *Breaking the Spell* (see note 38 above).

40. Cloninger notes that these measures of religiosity—such as frequency of church attendance or adherence to dogmatic beliefs—tend to be objective, and are potentially superficial. (Perhaps these studies best pick up James's healthy-minded religion). But Cloninger notes that this finding is "not true of the personal quest for communication with something beyond human existence, which is spirituality as measured by Self-Transcendence," which also has a genetic component in twin studies. He concludes, "This may explain why people have a personal need to understand their spiritual and existential position in life—otherwise they are not fully happy, regardless of their culture or family upbringing." (Personal communication, 2007) I might add that perhaps James's personalistic type of religion can be seen as partly genetic, while his healthy-minded variety can be seen as mostly environmental.

41. Abdolkarim Soroush, *Reason, Freedom, and Democracy in Islam* (Oxford: Oxford University Press, 2000).

42. Ibid., pp. 16–18.

43. Soroush, in an interview, said, "It was . . . Quine's theories on the philosophy of science that guided my explorations of the philosophy of religion. . . . His theory is that all science is interconnected and, as such, judged as a whole, not as a collection of individual discrete theories, in the tribunal of sense. . . . It was Lakatos who, with the help of Quine's ideas, developed the notion of 'research programs' in science: a whole family of theories, organized in a research program, enter judgment's court. In my book, *Contraction and Expansion of Religious Knowledge* [pp. 15–16], I have based one of my main arguments on this thesis."

44. Soroush, *Reason, Freedom, and Democracy in Islam* (see note 41 above), p. 21.

45. Jaspers, *Way to Wisdom* (see note 31 above).

46. Ibid.

47. Miguel de Unamuno, *The Tragic Sense of Life* (Princeton, NJ: Princeton University Press, 1978).

48. Martin Nozick, *Miguel de Unamuno: The Agony of Belief* (Princeton, NJ: Princeton University Press, 1982).

49. Unamuno, *The Tragic Sense of Life* (see note 47 above).

50. George Santayana, *Character and Opinion in the United States* (New York: Norton, 1920).

51. W. Montgomery Watt, *Muhammad: Prophet and Statesman* (London: Oxford University Press, 1961).

52. As Cloninger comments, it might be asked whether most terrorists might not be diagnosed as having personality disorders (with low self-directedness, cooperativeness, and self-transcendence), making them liable to the charismatic influence of sects—and thus potentially requiring attempts at replacing fear and hate with trust and unity (personal communication, 2007). This could be the case for some such individuals, but as James emphasized in his *Varieties*, the finding of a biological basis for different kinds of religious beliefs neither confirms nor refutes those beliefs. The question is not whether terrorist attitudes are right or wrong; most of us, based on purely moral considerations, can see their falsity. The question is this: Why do they occur in some individuals, in some religions, in certain times and places? The answer to that question is not purely biology or culture or theology,

nor can we wave our hands to say it is a mix. In our day and age, it is a specific mix, a peculiar mix, and I suggest that the enzyme that catalyzes the mix is poverty and political repression.

53. Niall Ferguson, *Virtual History: Alternatives and Counterfactuals* (New York: Basic Books, 2000).

COMMENTS ON SEYYED NASSIR GHAEMI'S ESSAY

RICHARD ANTOUN

I have just read "The Psychology of Islamic Fundamentalism." It is an interesting essay, written from the perspective of a Shi'i Muslim. I am more familiar with the Shi'i history than the William James psychology. The connections between the two are rather loose.

I am not an expert on religion or Shi'i Islam but the author's statement that Shi'i jurisprudence is more pluralistic than Sunni jurisprudence is in accord with what I know. On the other hand, between the four schools of Sunni Law, there are arenas of considerable disagreement on such matters as marriage, divorce, and custody of children. Modern Muslim secular states (the great majority in the world today) have a tendency to be eclectic in drawing on all of them to devise legal codes, thus introducing pluralism.

By the way, the author refers to these four schools as theological schools. That is incorrect. They are law schools. they are not engaging in discussions of salvation or the attributes of God, but of contracts, worship obligations, and family relations, for the most part. There were other Islamic schools, such as the Mutazilites and Asharites that could be rightly termed theological.

Of course, I don't agree with the author's definition of fundamentalism as a combination of a subjective, emotional, personalist attitude of faith, tied to a dogmatic religious doctrine. Rather I have viewed it as an ideal type with the seven attributes that can be found in my essay. Each of us fits somewhere on that continuum of attributes.

SEYYED NASSIR GHAEMI'S REPLY

I appreciate Professor Antoun's comments. The goal of my essay was to give Western readers a sense of the psychology behind the religious experience of some Muslims, particularly those in the Shiite tradition. This psychological approach has been most identified with William James in the West, though I also try to bring in more recent psychiatric studies of personality to see if they can be relevant to understanding Islamic fundamentalism. Readers can judge the extent to which this effort provides helpful insights. It is a rather exploratory effort — one meant to raise possibilities and fertilize our thinking from different sources — rather than an attempt to push forward or justify any single thesis.

Regarding the distinction between Islamic theology and law, it is relevant that this distinction is not as clear in the Islamic tradition as in the West. In the Islamic world, the law was Islamic law, and thus legal work meant theological work. In the West, the law has become secular and distinct from Christianity. In Islam it is important to distinguish *Kalam* (which is theology and law) from *Hikmat* (philosophy, which can attend to religious topics, like theology, or which can be pursued secularly; in either case, it is not necessarily concerned with law.) Islamic philosophy is often spoken about as if it is theology, whereas this is not the case. Furthermore, Islamic law cannot be approached without an appreciation of Islamic theology.

I think I would share Professor Antoun's insight that fundamentalism is not an all-or-nothing entity (that is, that one either is or is not fundamentalist) — rather, there are degrees of fundamentalism. His view of it from the ideal-type perspective, inaugurated by Max Weber in sociology, is useful. My attempt to approach fundamentalism from the psychological perspective is different from, and not necessarily in conflict with, an ideal-type sociological analysis. The notion that fundamentalism involves certain char-

209

acteristics (like a protest against modernism, activism, scripturalism, and so on) may be valid, but it still does not answer the question of *why* some persons are more fundamentalist than others. For that issue, some attention to the individual psychology of religious believers would seem to be needed. My essay was an attempt to begin to explore that topic.

CHRISTIAN ORTHODOXY, FUNDAMENTALISM, AND VIOLENCE

CRAIG NICHOLS

Tradition is the living faith of the dead;
traditionalism is the dead faith of the living.
— Jaroslav Pelikan

The above, oft-quoted epigram by the twentieth-century's foremost scholar of Christian doctrinal history highlights a paradox at the core of human existence that I wish to explore in this essay. The paradox is this: We can actualize our unique human potential (an authentic self), and hence bring something truly new into the world, only when we transcend the closed circle of the self within and by means of the continuity of a shared past that binds together a living community in the present. Overcoming isolated individualism requires a traditional, communal paradigm that has stood the test of time and the repetition of continual rejuvenation. Freedom from the perceived constraints of one's tradition is, ironically, a gift of tradition — but a gift that must be properly appropriated, for history has shown that there is a razor's-edge difference between the letter that kills and the spirit that gives life. Both are the potential inheritance of the past that conditions us and from which we take our bearings.

In an age when the education of youth is preoccupied with quasi-scientific modes of cognition that dogmatically reduce all phenomena to technological functions, the fact that we stand on the shoulders of those who have lived and thought before us cannot be taken for granted as self-evident, as it was for previous generations who bothered to study history in their youth. Global human thought, with but a few pockets of resistance, has descended en masse into a "dead faith," which believes dogmatically (in the negative sense this word now carries) that individual bits of knowable reality can be isolated here and now in the present, as though the whole context of lived human existence, including our collective past, were irrelevant to the meaning of these bits of data. This objectifying point of view has proven highly profitable (for some); conversely, the current global economic structure would likely crumble without it. But within this functionality and profitability is concealed the very essence of the will to power that results in violence.

Modifying Pelikan's epigram slightly (but within the general intention of his insight), I would like to suggest a point that may seem counterintuitive to those who have drunk deeply and uncritically from the well of modern "opinion" (the ancient, pre-Christian meaning of *doxa*). If we trade the word *tradition* for *orthodoxy* (in the Christian sense), and the word *traditionalism* for *fundamentalism* (a phenomenon appearing across a wide spectrum of religious and secular contexts), then a crucial distinction can be seen between the oft-confused phenomena of orthodoxy and fundamentalism. Fundamentalism, as I shall characterize it, manifests as an expression of the will to power of positivism, a will to power that has eclipsed the meaningfulness of tradition in the modern age. Hence, fundamentalism as a concept and in practice falls into the "dead faith" of ideology, which descends further into the totalitarian and tyrannical thinking of either left- or right-wing political fanaticism — the kind of thinking that ultimately envisages "final solutions" in the political sphere for perennial problems of the human condition.

Contrary to the expectations of those caught in this snare, historic Christian orthodoxy, I will argue, provides a vantage point for transcending the mutual pitfalls of fundamentalism, ideology, and the will to violence of totalitarian thought. But lest my argument fail before it begins (due to the possible misapprehension that I am merely longing for an ancient totalitarian and exclusivist vision due to my discontent with a modern one), allow me to stress at the outset (for any who conceive of orthodoxy as just another worldview, or ideology — hence, a self-imprisoning structure) that central to my argument is the paradox that orthodoxy transcends even itself. Consequently, my depiction of orthodoxy will hover between and above the fixed objectivity of a closed system on the one hand, and a simplistic (and deceptively poisonous) relativism on the other. In short, traditional Christian orthodoxy (distinguished from fundamentalism) makes possible a middle way of pluralism between relativistic inclusivism and objectivistic exclusivism.[1]

ORTHODOXY IS A HUMANISM

The highest truth is plural and one, and we participate in it. Nonetheless, it transcends even the synthesis of the one and the many.[2] Of the thousands of creedal variations in the history of Christianity,[3] this is the core epistemic and metaphysical idea, traceable to the first and most widely acknowledged ecumenical creed of Christendom, the Nicene Creed, ratified at the Council of Nicea in 325 and expanded by the Council of Constantinople in 381. The so-called Niceno-Constantinopolitan Creed set forth a benchmark definition of God as three-in-one, a trinity of distinct persons (*hypostases*), subsisting in one Godhead, unified in substance, or nature (*homoousios*). The central creed of historic Judaism, the *Shema* — "Hear, O Israel: The Lord our God is one Lord" (Deut. 6:4ff. RSV) — was recast through Greek metaphysical categories to make possible an extension of the Hebrew covenantal tradition to embrace the diverse Gentile cultures. This preserved at once their unique mythological and linguistic structures while transcending all particular mythological systems in the universality of a unified concept of God as absolute redemptive Source of being — by way of a fully ontologized culmination of the ancient mythology of the dying and rising God. The "othering" of God in the incarnation, death, resurrection, and ascension of Christ (defined as distinct from, yet fully one with, God the Father) is here understood to effect an absolute reversal of the entropy of the cosmos as a whole, including the human tendency toward moral decline, and to be a healing of the human condition accessible through the engagement of our freedom.

Standing *contra mundum* in the fourth century, when the whole Christian world was on the verge of descending into a lesser vision of the meaning of cosmic redemption, St. Athanasius described a "divine dilemma," the solution of which would be the incarnation of God and human participation in the divine life:

Man, who was created in God's image and in his possession of reason reflected the very Word [Logos] Himself, was disappearing, and the work of God was being undone. The law of death, which followed from the Transgression, prevailed upon us, and from it there was no escape. The thing that was happening was in truth both monstrous and unfitting. It would, of course, have been unthinkable that God should go back upon His word and that man, having transgressed, should not die; but it was equally monstrous that beings which once had shared the nature of the Word should perish and turn back again into non-existence through corruption.[4]

Notice how central humanity is to Athanasius's "orthodox" vision — central to God's concern. The angry God fueling so much medieval piety is far in the background of Athanasius's vision; in the foreground is a God of fatherly pathos, paradoxically at odds with his own impassability — a problem ultimately resolved in the passion of the Son. With fervent pathos, Athanasius intones the divine dilemma: "What then was God, being Good, to do?" The problem of evil and violence in human relations brings God to the point of ultimate sacrifice, the transcending of himself (which for the highest can only mean a descending to the lowest point of forsakenness and abandonment of the divine life through suffering as a human being). Through God's own humanization of himself, a mystical bridge is created for human beings to participate in the divine paradigm.

The Eastern Orthodox tradition preserves the language of the early Church Fathers in identifying this mystical participation as *theosis* — literally, "deification," which the Latin West developed under the heading of "sanctification". This ironically humanizing concept is presented perhaps nowhere so clearly as in Athanasius's formulation: "He, indeed, assumed humanity that we might become God."[5] God transcending, or descending from, himself (described as *kenosis*, a mysterious "emptying," in Philippians 2:5–8) creates the possibility for human beings to transcend their own downward tendency toward a violent will to power by actualizing the highest of human capacities, the freedom from self-enslavement, or ego-centered existence (through *theosis*, becoming divine by sharing in the divine life). This paradoxical conception of a fulfilled, empty self is remarkably similar to the *shunyata* concept found in Mahayana Buddhist metaphysics, and has a similar result: an ethics of compassion symbolized in a descending Savior figure (the bodhisattva). And yet the empty self envisioned in Christian orthodoxy is understood as a heightening of the self, a fulfillment through communal life with others and an absolute and personal Other. Hence, the goal is a perfected self (an eternal, relational process), rather than an annihilated self (a finally blown-out flame).[6]

Comparative religion, speculative philosophy, or social-scientific anthropology will search with difficulty for a higher vision of human potential. We may consider the matter, for example, within the frame of Paul Ricoeur's four categories for analyzing the major historical metanarratives of the human condition in his *Symbolism of Evil*.[7] The following is my assessment, using his terminology, of how an orthodox theological humanism ideally transcends the "servile will" that all religious-ritual and secular-political participation is intended to negotiate.

The "Adamic vision" of freedom in the Hebrew tradition is elevated to a freedom so free that it can lay down its life for another and thereby find it again. The "tragic vision" of Greek aestheticism is elevated to a perfected aesthetic deliverance by bringing the Creator of the human drama and the participants in the drama into absolute interrelation with each other; the human tragedy thus becomes a divine comedy in which death can be truly accepted as a defeated enemy rather than grimly borne through aesthetic displacement. The monistic and cyclical "ritual vision" of samsaric suffering, which underpins Indo-European myth and ritual, is transcended in a vision of individual and plural personal perdurance in the face of monarchical cosmology, a freedom to participate in the One, yet remain distinct from it. And finally, the ontological dualism between spirit and matter, achieved provisionally in Plato's metaphysical "Orphic vision," is given a mediating path for reconciliation, so that material being, including the human body, can be granted due dignity as fully real and good, an *incarnate* self,[8] neither mixed nor divided — distinct, but not separate. Orthodox Christianity thus conceived of a transcending humanism — an *Übermensch* traversing an abyss of nihilism, an elevated humanity higher than the gods of Hesiod or the heroes of Homer — long before Nietzsche's autopsy of the decadent, or "fallen" humanity and deity of the West. Is it possible that he overlooked a more profound vision of human potential than anything his own highly individual genius was able to imagine — or perhaps a vision more profound than the tradition of Western objectifying thought on the whole has grasped?

Nietzsche declared through his aesthetic prophet Zarathustra, "I should only believe in a God who knew how to dance."[9] And yet, he seems to have been oblivious to the orthodox God of *perichoresis*, a Dancer at once more wildly exuberant than Dionysus, more soberly rational than Apollo, and more authentically human than any aesthetic genius.

THE HUMAN NEED FOR CREED AND AUTHENTIC COMMUNITY

By preserving the distinction between Creator and creation, while deeming both essentially good, and envisioning a distinction within the very Creator, which provides the means for a beneficent exchange (*oikonomia*) between the distinct natures of Creator and creation, human beings are able to "become" God (*theosis*) while remaining forever distinct from God (perfectly finite and essentially human). Absolute difference and absolute unity are thus preserved in one transcendent vision. How is such an insight into the nature of being — and the transcending of the self implied by it — to be preserved and appropriated? Christianity provides two chief vehicles: the Creed and the Church. The Creed states a truth whose objectivity must be transcended through participation in that truth, just as the ego-self must be transcended. And the Church provides a living structure that preserves the meaning contained in the Creed through communal participation and authoritative — but not authoritarian — adjudication of interpretations of the truth, for finite authority structures are likewise to be transcended.

Returning to the concept with which we began, namely the need to preserve a living tradition, Pelikan points out that the "need for creed" entails a reciprocal need for dogma, which he defines as "the official public teaching of a community of faith."[10] But what of those who hold to a different creed, who are outside the fold of this or that particular community of faith? Pelikan acknowledges soberly the fact that among the three Abrahamic peoples of the Book, "the monotheistic creed has repeatedly become the text—or the pretext — for violence, coercion, and persecution against those who hold to another creed."[11]

To counter the resulting mentality of crusade, pogrom, jihad, and so on, the modern age, since the European Enlightenment, has proposed the general solution of giving up creedal affirmation in favor of a vague, non-dogmatic, relativistic faith, whether in God or human progress. Modern "tolerance" of a plurality of creeds depends largely on people holding no creed to be of any real significance. Nihilism is proffered as the rather unimaginative answer to the violence that holding on to one's creed with inordinate objectivity has occasioned throughout history. But this is both an unrealistic and a dehumanizing solution.

Etienne Gilson, whom Pelikan cites as his "principal scholarly guide to the intellectual history of the Western Middle Ages,"[12] identified the catastrophic descent of modern humanity into universal violence in the 1930s to be largely the result of the vacuum created by creedal indifference and the absence of specific belief.[13] Pelikan summarizes the point, and with it, the human predicament:

> The "will to believe" is so relentless — or, if I may put it this way, so insidious — that when it is denied or frustrated and when religious toleration, instead of being "justified by faith" (Romans 3:28), is justified by non-faith, belief will (in Dostoevsky's phrase) go around the locked doors and sneak in through a window, substituting Wotan for the God of Abraham, Isaac, and Jacob, the Father of the Lord Jesus Christ, and replacing the Shema and the Nicene Creed with the creed of *Blut und Erde*. With the disappearance of "the gods" or of the One True God, "the half-gods" may arrive, wearing a hammer and sickle or a swastika and bringing in their train a creed that is even more ready to persecute than any of the historic creeds have been.[14]

Modern history has demonstrated with remarkable clarity that a vague, free-floating notion of tolerance, based on nothing, opens communal human existence to the most dangerous possibilities of mass mentality.[15] When the historical fact of the human "will to power," which Kant, following the biblical tradition in general, described as *radical evil* stemming from the human will,[16] is dismissed as a perennial problem, then its unchecked operation mounts invisibly and sweeps over the globe with a vengeance previously unimagined. If the will to believe and the need for creed are in fact as strong a human impulse as Pelikan, Gilson, and the popular witness of human beings throughout history declare, then the most reasonable solution would seem to be to seek the overcoming of violence *through* creedal affirmation, rather than around it or without it.

We see this solution in part effected through the civil religiosity that binds citizens to the symbols and constitution of the modern nation-state. But patriotism of this sort is beleaguered by the same sort of nihilism that religious belief has suffered, and for largely the same reasons — caring too much about one's nation and culture over against "the others" can lead to hoarding of the earth's resources, wars of aggression, protectionism, and the like. The modern mentality thinks it best not to hold any supposed truths too dear — including, for example, the traditional biblical truth that human beings have a dignity above plants and animals due to their having been created in the "image and likeness of God" (Genesis 1:26–27), a paradigm which, when rightly construed, can ground both a humanistic vision and a consciousness of environmental responsibility.

Considering this text, St. Basil the Great implores us, "Learn well your own dignity."[17] He understands the essence of human dignity to be the freedom of shaping one's unfinished self, or one's open potential to be, which is a sharing in the divine prerogative of the Creator, fulfilled ultimately as an actualization of the life of the Creator. According to Basil, "Yet now he has made us with the power to become like God. And in giving us the power to become like God, he let us be artisans of the likeness to God."[18] Continued meditation, dialogue, and struggle for truth, striving for the fulfillment of this dignity *through* creedal affirmation, has eventually led a Church — at one time obsessed with confessional conformity to the point of Crusade and Inquisition — to the following binding creedal confession of the Second Vatican Council (as Pelikan quotes):

> The human person has a right to religious freedom. Such freedom consists in this, that all should have such immunity from coercion by individuals, or by groups, or by any human power, that no one should be forced to act against his conscience in religious matters, nor prevented from acting according to his conscience." The case for this freedom is said to be derived from "the dignity of the human person as this is known [first] from the revealed word of God and [second] from reason itself," so that it is not only a teaching of the Church but a universal human right.[19]

Creed, however, requires community — authentic community that emerges in the free recognition of the truth encoded in the creed. G. K.

Chesterton, in his book *Orthodoxy*, has commented on the highly democratic nature of such creedal recognition. "Tradition," he writes, "means giving votes to the most obscure of all classes, our ancestors. It is the democracy of the dead."[20] It is not the church hierarchy that is chiefly responsible for imposing a set of truths to be blindly accepted by unwitting masses. Rather, it is the communal recognition of a deep and mysterious truth in the succinct form of a creed that inspires assent (the creed itself being a distillation of the meaningfulness of a nuanced narrative tradition). And even though the preservation of the creed comes often through the assertion of an authoritative hierarchical claim, there is nevertheless the need for ordinary people, in the end, to validate the formulation of the historic theologians by becoming the "fourth wall"[21] of participation that makes the creed a living reality — a "living faith of the dead."

In point of fact, it is very difficult to identify the precise origins of the central creeds of Christendom. The ecumenical councils that have ratified and lent their authority to the creedal affirmations that have shaped all subsequent tradition in the West did not draw these formulations out of thin air, as otherwise uninformed readers of *The Da Vinci Code*, for example, might be tempted to think. Rather, underlying the theological debates of the professional dogma producers, whose explicit efforts resulted in official orthodox doctrine, there was a flowing lifeblood that bound clergy and laity together: the authority of the lived tradition of the liturgy, understood to be a direct inheritance of the apostolic witnesses who had beheld the Christ, who in turn was the *embodiment* of a living Messianic faith tradition.

The very meaning of *orthodoxy* stems from this vital undercurrent. The Greek word *orthos* lent the meaning of "straight," or "correct," to the compound term. But the meaning of *doxa*, which in classical Greek had meant "opinion" (as in the lowest level of Plato's Divided Line), subsequently developed to mean "laudatory opinion" — and hence "praise" or "glory," as it typically means in the Septuagint and New Testament. "Right doctrine" (an objectifying notion) is a secondary meaning of orthodoxy; "right worship" (an existential notion) is its primary meaning. Once again, Pelikan's statement of the point is most laudatory: "Creed is not in the first instance the business of the professional and learned theological elite; *it is meant to be prayed*, right alongside the Lord's Prayer, as an act of adoration and worship; and it has been a universal experience, far beyond the borders of Christendom, that the best way to preserve genuine spontaneity in the life of prayer is, paradoxically, to formulate fixed and traditional liturgical texts for recitation, on the basis that the spirit of devotion, individual and corporate, can then go on to improvise."[22] The collective affirmation, encoded objectively in the creed, thus indicates a dynamic, relational structure within truth itself — fixed, and yet fluid; clearly stated, yet mysteriously opaque.

The Communal Nature of Truth

We come round then to the crux of the matter: the communal nature of truth. A whole family of interrelated concepts is reflected in the term *communal*, at least three of which are essential for us as we seek to counter a modern bias concerning the meaning of truth: communication, community, and communion. The fundamental problem of fundamentalism, if I may put it this way, is an overestimation and oversimplification of one aspect of truth's multidimensionality — the objectification of being that allows individual consciousness to break apart the continuum of being into discrete units and then to correlate consciousness and "things" in binary opposition. Karl Jaspers's phenomenological metaphysics effectively sets forth the multidimensionality of truth as a corrective to this sort of reductionism.[23] At the highest level of truth, communality falls, on the one side, to philosophical or dialectical struggle for communication, and on the other side, to religious commitment to communion within a faith community. This can be seen through a brief analysis of his thought.

Jaspers's metaphysics progresses through several ascending (or transcending) stages. The first is world-orientation, in which the unity of Being-in-itself — the Encompassing Totality (*das Umgreifende*) — is intuited by being split into subjective and objective modes, thereby allowing individual bits of reality to be carved out of the Whole, which surrounds us. World-orientation itself divides into three levels: first, *the senses* apprehend a vague and indeterminate *environment*; this corresponds to instinctual animal existence, or in humans, the infant that has not yet emerged into self-reflective thought (as occurs through the developmental stage of object-permanence in the first several years of life). Second, as object-permanence develops and self-reflective thought matures, *consciousness* apprehends the surrounding world as a world of objects set over against the self, a world of things to be manipulated. Prior to this stage, everything just is, and just as there is neither truth nor falsity nor ethical deliberation for animals, self-reflection is required for truth to be possible in its nascent form. Truth at the level of the consciousness of objects now emerges as verifiable *correspondence* between the object and the concept of the object, the medium of which is logical explication. At this level, something either *is* or *is not* (*a* or not-*a*, with no tertium quid); the principle of noncontradiction reigns here for all truth claims that are posited.

But this level of truth must be transcended — not left behind, but, like the epistemic ground level of "sense-certainty," must be taken up into a higher relational dimension and preserved there. The truth that one consciousness, in one lifetime, could discern through individual observation of the world would be extraordinarily limited. Human beings would furthermore be stuck at the beginning stages of civilization, constantly reinventing the wheel if individual knowledge could not be communicated and combined amongst individuals to create integrated and collaborative systems of thought. As collective human *spirit* — or *mind* (*Geist*) — interprets the world, the third stage of world-orientation emerges as a systematic coherence of diverse forays into various domains of being. The various skeins of tradition, the collective and collected knowledge of the past and the present, are here woven together to form universal theories in the various natural and social sciences. Common knowledge is made possible at this level through communication, and communication will open the mind to several higher vistas as well.

Within world-orientation, rational communication elevates truth beyond the level of simply verifying posited facts (simple positivism)[24] to a kind of preliminary faith in a worldview built up around those facts. We begin to see here the radical limits of knowledge, for truth transcends knowledge, understood as mere factuality (although truth must never be wholly divorced from scientific factuality, lest we trade reality for fantasy). And yet, fixation upon the supposed objective factuality of worldly phenomena can cause us to misconstrue the full range of human experience, for the scientific mode of knowledge must be transcended in order to grasp a range of experience that eludes objective thought. This higher order of experience may be broadly construed as Transcendence, which appears on the one side as a transcending of the self (a transcending subjectivity), as the unique existence (*Existenz*) of human freedom that is conscious of the ability to choose whether or not to actualize its inherent potential. On the other side, Transcendence (*Transzendenz*) appears in the quasi-objective form of ciphers or symbols — a transcending objectivity that seeks to grasp the meaning of Being as a whole, and thereby situate the meaningfulness of one's existence (*Existenz*) within a coherent framework of Ultimate Reality, which serves to ground the meaning of human life and "save" it from absurdity, drawing out its hidden potential as it fervently seeks its Source. Such ciphers of ultimacy become idols when over-objectified, as though a statue or an idea could be the Absolute. But without them, ultimacy is transferred either to the self, making an idol out of the ego, or to natural phenomena or artistic creations, making idols out of things. Being in its totality can never be grasped objectively, and herein lies the fault of every fundamentalism. Fundamentalism claims to have knowledge — of the Absolute, or Transcendence, or the absolute meaning of Being, or the mind of God — which can only be apprehended obliquely, through faith.

Jaspers labors to distinguish philosophical faith from theological faith,[25] the former being the purview of philosophy, which restrains itself from dogmatic proclamations, and instead seeks to transcend objectification along the dialectical path of Socratic non-knowledge; the latter, however, he understands to operate within the claims of a special revelation that provides final dogmatic answers to the unanswerable questions of human existence. The "neo-orthodox," Protestant theologian, Rudolph Bultmann, writing in the 1950s, debated Jaspers on this point through a series of public discourses, trying to show that the language of theological faith must necessarily appear in dogmatic form, but that such theological endeavor, when properly understood, is aware of the ambiguity of all positive claims about absolute Reality.[26] Eastern Orthodox, Roman Catholic, and Protestant theologians — from Athanasius to Pseudo-Dionysius, from Augustine to Aquinas, from Luther to Barth and Bultmann — have recognized an apophatic dimension to theological language, an impossibility of saying finally what one cannot help but try to say as one attempts to transcend oneself.

And so, the line between philosophical and theological faith can be difficult to draw with precision. Jaspers, claiming to operate only within the nondogmatic uncertainty of philosophical faith, declares boldly, "The more authentically free a man is, the greater his certainty of God. When I am authentically free, I am certain that I am not free through myself."[27] The language of philosophical faith (rooted in reason) and theological faith (rooted in revelation) often overlaps to such an extent that the two faiths become virtually indistinguishable. And since a deep existential dimension can be discerned in the greatest theologians and philosophers, binding the endeavor of the philosopher and that of the theologian together, one can understand with sympathy that a Christian humanist philosopher like Erasmus, after reading Cicero and other classical Pagan moralists, could "hardly refrain from saying, 'St. Socrates, pray for me.'"[28] But the distinction Jaspers draws is instructive. The two faiths, philosophical and theological, are both *faith*, and so in some sense intertwine, but each finds its provisional fulfillment (provisional, since nothing is absolutely fulfilled in this world of limitation) through different means.

Philosophical faith overcomes the narrowness of the self (and hence finds a transcendent truth) through communication, the dialogue with other rational souls that provides a limited but crucial confidence that one is not alone in one's interpretation of reality. There is thus a provisional "certainty" that my existence is meaningful because it is a shared existence, ultimately receiving its contextualization through interaction, or participation, in the Source of all being. Theological faith overcomes the narrowness of the self (and thus experiences a transcendent truth) through communion, which can be understood broadly throughout all religious practice as common participation in the ritual (re-)enactment of a shared metanarrative. The central Christian sacrament of communion creates a mystical bridge within the context of the Church for transcending the individual self — both vertically in relationship with God, and horizontally in relationship with other communicants.

Jaspers specifically rejects the Church's traditional role as guarantor of the communion of souls through communion in large part because he does not want an objectified faith. And so he rejects confessional-creedal participation in the Church, arguing that faith in God "is not laid down in any definite articles of faith applicable to all men or in any historical reality which mediates between man and God and is the same for all men." Echoing Kierkegaard's Protestant existentialism, in this instance, he continues, "The individual, always in his own historicity, stands rather in an immediate, independent relation to God that requires no intermediary."[29] But does the mediation of the Church, which functions in large part to guarantee, through the preservation of tradition, a context in which a genuine communal experience can happen, necessitate an objectification of Transcendence? Further, without institutions of this sort (a comparable institution for the preservation of philosophical and scientific faith might be the university), would the truth experienced in authentic community be preserved at all?

John Zizioulas, writing from within the Greek Orthodox tradition, speaks to the concern of Jaspers that ecclesiastical authority may usurp and control the truth of communication through its control of the ritual of communion (as can be seen, for example, in the Medieval abuse of excommunication and interdiction for political purposes). Zizioulas, however, points to a more dynamic understanding of ritual communion than Jaspers seems ready to admit. Zizioulas argues that, for orthodoxy, the truth that manifests in communion and community is not dependent on an ecclesiastical authority objectively external to the event of revealed truth in the ritual. Rather, not unlike the supposed immediacy of philosophical faith, the authority that binds the community together stems from the event itself: "Because the Christ-truth is not only revealed but also realized, in our existence, as communion within a community, truth is not imposed upon us but springs up from our midst. It is not authority in the sense of *auctoritas* but is grace and love, embracing us in its being which is bound to us existentially. Yet this truth is not the product of sociological or group experience; it comes clearly from another world, and as such is not produced by ourselves."[30]

Communion in the orthodox Christian sense is thus a communion of God and human beings *beyond* time and space, and yet *within* time and space, being rooted in physical elements that "cast together" (as *symbolon*) spirit and matter. No matter how this is described (as Roman Catholic transubstantiation, Lutheran consubstantiation, or even Zwinglian memorialization), the root orthodox notion of *corporate* participation in a mystery existentially grounds the meaning of such dogmatic language. Orthodoxy, at its root, may thus be defined as a *corporate mysticism* that transcends the search for ecstatic experience known to individualistic mysticism.

The language of sacramental mystery, like the language of the creeds, is symbolic language — but symbol understood (as in Jaspers) as a higher truth than positivism comprehends, not a lesser. Without the preservation of textual and ritual possibilities of participation — as for example in the dynamic reciprocity, or living tradition, of creed and church — it is difficult to comprehend how any ciphers of Transcendence would be accessible *as a real possibility of faith* to a present generation in the face of the leveling tendency of modern, technologized mass society.

Further, one cannot *commune with* a generic God any more than one can marry a generic spouse, for as Jaspers points out, "Man's supreme achievement in this world is communication from personality to personality. Accordingly, our relation to transcendence, if we may speak in paradox, becomes sensibly present in our encounter with the personal God."[31] But faith in a personal God (which, according to Jaspers, is a culminating recognition of philosophical faith) implies a reversal in which this God speaks *to me* through revelation. Faith that genuine communication between persons is possible and even necessary for human existence to be meaningful (the core of philosophical faith) leads naturally to the genuine possibility of a faith in which communication is both vertical and horizontal simultaneously — a revelatory faith (meeting the approaching "Other") manifested in and through a communal body. For such a possibility to be realized, both faiths, theological and philosophical, must be entered into *existentially* by the person seeking to overcome objectifying thinking.

Just as meditation on Trinitarian theology reveals a perpetual motion within the Godhead itself, philosophical reflection on the nature of truth reveals a perpetual motion between various levels of faith and knowledge. The highest truth is participation in this dialectical motion, not fixation on any particular static concept. Platonic dialectic, aimed at obtaining the Good, and *perichoretic theosis*, aimed at communing with God, thus dance together at the highest level of truth without collapsing into each other. The orthodox link between the two faiths was worked out by the early Church Fathers as a *Logos* Christology that bridged the concepts of reason and revelation, and yet transcended both in the recognition that all kataphatic language is only meaningful in apophatic experience.

OBJECTIFICATION, FUNDAMENTALISM, AND VIOLENCE

Objectification of Transcendence is the essence of fundamentalism; the inevitable result is violence, either toward mind or body. Christian orthodoxy emerged in the first several centuries through a hard-fought struggle against a multitude of gnostic rivals, all of which sought to reduce the apophatic Unknowable to a kataphatic Known.[32] Orthodoxy strove to preserve a notion of truth perfectly balanced between the objectivity of the symbol which would maintain it in immutable form, and the free potential of the mind to conceive of the Absolute in the full spectrum of symbolic possibility. That it often fell short of this ideal in practice is a lamentable fact of history, as the violent persecution of heretics shows (especially after Christianity experienced the radical reversal — moving from persecuted faith to imperially sanctioned religion). This is a problem with every communal ideal, the source of the problem lying not so much with the ideal as with the will to power of the human condition. Christianity sought to preserve a delicate balance between immanent authority structure (the visible Church) and transcendent meaning (the invisible "body of Christ") through the liturgical use of creeds, the earliest of which were hammered out in the struggle to preserve the unity of the faith over against the schismatic nature of the gnostic cults.

Although there are a multitude of groups lumped together as "gnostic," the very term helps to identify what is common to them. Simply put, gnosticism claims to *know* that which can only be grasped through faith. Hence, the creeds that were developed to oppose gnosticism should not be interpreted in gnostic fashion, as they typically are understood by the modern positivistic mindset that rejects them as an objectification of the Absolute. Gnosticism, for example, typically claimed to have an alternative revelation, stemming from Christ — a secret gospel that would allow only a select few into the inner sanctum of salvation, that is, those *possessing* the secret knowledge of the mind of God.[33] It is interesting to note how anti-Semitic most gnostic teaching was; it was orthodox thought that insisted that the God and Father of Jesus Christ was the same God who created all things and pronounced them good in Genesis I — and therefore, the emerging New Testament canon, according to the orthodox, should not displace the Old, but should be read as its fulfillment. Something new had emerged, but within the continuity of an ongoing tradition.

Gnosticism, furthermore, was typically *docetic*, considering the appearance of God in human flesh to be a mere appearance, for the gnostics found intolerable the paradox that the Savior, who was spiritual and good, could suffer and die within the prison of a material body, which was deemed evil — so Christ only *seemed* to die in the flesh. Gnosticism thus resolved the paradox of spirit and matter (a paradox which every incarnate human soul intuits in itself as a limited freedom, or *Existenz*) by rejecting the legitimacy of human (and divine) participation in matter. Orthodoxy fought for the full acceptance of bodily reality, and hence opened itself to a radical humanism, as I have argued above.

Orthodoxy dealt with the paradox of the coexistence and dynamic relationship between spirit and matter by grasping the problem from the perspective of the whole, rather than trying to build up to the whole by adding together disparate parts. For example, the procedure of constructing a god-man from the ground up always resulted in a half-god, half-man. Such a creature would be neither fully the one nor the other, but a unique hybrid, like a Centaur or Chimera. Such conceptions allow for a partial transcendence of the self, but they also obscure the full paradox of the human being's integration of spirit and matter, or freedom and necessity. Orthodoxy sought a higher conception of Christ (and fought hard not to lose it): a paradoxically whole God and whole human being in one cipher of Transcendence, a perfect unity of transcendence and immanence, mediated in a single symbolic manifestation. Such a conception defies objectification, yet it must be set down in creedal and doctrinal form for two chief reasons. The first is simply to preserve the precise form of the concept so that the attainment of thought would not be lost to subsequent generations. But the second and most important reason is to provide a means by which the truth encoded in the doctrine may be appropriated through participation in the archetype — for a symbol is only meaningful when a participant participates in its meaning; it is a dynamic reciprocity.[34]

Fundamentalism, a modern form of gnosticism, focuses narrowly on the first of these impulses and tends to forget that the second drives the interpreter toward a transcending of the first. The first tendency anchors the symbol in objectivity, the mode of truth proper to world-orientation. The second transcends objectivity (while necessarily speaking in quasi-objective language), and presses the interpreter (or better, the *participant* in symbolic meaning) toward a mystical grasping of an apophatic whole, which can never be fully objectified, lest it become an idol. The cultivation of a mystical transcending of objectivity further implies the humility of "non-knowledge." It is an ironic "knowing that I do not know" the absolute truth (the chief characteristic of Socratic wisdom), and hence I am pressed toward humility, recognizing that I do not have the Absolute as a mental possession. It always eludes my control, and yet, I have it as I participate in it. It presses me toward the humble acknowledgment that someone else's cipher of transcendence, someone else's creed *may* be a participation in the truth as well, for I do not *know* that it is *not* so, regardless of how strongly I may adhere to the truth of my own creed.

I have described fundamentalism in terms of a general epistemic tendency that has threatened to narrow orthodox thought throughout its history. The label itself emerged into the mainstream of American consciousness in the first decades of the twentieth century as a conservative faction of the Presbyterian Church (grounded in the activity of Princeton Theological Seminary) sought to shore up the relativistic erosion of the faith from the encroachment of modernist thought.[35] The irony of the movement, in retrospect, was and is its use of a modernist philosophical underpinning (a largely de-ontologized modern nominalism) to ground a hermeneutic and theology that could be set up in opposition to the "modernist," or "liberal," theology of the nineteenth century. The contrasting positions, much as in the creationist-evolutionist debate, rest on the same modernist foundations of philosophical positivism.

Consider, for example, the "five fundamentals" of the faith that were posited by the General Assembly of the northern United Presbyterian Church in the United States of America in 1910 as essential to "Protestant Orthodoxy."[36] They consisted of a literal, or objective, belief in (1) the inerrancy of the Bible, (2) the virgin birth of Christ, (3) juridical atonement through the sacrificial death of Christ, (4) the bodily resurrection of Christ, and (5) the historicity of Christ's miracles. The positivism that modernist thought had applied to natural phenomena, admitting as relevant only what can be known objectively, was applied to the faith tradition of Christianity, arguing, in effect, that the symbols of faith must be accepted according to the same standard as the positivistic sciences. They had bought into the modernist either-or standard of truth that can only admit of an exclusivistic orientation to what is real and meaningful. Traditional symbols are thereby reduced to "mere symbols," which are opposed to objective reality. The Bible then must be either true or false; the virgin birth, resurrection, atonement, and miracles either happened or they did not. As fundamentalism subsequently combined with dispensationalism, the literal interpretation of eschatological language further insisted on a de-symbolification and de-mystification of the most symbolic of all biblical discourse, apocalyptic prophecy. There is no middle ground when the standard is definite knowledge.

But what sense can this approach make out of the doctrines of the Trinity or the two natures of Christ? How can God be three-in-one? How can the impassable God become human so as to suffer a passion? How can God empty himself (*kenosis*) so that human beings might become divine (*theosis*)? How can Christ be completely human and completely divine in one instantiation? How can God be *literally* a Father and a Son to himself at the same time? This sort of language demands a movement toward apophaticism and mystical appropriation; objectification can only obscure its meaning, rendering the transcendent reality ultimately inaccessible. Ironically, the attempt to preserve orthodoxy with modern philosophical presuppositions resulted in a new gnosticism, a new resolution of the paradox of faith.

From within the ranks of the Reformed Calvinist tradition (on the Germanic side), a much more productive counterposition to the nineteenth-century liberal theology born of Schleiermacher and the European Enlightenment emerged in Karl Barth's "neo-orthodoxy," which represented a return to the tradition of ongoing clarification of biblical revelation as a historical "church dogmatics." Even with a Reformed distrust of philosophical speculation (although he himself was highly influenced by Kant and Kierkegaard, among other philosophers), Barth nevertheless managed to forge a middle way between liberalism and fundamentalism by transcending both in the recovery of a transcendent conception of the revealed *Logos* (forming an implicit link with the *Logos* Christology of the early Church Fathers). Consider, for example, the implications of Barth's nonobjectivist understanding of divine-human reconciliation in Christ: "Our starting-point," he writes in the *Church Dogmatics*, "is that this 'God with us' at the heart of the Christian message is the description of an *act of God*, or better, of God himself in this act of his. It is a report, not therefore a statement of fact on the basis of general observation or consideration. God with us, or what is meant by these three words, is not an object of investigation or speculation. It is not a state, but an *event*."[37]

Barth, like the modern fundamentalists, emerged from within a tradition of *sola scriptura* (a Protestant anti-tradition tradition), but with his understanding of participation in the Word (*Logos*) in and through the words (*logoi*) of the text of Scripture, his theology opened to an existential dimension that, like classical orthodoxy, transcended both subjectivism and objectivism. For Barth, as in classical Christian orthodoxy, God is not an object, nor is God's revelation. Knowing God is a *present* existential event, not a datum of the past — an event that is made possible in and through the living tradition of canon, creed, and church.

CULTIVATING TRUTH AS MYSTERY AND COMPASSION

To the extent that orthodoxy remains true to its essence as a cultivation of mystery, it naturally opens itself in humility to dialog with other traditions, for ultimate truth is no one's possession. A significant clue to understanding this plural dimension of truth (and yet, also a clue for maintaining truth in a particular tradition, rather than abandoning all truth in bland relativism) can be seen in the Dalai Lama's discussion of the world religions:

> One could say that the ethical teachings of a faith tradition are the conclusions supported and validated by the process of the metaphysical or philosophical thinking. Although the world's religions differ widely in terms of metaphysics and philosophy, the conclusions these differing philosophies arrive at — that is, their ethical teachings — show a high degree of convergence. In this sense, we can say that regardless of whatever metaphysical explanations religious traditions employ, they all reach similar conclusions. In some form or another, the philosophies of all world religions emphasize love, compassion, tolerance, forgiveness, and the importance of self-discipline. Through interfaith and interpersonal communication, sharing, and respect, we can learn to appreciate the valuable qualities taught by all religions, and the ways in which all religions can benefit humanity.[38]

Nevertheless, as he goes on to say, "if one pursues any path deeply enough, it eventually becomes necessary to embrace one spiritual path together with its underlying metaphysics."[39] Only by actually walking a specific *traditional* path in common lot with the "democracy of the dead" (to recall Chesterton's phrase) can anyone make any sort of spiritual, intellectual, or ethical progress. One cannot cultivate oneself in theory, nor in isolation. Commitment to specific metaphysical symbols is required for actual participation in the higher levels of truth. The Dalai Lama thus rightly contends that it can make a big difference whether one embraces a personal Absolute, as in the Western "religions of the book," or an impersonal Absolute as in various forms of Hinduism, Buddhism, or Daoism, although in humility he refrains from declaring any one religion (including his own) to be the only objectively right one. If truth is to be grasped as a reality, a struggle against untruth is required, but the struggle for truth must be a loving struggle, lest the will to *possess* the truth overshadow compassion for the human predicament. Love and compassion for others is thus revealed to be the existential meaning of truth at the highest levels of non-knowledge.

The mediation of the infinite and the finite always yields a paradox upon which every attempt at literal understanding ultimately suffers shipwreck. The gospel, the creeds, and orthodox thought as a whole — at its highest level of meaning — is obscured by literalism; it was *traditionally* meant to be appropriated through mystical participation in a sacramental life practiced in a community of shared faith. For this reason, the mystery (Greek *mysterion*, or Latin *sacramentum*) of communion was always the central ritual practice of the nascent Christian community. Common creedal confession likewise formed a central part of liturgical worship, indicating a continuity between the two practices.

To see the mystical nature of the orthodox use of the creed, one might further compare its liturgical recitation to the use of the *koan* in Zen Buddhist practice. In Zen, the *koan* is a "public case," a puzzle or story transmitted from master to pupil (compare apostolic succession) that ultimately has no solution, except the existential illumination of the practitioner. The point of the *koan* is to transcend the objectifying ego. A literal answer is always a mistake. The same holds true for orthodox creedal affirmation. Of course, a key difference certainly lies between the two traditions insofar as Christian orthodoxy promotes a corporate, communal mysticism, whereas Zen leans toward individual mysticism (despite its traditional preservation in monastic communities).

Yet parallels abound. Reminiscent of Daoism, which helped transform Chinese and Japanese Buddhism into its unique forms, the Greek Orthodox theologian, Bishop Kallistos Ware, cuts against the Western tendency to objectify faith by describing orthodoxy (contra fundamentalism) as a *way* rather than a possession or mental content, a *path* of meditation and loving struggle that must be lived in order to be known — existential terms that mirror the actualization of existence (*Existenz*) described by Jaspers. It is instructive that Ware begins his primer on orthodoxy[40] with a chapter on "God as Mystery" before setting forth chapters on the more objective determinations of God (God as "Trinity," as "Creator," as "Man," and as "Spirit"), and concludes with a chapter specifically dealing with participation in Transcendence, "God as Prayer." At every step, cultivation of the Trinitarian doctrine, preserved in the creed, is meant to bring the practitioner, like the Zen disciple, past the objective form to a lived reality of compassion for all living beings. Like Buddhism, orthodoxy espouses wisdom (compare Buddhist *prajna*) through compassion (compare Buddhist *karuna*). The ciphers of Transcendence are different between the two religions, but the methods and goals are remarkably similar, namely, pressing through the mystery of being to realize (that is, to make real) compassion. Consider Ware's description of Trinitarian life:

> A genuine confession of faith in the Triune God can be made only by those who, after the likeness of the Trinity, show love mutually towards each other. There is an integral connection between our love for one another and our faith in the Trinity; the first is a precondition for the second, and in its turn the second gives full strength and meaning to the first. . . . Because we know that God is three in one, each of us is committed to living sacrificially in and for the other; each is committed irrevocably to a life of practical service, of active compassion. Our faith in the Trinity puts us under an obligation to struggle at every level, from the strictly personal to the highly organized, against all forms of oppression, injustice and exploitation. In our combat for social righteousness and "human rights," we are acting specifically *in the name of the Holy Trinity.*[41]

The collective confession of the creed, understood as participation in an archetype of love and self-sacrifice, grounds a collective commitment to an ethical orientation in the world, wherein the loving struggle for truth expands into a loving struggle for social justice and human rights. The way of orthodoxy is thus an expanding horizon that opens to "the other" in compassion and dialogue, aware that all human beings share the same plight, the same condition, the same limitation of understanding. It nevertheless maintains itself against the collapse of all truth, by preserving in genuine faith a commitment to the quest for truth as mediated through its own traditional symbols. The One thus opens itself to plurality — without dissolving in irretrievable difference. The way of fundamentalism, by contrast, is a narrow tunnel vision that believes Transcendence can be possessed as a mental content, and since this content is believed to be held uniquely by one group, all others must be wrong. What will toward genuine communication, or open dialogue, can come from such an understanding? In its more benign forms, fundamentalism engenders indifference toward other belief systems, a kind of protectionism. In its more malicious forms, it seeks to coerce others into conformity — to the point of mental or physical violence. This pattern holds whether one is speaking of secular-progressive political forms of fundamentalism or traditionalistic religious forms.[42]

The cultivation of Transcendence, through appropriating an "objective" creed, in a process that allows for a transcending of the creed's objectivity in mystical participation, opens collective human potential to a loving struggle for truth that hovers between the negative extremes of violent mental coercion and apathetic nihilism. The key to overcoming violence, perhaps ironically, is to struggle for truth from the basis of one's own tradition (so that a nihilistic rootlessness does not sweep away the entire endeavor) while simultaneously, in communication with traditions other than one's own, cultivating awareness of the mysterious nature of truth. The meaning of one's own existence (or one's tradition as a whole) can only be clarified in the eyes of an "other," for truth is a *shared* reality, and only in sharing it does it emerge at all—in the nexus of communication, community, and communion with the Source of one's being.

EPIGRAM: Jaroslav Pelikan, *The Christian Tradition: A History of the Development of Doctrine, Vol. I: The Emergence of the Catholic Tradition (100–600)* (Chicago: University of Chicago Press, 1971), 9. See also, Jaroslav Pelikan, *The Vindication of Tradition* (New Haven, CT: Yale University Press, 1984) pp. 65ff.

NOTES:

1. I should further add that *orthodoxy* in this essay is meant in a fairly broad sense and is intended to indicate an essential theological and existential orientation that can be found as the lifeblood flowing through Eastern Orthodoxy, Roman Catholicism, and Protestantism, despite the dogmatic differences that have emerged in these major branches of historic Christianity. I do not wish to minimize the importance of doctrinal differences, but rather to locate a common ground from which to make a greater point concerning identity and difference in the determination of the meaning of truth, and the ethical implications of "orthodox" metaphysics, broadly construed.

2. Vladimir Lossky describes well how the orthodox Christian theology of Pseudo-Dionysius (ca. fifth or sixth century), a paradigmatic mystical theologian for both the Eastern and Western churches, transcends the synthetic, primordial "God-Unity" of the neo-Platonists, and Plotinus in particular. See Vladimir Lossky, *The Mystical Theology of the Eastern Church*, trans. Members of the Fellowship of St. Alban and St. Sergius (Crestwood, NY: St. Vladimir's Seminary Press, 1957) pp. 29–33.

3. For a definitive guide to the meaning and function of creeds in the history of Christian thought and experience, see Jaroslav Pelikan, *Credo: Historical and Theological Guide to Creeds and Confessions of Faith in the Christian Tradition* (New Haven, CT: Yale University Press, 2003).

4. St. Athanasius, *On the Incarnation (De Incarnatione Verbi Dei)*, trans. by A Religious of C.S.M.V. (Crestwood, NY: St. Vladimir's Seminary Press, 1993) pp. 31–32 [§6].

5. Ibid., p. 93 [§54].

6. It is striking to consider the parallel between orthodox "theosis as kenosis" and the Zen notion of enlightenment as "suchness" (*tathata*), which identifies *shunyata* as "something" transcending the being/non-being duality, but a detailed analysis lies beyond the scope of this essay.

7. See Paul Ricoeur, *The Symbolism of Evil*, trans. Emerson Buchanan (Boston: Beacon, 1967).

8. Cf. Gabriel Marcel's notion of "incarnate being," based on the orthodox Christian archetype of the incarnation, as a reconciling category between idealism and materialism, or Cartesian mind-body dualism; see chap. I, "Incarnate Being as the Central Datum of Metaphysical Reflection," in his *Creative Fidelity*, trans. Robert Rosthal (NY: Fordham University Press, 1964).

9. Friedrich Nietzsche, *Thus Spoke Zarathustra*, trans. Graham Parkes (New York: Oxford University Press, 2005) p. 36 [Part I, §7].

10. Jaroslav Pelikan, "The Will to Believe and the Need for Creed," in *Orthodoxy and Western Culture: A Collection of Essays Honoring Jaroslav Pelikan on His Eightieth Birthday*, ed. Valerie Hotchkiss and Patrick Henry (Crestwood, NY: St. Vladimir's Seminary Press, 2005) p. 166.

11. Ibid., p. 170.

12. Ibid., p. 171.

13. Etienne Gilson's call for a dogmatic basis for tolerance can be found in his *Dogmatism and Tolerance* (New Brunswick, NJ: Rutgers University Press, 1952).

14. Pelikan, "The Will to Believe and the Need for Creed" (see note 11 above) p. 171.

15. Gabriel Marcel, again informed by his "creative fidelity" to orthodox Catholic tradition, together with an openness to existential philosophical speculation, is further instructive on this point in his *Man Against Mass Society*, trans. G. S. Fraser (Lanham: University of America Press, 1985).

16. See Book I: "Concerning the Indwelling of the Evil Principle with the Good, or on the Radical Evil in Human Nature" in Immanuel Kant, *Religion within the Limits of Reason Alone*, trans. Theodore M. Greene and Hoyt Hudson (New York: Harper & Row, 1960).

17. St. Basil the Great, *On the Human Condition*, trans. Nonna Verna Harrison (Crestwood, NY: St. Vladimir's Seminary Press, 2005) p. 33.

18. Ibid., p. 44.

19. Pelikan, "The Will to Believe and the Need for Creed" (see note 11 above) p. 172.

20. G. K. Chesterton, *Orthodoxy*, in *The Collected Works of G. K. Chesterton*, ed. David Dooley (San Francisco: Ignatius, 1986) p. 51.

21. I am here applying Gadamer's analysis of "aesthetic play" to the "play of communion," so to speak. Consider his description of the ambiguous phenomenon of "play": "All presentation is potentially a representation for someone. That this possibility is intended is the characteristic feature of art as play. The closed world of play lets down one of its walls, as it were" [Hans-Georg Gadamer, *Truth and Method*, 2d. ed., trans. Joel Weinsheimer and Donald G. Marshall (New York: Crossroad, 1992) p. 108]. Applying metaphysical "play" to the specific case of a theatrical "play," he continues: "It is not really the absence of a fourth wall that turns the play into a show. Rather, openness toward the spectator is part of the closedness of the play. The audience only completes what the play as such is" [Ibid., p. 109]. Liturgical ritual is more obviously participatory than a theatrical drama; but the point concerning metaphysical participation in the symbolic "play" of meaning is largely the same.

22. Pelikan, "The Will to Believe and the Need for Creed" (see note 11 above) pp. 179–80.

23. The definitive statement of Jaspers's metaphysics can be found in his *Philosophy*, 3 Vols., trans. E. B. Ashton (Chicago: University of Chicago Press, 1969, 1970, 1971). For a more succinct version of the key elements of his thought progression, see Karl Jaspers, *Reason and Existenz*, trans. William Earle (New York: Noonday Press, 1955); especially pertinent to the present discussion is the Third Lecture in this text on "Truth as Communicability."

24. I employ the term *Positivism* throughout this essay rather broadly, and in a sense consistent with Auguste Comte's nineteenth-century coinage. As such, it refers to the modern mode of scientific inquiry (born of late Medieval nominalism) that has divorced itself from traditional theology and metaphysics, setting in their place the methodology of empirical verification of the properties and relations of natural phenomena. Positivism may be seen as a common denominator in the modern movements of sociology, psychology, economics, and political theory, as well as analytic philosophy and the hard sciences.

25. See Karl Jaspers, *Philosophical Faith and Revelation*, trans. E. B. Ashton (New York: Harper & Row, 1967).

26. See Karl Jaspers and Rudolph Bultmann, *Myth and Christianity: An Inquiry into the Possibility of Religion Without Myth*, trans. Norbert Guterman (Amherst, NY: Prometheus, 2005).

27. Karl Jaspers, *Way to Wisdom: An Introduction to Philosophy*, trans. Ralph Manheim (New Haven, CT: Yale University Press, 1954) p. 65.

28. Quoted in Jacob Bronowski and Bruce Mazlish, *The Western Intellectual Tradition, From Leonardo to Hegel* (New York: Harper & Row, 1960) p. 67.

29. Jaspers, *Way to Wisdom* (see note 28 above) p. 47.

30. John D. Zizioulas, *Being as Communion: Studies in Personhood and the Church* (Crestwood, NY: St. Vladimir's Seminary Press, 1985), 115.

31. Jaspers, *Way to Wisdom* (see note 28 above) p. 71.

32. For an excellent guide to the diverse forms of gnosticism, see Kurt Rudolph, *Gnosis: The Nature and History of Gnosticism*, trans. Robert McLachlan Wilson (New York: Harper & Row, 1983).

33. The secret gnosis of the gnostics consisted generally of newly invented Neoplatonic mythology, involving the descent of a Savior through many metaphysical levels, or aeons, to rescue the divine-human souls who have been imprisoned in material bodies by a malicious demiurge creator — that is, Yahweh, the god of the Old Testament. Bentley Layton describes the "classic gnostic myth," using The Secret Book According to John as a chief paradigm, in his "Historical Introduction" to *The Gnostic Scriptures: A New Translation with Annotations and Introductions* (New York: Doubleday, 1987) pp. 5–22.

34. It should be noted that orthodox theologians ultimately claimed the term *gnosis* for themselves, while condemning the use to which it was put by "gnosticism." As Pelikan points out, the ante-Nicene Alexandrian school, including Clement and Origen, shared much in common with gnostic Neoplatonism, although they were considered orthodox in their time. He adds that the term *gnostic*, particularly in Clement "was used as a title for the Christian intellectual" [Pelikan, *The Christian Tradition*, Vol. I (see note 11 above) pp. 95–96]. However, the orthodox meaning of *Christian gnosis* developed as an apophatic Trinitarianism with emphasis placed on the personal (hypostatic) relationality of "knowing another" rather than knowing a cognitive content. Lossky, representing Eastern Orthodox mystical theology, states, "This awareness of grace and of God's presence in us, is generally called gnosis or spiritual understanding (*gnosis pneumatike*), defined by St. Isaac the Syrian as 'the knowledge of eternal life' and 'the knowledge of secret realities.'" [Lossky, *Mystical Theology of the Eastern Church* (see note 3 above) pp. 246–47]. But the "secret" to be "known" is that all objective knowledge must be transcended, for "the more one is united to Him, the more one becomes aware of His unknowability, and, in the same way, the more perfect one becomes, the more one is aware of one's own imperfection" [Ibid., p. 205].

35. A good orientation to the roots of fundamentalist thought in America can be seen in J. Gresham Machen's book *Christianity and Liberalism* (New York: Macmillan, 1923). There are many side issues in fundamentalism, but the key issue, as this text shows well, is the fundamentalist opposition to "modernism" (or "liberalism") and the literalist hermeneutic used to counter it. This, in my view, is the key to "fundamentalism." It should be noted, however, that Christian fundamentalism later came to be intimately connected with dispensationalist eschatology, and because Machen, along with B. B. Warfield, of the

Princeton School of fundamentalist Calvinism, opposed the growing trend of dispensationalism in the ranks of the fundamentalists, many fundamentalist Christians today do not necessarily claim him as their own.

36. See C. T. McIntire, "Fundamentalism," in *Evangelical Dictionary of Theology*, ed. Walter A. Elwell (Grand Rapids, MI: Baker Book House, 1984) p. 433.

37. Excerpted from the Church Dogmatics in Clifford Green, ed., *Karl Barth: Theologian of Freedom* (Minneapolis: Fortress, 1989) p. 207.

38. Tenzin Gyatso, *Essence of the Heart Sutra: The Dalai Lama's Heart of Wisdom Teachings*, trans. Geshe Thupten Jinpa (Boston: Wisdom Publications, 2005) p. 10.

39. Ibid., p. 19.

40. Kallistos Ware, *The Orthodox Way* (Crestwood, NY: St. Vladimir's Seminary Press, 1979).

41. Ibid., pp. 38–39.

42. Similarly, a "dogmatic" epistemology of positivism taints much of contemporary scientific discourse by insisting on a uni-dimensional understanding of truth — a view which is not even tenable among the natural sciences, for each distinct field of scientific endeavor presupposes a Whole that cannot be grounded from within itself.

COMMENTS ON CRAIG NICHOLS'S ESSAY

JAMES CAREY

I have found the essay "Christianity, Fundamentalism, and Violence" to be interesting, forceful, and engagingly written.

I have reservations about speaking of fundamentalism as something that points toward "final solutions." Unlike most contemporary critics of fundamentalism, you commendably anchor this concept in its historical origins. But you seem to occasionally employ the term *fundamentalism* as a synonym for religious fanaticism, when the latter expression would have been more accurate and less tendentious. Similarly, I think that linking fundamentalism with "the will to violence in totalitarian thought" is too extreme. It might not even adequately express your real intention. You *characterize* fundamentalism as "an expression of the will to power of positivism," but — unless I've overlooked it, which is certainly possible — you do not *define* fundamentalism until later, and there the historically precise definition is not fully in accord with the earlier characterization. Or so it seems to me.

I don't know what earliest creeds you have in mind. The Church certainly struggled with Gnosticism, but the first two-thirds of the Nicene Creed, composed at the Council of Nicaea were directed not against Gnostics but against Arius and his followers. The last third, composed at the First Council of Constantinople, was directed against those who denied the divinity of the Holy Spirit. The formulations of the third council, at Ephesus, were directed against Nestorius and his followers, while those of the fourth Council, at Chalcedon, were directed against the Monophysites. You know all this, I feel sure. I only wish to point out that none of these groups, as far as I am aware, were traditionally thought of as Gnostics. That having been said, I do think that there is a similarity between these heresies and those of the Gnostics. For, in all these cases, the Christian faith was disfigured and transformed into something that one could intellectually comprehend in worldly terms — thus obviating its mystery.

If I understand Jaspers's use of the term *cipher*, I would have thought that the cipher, or mysterious union of the apparent irreconcilables, (divine) transcendence and (human) immanence, would more clearly be expressed by *Incarnation* or by *theosis* than by *Transcendence*, at least in the context of Christian orthodoxy. I do realize, however, that the term *Transcendence* (with a capital "T") may be doing double duty for both *Incarnation* and *theosis*, which you, following the lead of St. Athanasius, correctly recognize as two sides of the same coin.

Although this or that fundamentalist might claim to *know* what he only *believes*, fundamentalism, certainly Christian fundamentalism, understands itself to be faith and *not* knowledge — least of all, *esoteric* knowledge. So I don't know why you call fundamentalism a form of Gnosticism. Is it perhaps your opinion that any opinion, thought, or belief that claims to be objectively true, and not just a matter of subjective perspective — whether the subjective perspective of a particular individual or the subjective perspective of a particular community — is, even if unbeknownst to itself, thereby Gnostic? If so, then orthodox Christians are at least as Gnostic as fundamentalists.

You attribute to Christian fundamentalism the presupposition that "the virgin birth, resurrection, atonement, and miracles either happened or they did not." This "either-or," however, has been the presupposition of virtually all serious thought about Christianity prior to the twentieth century. That you can't have it both ways has been the presupposition of both Christian thought and anti-Christian thought. This is the presupposition of Christian orthodoxy, most definitely of Christian Orthodoxy, as well as of fundamentalism.

Regarding the reports of miracles, I fully agree that there is no "definite knowledge," regarding those questions. But none of the beliefs that you refer to are frank contradictions. (They do, of course, contradict natural science. But natural science, unlike logic and mathematics, necessarily depends on empirical generalizations, and so it lacks the indubitable certainty that it is wont to claim for itself these days.)

Now, there would indeed be a contradiction if orthodox Christians said there was only one God, but that there were really three Gods, or that there were three divine persons, but that these three were only one divine person. No one can truthfully claim to believe these things because they violate the nature of the mind itself. The Church teaches, instead, that God is one Being subsisting in three divine persons—a truth that does not contradict our reason, but which cannot be fully comprehended by our reason either.

The same is true of the Incarnation. Orthodox Christians do not say the Christ has two natures but that these are really only one nature. Nor does it say that Christ is one person but that he is also two persons. Such things would be frank contradictions and, again, could not be considered by the mind, no matter how hard one was trying to be pious or, for that matter, mystical. The Church does not teach such contradictions but, rather, that Christ is one person with two natures. And that is not a contradiction but, like the Trinity, a revealed mystery that calls for the response of faith, not of knowledge.

Of course one might say that the Incarnation is a contradiction, because everything in the world that we know about has only one nature, and one might say something similar about the Trinity. But then one would be essentially voicing the Church's own claim that the doctrines of the Trinity and the Incarnation pertain to truths that, because they transcend our experience of the world, cannot be refuted by appeal to what we know, or think we know, about the world.

I thought, perhaps wrongly, that Barth's "non-objectivist understanding" expressed a commitment to regard God not as an object (a *thing*), and thus adequately graspable by the ostensibly disinterested intellect, but as a subject (a *person*), and hence to be encountered rather than grasped. I sense — and maybe it's my misreading — an equivocation in your use of the term *objective*. God's being with us is certainly not objective, if *objective* means "in the manner of an object." But I thought that Barth would hold that God's being with us is objective in the sense of his being objectively (that is, *really*) with us, and not just with us subjectively (as a matter of subjective interpretation or perspective). In other words, *statements* about God (or about any person) can be objective, in the latter sense, without implying that God himself is an object rather than a person. The statement, *God is with us*, is objectively (that is, *really*) true, so much so that the contradictory claim, *God is not with us*, is objectively (that is, *really*) false. God is with us whether we like it or not. He is with us even when we deny his existence, for he continues to call us to himself. Maybe you did not intend to imply that Barth thought otherwise, but I do think that your usage of the word *objective* is ambiguous, which leads me now to my final observation.

Unless I am seriously misunderstanding the concluding pages of your paper, you seem to be saying that it might be possible to get beyond exclusivist ways of regarding truth. You seem to concur in the Dalai Lama's claim: "If one pursues any path deeply enough, it eventually becomes necessary to embrace one spiritual path together with its underlying metaphysics." The Dalai Lama speaks rightly about the remarkable similarities that one can find in the *moral* teachings of the different world religions. (A Thomist or a Kantian would say that this congruence is not fortuitous, and that it reinforces their claim that the natural/moral law is a native endowment of human reason.) But the Dalai Lama stops short, at least in the cited passage, of saying that the underlying metaphysics, or the visions they are thought to culminate in, are similar, much less equivalent.

Your formulation —"Only by actually walking down a specific traditional path . . ."— makes me think of the teaching of Fritjof Schuon. I don't wish to argue here that Schuon's teaching is unsound — though that is indeed my opinion — only that it is not orthodox.

Every orthodoxy that I am familiar with understands itself, qua *ortho*-doxy, to be *ipso facto* the only genuine orthodoxy. In the Gospel of John (14:6), for example, Jesus says, "I am the way, the truth, and the life; no one comes to the Father unless (literally, "if not") through (*dia*) me." Now, *one* deep orthodoxy insists on this, claiming that one person, Jesus of Nazareth, was the Son (begotten according to the flesh) of a Jewish virgin and ("eternally begotten before all worlds," Nicene Creed) of the eternal God and Father. But *another* deep orthodoxy denies this. How can both orthodoxies be thought (especially in light of John 14:6) to lead equally to "participation in the higher levels of truth" unless, one holds, contrary to Christian orthodoxy in *any* of its forms, that the Trinity does not exist at the "higher levels of truth"?

Maybe the tension between conflicting orthodoxies can be relaxed by understanding *truth* in a new way, though I doubt it. My immediate question, however, is this: Why would one think that this novel way of regarding truth — which in all frankness appears, to me at least, to be *itself* "an attempt to preserve orthodoxy with modern philosophical presuppositions"— is bound up with Christian orthodoxy? You might respond that your entire essay answers this question. If so, all I can do is promise to read the paper again and to ponder it more carefully so as to understand the answer. But I do think that *truth* is considered by all orthodox Christians not as "a reality" but as reality *simpliciter* — *reality* being convertible with *truth* only because it is eternally present in its ultimate intelligibility to the mind of the omniscient God, in whose image we are made and in whose understanding we are therefore able to have some small share.

To repeat, though we differ on some things, I do think that your essay is a strong contribution.

CHRISTIANITY AND FORCE: THE JUST WAR TRADITION

JAMES CAREY

The problems of force in general and of war in particular have been vexing ones for Christianity from the beginning. The New Testament does not offer an unambiguous teaching on this matter. On the one hand, there are Christ's[1] well-known injunctions to "resist not evil" and to love not only one's neighbors, but one's enemies as well. To these should be added his statement that those who live by the sword shall die by the sword.[2] On the other hand, there is Christ's perhaps surprising command to his disciples to "procure a sword, if you don't have one" as well as his remark about the necessity of rendering unto Caesar that which is Caesar's.[3] Christ calls the faith of a Roman centurion exemplary.[4] He does not counsel, much less command, the centurion to forswear the profession of arms. Nor does John the Baptist counsel such a thing in a similar situation.[5] Paul says that secular rulers do not bear the sword in vain, for they are ministers of God executing wrath on those who do evil. His insistence on obeying the secular authorities would seem to hold even when they command service in the military.[6]

Much has been written on the question of what the New Testament teaches, or intends to teach, regarding the employment of force as a last resort in self-defense and in defense of the innocent and defenseless. Pacifists and nonpacifists have combed through the New Testament assiduously searching for passages that support their respective positions, usually turning a blind eye to passages that do not, or interpreting them metaphorically while insisting on the literal meaning only of what they find congenial. To this extent, disputes regarding what the New Testament teaches about war follow the familiar and dreary pattern of disputes regarding what the New Testament teaches about other controversial matters.

These disputes are not our theme. Our theme is what the Church teaches about war. By framing the matter this way, we adopt a Catholic perspective, a perspective according to which the Church — understanding itself to be illuminated by the Holy Spirit, the "Spirit of Truth,"— is *the* interpreter of Scripture.[7] It was, after all, the Church that, around the fourth century, established the canon of the New Testament, accepting only a limited number of texts from among those that claimed authenticity and authority, and rejecting the rest. This canon, established by the Church, is accepted by Catholics and mainstream Protestants alike. If the New Testament is divinely inspired, then the Church must have been divinely inspired as well, at least when deciding which texts would be in the canon and which texts would not.

In addition to establishing the canon of the New Testament, the early Church formulated certain nonnegotiable articles of faith. It also laid the foundation for a comprehensive theological and moral teaching on man's relation to God and to his fellow men, including the question of when, if ever, going to war is justified — that is, when, if ever, going to war is the lesser of two or more evils — and how war ought to be conducted once entered into. We cannot recount here the full history of the Church's teaching on just war, neither the precedents of this teaching and its first appearance, nor its evolution (or devolution) over the centuries. We concentrate, instead, on the concept of just war as articulated by Thomas Aquinas in the *Summa Theologiae*, where just war theory occurs in its classic form, and, in spite of important modifications, continues to shape policy decisions in the conduct of military operations. Then we shall turn to contemporary just war theory and to current challenges which, as we shall see, contemporary theory is poorly equipped to meet.

The issue of just war is worth our attention for several reasons. Technological advances over the last two centuries have made war fighting paradoxically both more destructive and more discriminate. Highly divergent, even mutually antagonistic philosophies, going by the names of *pacifism* and *realism*, call the very concept of just war into question. The question of whether war can ever be just, or, for that matter, unjust, is in fact part of the more general problem of what justice itself is. Reflecting on this question leads us to take seriously the possibility of a standard of justice that transcends positive law, even positive international law. We realize that such standards can be found in revealed religion, but our hope is that a transcendent standard can be found that does not presuppose theological claims on which one cannot expect to find consensus, least of all in the West. Our hope is not disappointed.

Early in the *Summa Theologiae*, Thomas Aquinas makes a distinction, capital for his entire project, between those things that can be known through our natural powers — by reason and ordinary human experience — and those things that are revealed by God himself and must be taken on faith.[8] Thomas's natural law teaching, of which his teaching on just war is an extension and specification, falls within the context of the former. It is a rational teaching and therefore accessible to rational beings regardless of sectarian or confessional allegiance. It is accessible to unbelievers as well as to believers. Assuming it is sound, it is binding on both.

Natural law is viewed with suspicion today. What is said to be authorized or prohibited by it has been occasionally advanced by Roman Catholic clergy and apologists not so much with an appeal to reason and ordinary experience alone as with an appeal to authority. "Because *the Pope* says that x is a matter of natural law, it must be accepted as such," one sometimes hears. This way of speaking, which is at odds with the deepest stratum of the Roman Catholic theological tradition, is curious, since *natural* law is supposed to be accessible to all human beings, not only to ecclesiastical authorities.[9] Not surprisingly, many have inferred that the language of natural law is only a cloak for what is a matter, at best, of revelation — at worst, of papal *fiat* merely. When natural law is invoked as the authority for papal declarations that are contested even among Roman Catholic theologians, it is not surprising that its authority would come to be distrusted or categorically denied by those who are not loyal Roman Catholics. This rejection of natural law, however, is rash, based as it is on a profound misunderstanding.

The foundational principle of natural law, Thomas says, is that "good is to be done and pursued, and evil avoided."[10] This principle is self-evident and everyone who acts — does something on the basis of even the slightest deliberation — necessarily makes use of it, even if he does not vocalize it (just as everyone who *thinks* makes use of the self-evident principle of noncontradiction, even if he does not vocalize it). By attending to our natural inclinations and their order, Thomas shows how the otherwise merely formal principle — good is to be done and pursued, and evil avoided — acquires specific content and obligatory force. We have an order (or rank —

ordo) of inclinations and a corresponding order of goods. We have an inclination to self-preservation, which we share with even inanimate objects, and we have inclinations to procreate and to provide for our young, which we share with irrational animals. As human beings, however, we have additional inclinations that are proper to our specifically rational nature, the chief of which are to know the truth about God (or whatever first cause or first causes things may have) and to live in society.[11] The inclinations to rational inquiry and rational sociability express the good of reason. The good of reason, which has the character of an end, is a higher-order good that takes precedence over the goods we share with irrational animals and mere things. The inclinations that direct us to this higher-order good give rise to the two primary precepts of natural law, "to shun ignorance and not offend others, among whom we are bound to live."[12]

In the precept that we not offend others is contained the germ of Thomas's teaching on justice. It is significant that this precept does not say that one should not inconvenience, hurt, or kill others. This precept does not forbid every kind of harm. The precept says only that one should not offend. The Latin word *offendere*, as Thomas uses it, is broad enough to include everything from minor acts of deliberate annoyance to premeditated murder. An offense differs from other types of harm not in degree but in character. When an individual protects himself or another innocent person from assault, he does not offend his assailant. Similarly, when the state awards the death penalty to a criminal — "the offender" as we call him — who has, say, killed a family in cold blood, it does not offend him.[13] An offense is a harm inflicted by a human being — irrational animals cannot offend — on another human being, deliberately and either without provocation or out of proportion to a prior offense suffered.[14]

Thomas treats justice as the virtue of rendering to each his due.[15] Injustice, on the other hand, is the vice of not rendering to each his due. It can include giving to others bad things that they do not deserve. To commit an injustice is to offend in the technical sense spelled out above. The question as to whether there can be a just war turns, then, on the question of whether war, which surely harms the enemy, in every case offends him. The answer is that it does not. It would be preposterous for a country that has initiated offensive and unprovoked actions against another country to admit doing so (which is, of course, rare) and then complain that it is offended by the invaded country's attempt to defend itself.[16]

In the *Summa Theologiae*, the question, "On war," commences with the article "Whether it is always sinful to wage war." The title of this article is revealing.[17] The qualifier *always* suggests that war is usually sinful. Thomas argues that it is nonetheless not always sinful. He spells out three conditions that have to be met for the waging of war to be just.[18] War may be declared only by the individual or individuals who bear sovereign authority in the political community, which of course varies from regime to regime. There must be a just cause. And those waging war must have a right intention.

The first condition is that war may only be authorized by the sovereign. This condition rules out the possibility of a private individual's justly waging war on his own, or along with another group of like-minded private individuals. This condition had to be specified in the medieval period, when a nobleman, whose estate might be at the border of his sovereign's territory, might be tempted to wage war against those on the other side of the border without the consent of his sovereign. For some time it received attention by just war theorists mainly as an archaism. Its pertinence is incontestable today, in an age of nonstate actors operating out of countries whose governments are either tacitly complicit with them or too weak to expel them. When sovereign authority is distributed across different branches of the government, some confusion can result, particularly if war is not expressly declared but is otherwise authorized by the government. In such cases, Thomas's first condition is met, but just barely.

The second condition is that the cause must be just. Self-defense would seem to be the obvious cause. But Thomas mentions something different, namely, "that those who are fought against deserve being fought against on account of some fault."[19] If one country undertakes a war of aggression against another, the self-defense of the latter country is interpreted by Thomas as deserved punishment of the first, the presumption being that any war of aggression is *ipso facto* unjust. But punishment of the enemy is not limited to self-defense against him. If a country defeats an aggressor at its borders, or at a later point in the course of hostilities drives an invader from its territories, it may justly invade in turn with the intent of punishing the enemy for his original aggression. It may do so even if it is no longer in danger of being invaded itself, the enemy having supposedly learned his lesson. If in WWII, for example, Hitler had withdrawn his troops from Poland after exterminating large numbers of Poles, Poland could have justly invaded

Germany in turn, for punitive reasons exclusively. In the first Gulf War, Iraqi troops were pursued and attacked on Iraqi soil even after having retreated from Kuwait and when the self-defense of the latter had already been achieved. Just cause is the righting of a wrong, and for this reason it is not limited to justifiable self-defense.

The third condition, right intention, must be distinguished from the second. A nation can justly wage war even, as we noted, to the point of invading the country of an aggressor who has retreated back into it. But, in so doing, its goal must be the promotion of good and the avoidance of evil. It is striking that Thomas permits the prosecution of war for the sake of punishing evildoers, but expressly rules out the cruelty of vengeance (*ulciscendi crudelitas*). Punishment must be restricted to those who started the war and those who prosecuted it inhumanely — those whom today we would call war criminals. Noncombatants and ordinary prisoners of war must not be cruelly abused, even if their country was in the wrong.

In his question treating just war, Thomas does not explicitly and by name distinguish *jus ad bellum* (the right to go to war) from *jus in bello* (right conduct in the course of war). But the distinction comes to the fore in his elaboration of the relation between right intention and just cause. By emphasizing the inner intention of the combatants, and not their actions merely, Thomas treats the question of just war from the perspective of ethics broadly considered. It is not only how the combatants act, but what motivates their actions, that has a bearing on the justice or injustice of their actions, both *ad bellum* and *in bello*.

As one can surmise, and as Thomas makes clear elsewhere, prudence and sound judgment are indispensable for the correct application of principles to concrete circumstances throughout the ethical sphere.[20] And nothing in the article under consideration relies on Christian theology or on any other theology. Thomas cites Holy Scripture and doctors of the Church only by way of responding to objections that also cite these authorities, or in order to show that his rational teaching accords with the revealed theology of the Church without logically presupposing it.

The article, "Whether it is always sinful to wage war," is followed by three more articles. Unlike the first, the second article, "Whether it is permissible (*sit licitum*) for clerics and bishops to fight," does rely on the theology of the Church. Thomas's answer to this question is no. He does not claim, however, that it would be unjust for clergy to fight, only that it would be impermissible for them to do so, for two reasons in particular. In the first place, warlike pursuits hinder the mind from contemplating divine matters, from praising God, and from offering prayers for the people. Fighting thus interferes with the office and duties proper to clerics. Killing and shedding blood is particularly at odds with the clergy's "ministry at the sacrament of the altar." It is impermissible for clerics to fight, not because doing so would be unjust or sinful, but because it would be incongruous (*non congruit*) with their specific calling.

And yet it is a positive duty for clerics to exhort others to participate in a just war. The standard that Thomas appeals to here is divine law as interpreted by the Church, and not just to natural law. The same is true of the fourth article, "Whether it is lawful to wage war on holy days," to which Thomas answers yes. Physicians may heal an individual on the Sabbath. Providing for the safety of the whole commonwealth is, however, much more important than providing for the health and safety of a single individual. If fighting on the Sabbath is necessary for the prosecution of a just war, it is lawful to fight on the Sabbath and on other holy days as well.

The context of the third article, "Whether it is lawful to make use of ambushes in war," is, like that of the first article, natural law rather than divine law.[21] An ambush is a kind of deception and might seem to violate the precept of justice that forbids lying. Thomas argues, however, that to refrain from revealing the whole of one's thoughts to others is not intrinsically unjust. An ambush is this sort of deception. Moreover, no one conducting an ambush would claim that his enemy should not be permitted to do the same thing. One can assume then that if there were a treaty, or verbal agreement, forbidding ambushes, violating the treaty and conducting an ambush would be unjust, inasmuch as it would be a breach of faith. Thomas forbids both breaking a promise and frank lying as always unlawful, even in the prosecution of a just war.[22] Regarding Thomas's rigor on this point, it should be remembered how outraged we become when we hear that solders have used a white flag to pretend surrender and then have killed those advancing to accept their surrender. Our outrage makes sense only on the assumption that even war should be governed by moral principles. On the other hand, it should be noted that when Thomas treats lying more generally he says that, though every lie is a sin, not every lie is a mortal sin.[23] In extreme circumstances, a certain kind of lie should be regarded with indulgence, if not looked upon as a necessary evil.[24]

Thus far we have been considering only the teaching of the Roman Catholic Church on just war, as represented by its classic expositor, Thomas Aquinas. The teaching of the Orthodox Church, which is also Catholic, is neither as developed nor as comprehensive as that worked out by Thomas and his successors. But several features are worthy of note. In the frequent litanies that occur in the services of the Orthodox Church, "this land and its armed forces" are explicitly prayed for. These prayers are not simply for military success in a just cause, but for the salvation of the souls of those engaged in military activity.

An early canon prescribes that soldiers who have shed blood be barred from communion for three years.[25] This practice has been relaxed with the passage of time, but the canon is nonetheless revealing. While not simply forbidding military service in general or the killing of enemy soldiers in particular, it recognizes that engaging in war is nothing but the least bad alternative available. Orthodox theologians tend to be uncomfortable with the concept of just war, perhaps out of concern that self-congratulation on the justice of one's cause *ad bellum* can be conducive to excesses *in bello*.[26] Part of the justification for the firebombing and dropping of nuclear bombs on German and Japanese cities in World War II seems to have been that "*they* started this war, we didn't." But demonizing civilians as well as ordinary soldiers fighting for their country — "Japs and Nazis, *all* of them!" — disregards their humanity.

Even in strict combatant-to-combatant contests, there are moral problems. It is not possible to achieve a difficult victory without a sense of accomplishment, which can easily metamorphose into elation. But elation at killing enemy soldiers, whose only moral defect may be that they are citizens of a country that has not met all the criteria of *jus ad bellum*, is hardly commendable.[27] It may be psychologically unavoidable, however, and, to that extent only, excusable. Those who have entered the profession of arms — particularly in the West — are required to scrutinize the moral quality of their acts more frequently and more closely than the members of any other profession. If war is a *necessary* evil, it is also a necessary *evil*. Its effect on the souls of those who are engaged in it is hardly salutary.

Still, few Orthodox theologians would agree either with unqualified pacifists in holding that going to war is never permissible or with so-called realists in holding that, in war, "anything goes."[28] The practical consequences of the Orthodox position, both in the conduct of foreign policy and in the conduct of military operations, are closer to Thomas Aquinas's teaching than to either of the extremes opposed to it.

Thomas's teaching on just war got further elaboration in the Western theological tradition and in secular, international jurisprudence as well. The consequence of this development, the convoluted course of which we shall not attempt even to sketch, is that a consensus has emerged, at least in the West, that certain criteria must be met for a war to be rightly entered into and rightly conducted. By broad international consensus, they are the following:[29]

JUS AD BELLUM

1. Just Cause
2. Right Authority
3. Right Intention
4. Proportionality of Ends
5. Last Resort
6. Reasonable Hope of Success
7. Aim of Peace

JUS IN BELLO

1. Proportionality of Means
2. Noncombatant Protection/Immunity

The first three *jus ad bellum* criteria are the ones that Thomas himself explicitly names, and the remaining four are little more than logical elaborations of the first three. The criterion that ends must be proportional requires that any goal to be attained by the killing and maiming of large numbers of human beings be worth it. This criterion is implicit in Thomas's just cause condition. The criterion that peace be aimed at is explicitly mentioned by him in his discussion of right intention.[30] Peace is not, however, the only permissible aim. If a country is invaded, peace might be best secured by immediate capitulation, and even acquiescence in enslavement. An attacked country, however, can justly aim at preserving its liberty instead of settling for "peace at any price." The criterion that there be a reasonable hope of success would seem to be a sine qua non for waging war. The difficulty, however, lies in assessing what is reasonable to hope for given that the fortunes of war are notoriously unpredictable. And the question of what constitutes success is similarly problematic.[31] According to the criterion of last resort, peaceful means of resolving a crisis must be attempted first. Going to war is justified only when further negotiation is reasonably judged to be futile, when, as is said, "diplomatic channels have been exhausted."

Applying these criteria to concrete circumstances obviously requires judgment. It does not lend itself to precise calculation. None of the criteria are merely subjective, but it is clear that the objective evidence that must be weighed varies from criterion to criterion and from case to case. In his own account, Thomas specifies the condition of rightful authority first because it is least subject to interpretation. He then specifies just cause and right intention, in that order, because the former is subject to public examination whereas the latter has to do with motives that can be hidden. Of the four remaining *jus ad bellum* criteria in the above list, two are contained in Thomas's three conditions and two are "judgment calls." The current list of seven criteria for *jus ad bellum* marks little if any advance beyond the three conditions that Thomas lays down.

Whereas *jus ad bellum* criteria are the concern of statesmen, *jus in bello* criteria are the proper concern of the military. Before considering the latter, it is worth noting an implication of Thomas's argument. Two countries cannot go to war with each other if both meet all the above *jus ad bellum* criteria.[32] One of these countries is violating at least the criterion of just cause, assuming that two countries cannot with equal right attack one another. Strictly speaking, every war is unjust inasmuch as one or more of the parties cannot have met all the *jus ad bellum* criteria. That means that all the soldiers fighting on one of the two sides, and possibly all the soldiers fighting on both sides, are fighting on behalf of a country that has entered into war unjustly. What is a soldier to do when he has become convinced that his country is waging an unjust war?

Thomas concurs in Paul's injunction to Christians that they obey their rulers.[33] If a citizen thinks that his government is levying taxes unjustly, or using them to fund activities he is opposed to or even holds to be unjust, he nevertheless has a general obligation to pay his taxes. Similarly, if a soldier thinks his government is waging a war that does not meet one or more of the *jus ad bellum* criteria, he is nonetheless obliged to fulfill his military obligations. But Thomas argues that tyrannical governments have only the appearance of legitimacy, and that a tyrannical law is not really a law at all. Accordingly, the obligation to obey such a law is not absolute.[34]

This having been said, it must be added that the contemporary disjunction, "either democracy or tyranny," is from the perspective of Thomas a false disjunction (and one with ominous implications in the conduct of foreign policy). He follows the classical tradition of distinguishing between kingship and tyranny, and between aristocracy and oligarchy. Kingship and aristocracy are every bit as legitimate as democracy. And so are mixed regimes that combine monarchical, aristocratic, and democratic elements. The illegitimacy of a tyrannical regime consists not in its autocracy but in the fact that it does not pursue the common good.[35] Of course, how single-mindedly a given regime pursues the common good is an open question. Even democracies have been known to pursue the good of the majority only, greatly to the detriment of the minority — sometimes a disadvantaged racial, ethnic, or religious group, and sometimes the wealthy few. A "tyranny of the majority" is very much a possibility.

A citizen does not have an unqualified duty of obedience to a tyrannical regime. He may even attempt to overthrow it. Since a tyrant already rules by force, a successful revolution will have to employ force or a credible threat of force as well. The consequences of revolution, however, are difficult to predict. There is always the possibility that revolution will result in a violent anarchy, civil war, and a new tyranny presided over by a ruthless opportunist or a bloodthirsty mob more savage than the tyrant overthrown.

We can deduce a general principle from these considerations. If a citizen is convinced that the regime he lives under is a tyranny, and that its laws and policies are so unjust that revolution, with all its imponderables, is preferable to continued submission, he may justly refuse to obey the political authorities. If a soldier is convinced that the regime he lives under is not only tyrannical but is conducting a war so unjust that it would be better for his country to suffer defeat, with all *its* imponderables, he may refuse to fight. And if he judges that revolution has a reasonable chance of success and will result in the installation of a nontyrannical regime, then he may engage in armed insurrection. Indeed, he has a duty to do so.[36] He has a moral and truly courageous alternative to obedience. But it is an extreme one. If the soldier is unwilling to pursue the course of armed insurrection, his only reasonable alternative is to do his military duty, rigorously adhering to the *jus in bello* criteria himself and mitigating, when possible, the excesses of others. In performing his military duty both courageously and honorably, he can advance the cause of nobility even in a cause that is less than noble.

On the assumption that, in a given conflict, all the *jus ad bellum* criteria have been met, going to war is justifiable if not obligatory. And yet, in itself, war remains something bad. Otherwise, it would not be a last resort. War does not suddenly become good simply because it is not as bad as the alternatives. Harm is always done, not only to combatants, but to noncombatants as well. Wives are deprived of their husbands, and vice versa when women are combatants; children are deprived of their parents, and parents are deprived of their children. Collateral damage inevitably occurs, and psychological damage is often worse than physical damage. Many a noncombatant would prefer the loss of his own arm or leg to the death of a combatant family member.

The proper end of specifying the strictures within which war should be fought is not to sanitize or sugarcoat the horrors of war, but to mitigate them.[37] Those who follow the profession of arms have an interest in distinguishing what they do from murder. They make a distinction comparable to the distinction between the guilty and the innocent in civilian life. This is the distinction between combatants and noncombatants. It is the distinction that underlies and gives meaning to the *jus in bello* criteria of noncombatant immunity and proportionality of means.

Soldiers are under a strict obligation not to target noncombatants. The purpose of the Allied bombing of German and Japanese population centers during World War II seems to have been to inflict so much misery on civilians they would pressure their governments to sue for peace. The bombing of Hiroshima and Nagasaki, in particular, is plausibly claimed to have saved countless lives, not only countless lives of Allied troops who would otherwise have had to invade the Japanese homeland, but countless lives of Japanese soldiers and Japanese civilians as well, who would have been killed when called upon to resist that invasion. For these reasons, some say that the deliberate targeting of noncombatants can, on occasion, be morally justified.

But one could also say that the Mi Lai massacre during the Viet Nam War, or an event like the Mi Lai massacre, was similarly intended to pressure the enemy to capitulate or enter into a truce, with more lives saved in the long run. The aim of saving a greater number of lives, which was the rationale for the deliberate targeting and bombing of civilian population centers during WWII, could be invoked to justify virtually all excesses in war. That bomber crews could not see the faces of their civilian victims hardly renders their actions less objectionable than those of ground troops who *could* see the faces of their civilian victims — and have had to live with the memory of those faces. The notion that good ends justify grave and intrinsically evil means is generally rejected by contemporary just war theorists, as it was rejected by Thomas Aquinas 750 years ago.

Quite different from the deliberate targeting of noncombatants is the military application of the principle of double effect. What is referred to today as collateral damage is bound up with this principle. To understand double effect, it is helpful to consider its application in a situation that has nothing to do with war. According to current Roman Catholic teaching, the one place where something resembling abortion may be permissible is when a pregnant woman needs a lifesaving medical procedure — such as a hysterectomy that will remove a highly malignant tumor — and the fetus will be killed in the process. In such a case, the physician is not trying to kill the fetus. He even has an obligation to preserve its life if at all possible. The death of the fetus is an unintended, even if foreseen and unavoidable consequence of a medical procedure that is necessary to achieve a good end. The medical procedure then has a double effect, only one of which is actually intended. Quite different is the case of an abortion in which the death of the fetus is actually intended. One might respond that the distinction is moot since in both cases the end result is the same: a pregnancy has been terminated, a fetus has been killed, and a woman who was pregnant is alive but no longer pregnant. All this is, of course, true. The difference consists solely in the intention, that is, in the disposition of the will. It is therefore a moral distinction, like the distinctions between war and murder and between pacifism and cowardice.[38]

The principle of double effect is invoked in war when a genuine military target, for example, an enemy artillery battery, cannot be neutralized without the possibility, or even the likelihood, of civilian casualties. The intention in such a case is not to kill the civilians, not even in the interests of bringing about a swift cessation of hostilities, sparing the enemy further loss of life, achieving victory in a just cause, establishing a lasting peace, and so forth.[39] The intention, rather, is to neutralize the artillery battery — that is, to render it militarily useless — and every reasonable effort should be made to minimize civilian casualties. Here the *jus in bello* criteria of proportionality and noncombatant immunity complement one another, and both must be adhered to. No more force should be employed than is required to neutralize the battery, and anticipated collateral damage to noncombatants must not be disproportionate to the military benefits of taking out the actual target.[40] On the other hand, if noncombatant casualties are not anticipated, this stricture may be relaxed. A commander might apply much more force than required to neutralize an artillery battery if he has reason to think that enemy infantry might also be in the vicinity of it.

The criterion of proportionality of means applies not only to situations in which noncombatant casualties can be anticipated, as a check on abuse of the principle of double effect; it also applies to dealings with enemy combatants. For example, there are internationally recognized bans on certain weapons, such as poisonous gas and small arms equipped with silencers. Of course, if one side refrains from a certain action *only* because of a mutual agreement that the other side has chosen to violate, the former is no longer bound by the agreement. The case is quite different with noncombatant immunity. The deliberate killing of noncombatants is intrinsically at odds with *jus in bello*, even as a response to the enemy's doing the same thing.

Whereas it is commonly granted that application of the principle of double effect in military situations, at least when complemented by the principle of proportionality, is different from deliberately targeting noncombatants and thereby treating them as mere means to some other end, some would say that refraining from treating them as mere means still falls short of treating them as ends-in-themselves.[41] But the very fact that a military commander attempts to limit collateral damage, and that he does so at some risk not only to his mission but to himself and his troops as well, is evidence that he is treating noncombatants as ends-in-themselves. Otherwise, why would he give any thought at all to the principle of proportionality?

He could ignore this principle entirely without thereby reducing the non-combatants to the status of mere means. By attempting to minimize collateral damage, he takes a step beyond not treating the noncombatants as mere means. To be sure, he is not doing everything he can to prevent collateral damage, for then he would not order an attack on a target that has been placed, perhaps deliberately, in the midst of noncombatants. But in a war that has been justly entered into, victory is a good. Due precaution must be taken to minimize collateral damage, but protecting noncombatants from every adverse collateral effect of combat is not the single good that trumps all others, nor is it even possible.

Among noncombatants, one must include prisoners of war. Because they have ceased fighting and have laid down their arms, they are no longer combatants. Now, it is popularly said that the purpose of combat is to kill the enemy. If that were the purpose, however, there would be no compelling reason to refrain from killing enemy prisoners. There might well be an agreement between the belligerent parties not to do so. But if this agreement were the sole basis for the decision not to kill them, then if one side breaks the agreement, there would be no reason for the other side not to respond in kind. After all, accepting the surrender of enemy soldiers and escorting them to the rear has to be done by troops who could otherwise be contributing directly to frontline fighting. The guarding, feeding, and housing of prisoners of war requires further redirection of troops and resources away from the actual and urgent business of fighting an enemy who remains a deadly threat. Refraining from killing prisoners, not to mention providing for their welfare and treating them in a generally humane manner, makes sense only if the purpose of combat is something other than killing the enemy.

The purpose of combat is, in fact, to defeat the enemy. If it were practicable to defeat him without killing him, it would be obligatory to do so. Defeating the enemy means overcoming the enemy's will to resist, a vastly more humane conception of the goal of combat than killing the enemy. Of course, in practice it is usually impossible to preserve this distinction. It pertains to the nature of war that many of the enemy must be killed, or at least wounded, before their will is broken. Still, the distinction is real. Without making it, there is no reason to spare the lives of enemy soldiers who have surrendered, especially when their leaders do not honor this principle.

A question arises as to whether this distinction could play a role in the course of combat itself. *Jus in bello* clearly requires protection of enemy noncombatants. But what about protection of enemy combatants? Where interest is involved in the application of judgment to concrete situations, it is easy for specious reasoning and self-deception to enter the picture. Regarding *jus ad bellum*, a government almost never declares war without advancing reasoning to the effect that its cause is just. What this means is that soldiers, who, as we noted, have an obligation to serve their country except when its cause is so unjust as to warrant armed revolt, are often in the same moral position as the soldiers they are fighting. Soldiers respect the bravery and tenacity of worthy opponents. They, too, recognize that the proper end of combat is not to kill the enemy but to overcome his will to resist.[42]

To speak of an obligation to protect the enemy while defeating him may seem to be an exercise in academic preciosity. Still, one can hope that military technology might at some point develop not only munitions of greater and greater precision that will increasingly limit collateral damage, but also munitions that could incapacitate the enemy and defeat him without killing him. After all, when a criminal who has been disarmed continues to resist arrest, police are obliged to use no more force than is needed to subdue him. A similar situation could occur on a battlefield, especially when the enemy has been routed and is in headlong retreat, but has nonetheless not yet thrown down his weapons and surrendered. That one might be able to stun and then disarm an enemy soldier without killing him outright is at least conceivable. Of course, it might not be practicable, given the duress of battle, the need for instantaneous decisions, and the obligation to protect both one's fellows and oneself in the interest of accomplishing the mission at hand. Still, that it is conceivable at all, even as something that can only be hoped for, is a further sign that the purpose of combat is not simply to kill the enemy.

Our treatment of the finer points of just war theory may seem to have taken us rather far from anything having to do with Christianity. We repeat, however, that Thomas Aquinas presents his teaching on just war, from which contemporary just war theory differs less in terms of details than of foundation, as fully accessible to reason quite apart from revelation. But that presents us with a puzzle. If the teaching on just war is accessible to reason, why do we not find anything comparable to it in classical Greek philosophy, particularly in the philosophy of Plato and Aristotle?[43]

For Plato and Aristotle, justice, a concept problematic enough even when applied to relations between citizens, is even more problematic when applied to relations between cities—or, as we would say today, between states. To be sure, we can find suggestions in the writings of these two philosophers and their followers implying that justice is a concept that is *not* simply *in*applicable outside the walls of the city.[44] But these passages do not refer back, even ultimately, to a trans-political, natural law, such as we find in Thomas Aquinas.[45] Plato and Aristotle may have had doubts about whether the existence of a binding trans-political law, distinct from the laws of particular communities, could be established without introducing theological claims that go beyond what natural reason can establish on its own.[46] Foreign policy is, in any case, not so prominent a theme in their writings as is domestic policy.

Thucydides, of course, writes extensively about foreign policy, and his characters speak of justice in this context as well as in matters of domestic policy. But none of them elaborates anything resembling a developed just war teaching, nor does Thucydides himself. Indeed, he rarely speaks in his own name regarding moral matters.[47] He does not tell us, for example, what he thinks of the Athenian decision to execute the entire adult male population of Melos, enslave the rest of the population, and repopulate Melos with colonists from Athens as a "reward" for the efforts of the Melians to preserve their political neutrality and liberty. Plutarch, though not Thucydides, reports that the severity of Athenian policy regarding Melos was endorsed by Alcibiades. And Alcibiades was a pupil, even if a refractory pupil, of Socrates. Socrates, of course, can hardly be held responsible for Alcibiades's excesses, as Plutarch, no less than Plato and Xenophon, makes clear.[48]

In fact, one can construct an argument against the Athenians' treatment of the Melians on the basis of reasoning that Socrates advances in the *Republic*. Greek cities should practice restraint and act with a view to eventually restoring amicable relations when they are at war with each other, though not necessarily when they are at war with barbarians. Greeks and barbarians are "enemies by nature." Greeks cities should always be able to form a united front in the face of a potential invasion from without.[49] We note that the reasoning used by Socrates here is prudential merely. He does not appeal to any concept of natural law.

Cicero, however, does appeal to a concept of natural law. He also advances a teaching on just war that anticipates Thomas's teaching.[50] The connection between the concepts of just war and natural law in the tradition is intimate. It is, in fact, so intimate as to raise the suspicion that a coherent and developed just war theory cannot dispense with the concept of natural, trans-political law. This suspicion is confirmed when we turn to modern philosophy.

Unlike ancient Greek philosophy, modern philosophy does have a developed just war teaching. And it is based on a concept of trans-political law, just as Thomas's teaching is. But for modern philosophy, trans-political law comes more and more to be interpreted as positive international law — that is, what the international community has agreed upon[51]— rather than a law rooted in the very nature, or essence, of man as a rational animal. The seeming advantage of this shift from natural law to international positive law is the dissociation of just war theory from metaphysical assertions about the essence of man. The disadvantage of this shift, however, is that positive international law can be construed as morally binding — that is, binding independently of the bad consequences entailed by its transgression — only if agreements as such are morally binding. That agreements as such are morally binding is, however, not a tenet of international positive law but of natural law.[52]

The teaching of Thomas Hobbes is illuminating here because of its exemplary clarity. Hobbes argues that in a state of nature, prior to the establishing of a social contract, there is no such thing as justice and injustice. The social contract establishes a common power in awe of which the various parties to the contract abide by their agreements. Now, in an agreement, one binds oneself to do something, and Hobbes says that it is only reasonable to abide by what one has bound oneself to do. But the contract derives its strength from fear,[53] so much so that it is actually void without a common power terrifying the parties into compliance with its terms.[54]

One cannot contract away one's right to defend oneself against physical threats.[55] Hobbes repeatedly calls the state of nature a "state of war," and he notes that war consists not just in actual conflict but in "an inclination thereto."[56] The same relation holds between nations as holds between individuals in the state of nature. In neither case is there a common power in awe of which they feel compelled to abide by their agreements. On the currently pressing question of whether a nation should abide by the principles of *jus in bello* when its enemy has abandoned them, it is not difficult to guess what Hobbes's answer would be.

Hobbes's teaching on these matters is rarely appealed to in contemporary just war discussions. It seems too harsh, if not too frank. Embarrassed by the poverty of their resources, many contemporary theorists have taken recourse in the apparently precise but, in fact, obfuscating terminology of "stipulation." We *stipulate* that agreements are morally binding. We also stipulate that international positive law must be followed, we stipulate that there are basic human rights, and we stipulate that the precepts of *jus ad bellum* and *jus in bello* are obligatory. But to stipulate can mean in these contexts only to specify by way of an agreement. And it is arguing in a circle to claim that we should abide by our agreement to do something because we have stipulated — specified by agreement — that we will do so.[57]

From the moral fervor with which many just war theorists speak, one gets the impression they would like to say that, regardless of international agreements, it is *intrinsically* wrong to target enemy noncombatants deliberately. It is so wrong that we should not do so even if we are confronted with an enemy who deliberately targets our noncombatants. Contemporary theorists by and large say that we should not respond in kind, but few of them are able to provide compelling moral reasons — as distinct from prudential reasons — for why we should not do so. Their response would be much stronger if it were founded on the concept of natural law. But the appeal of this concept is dampened for them because of its connection with Catholic theology. The character of this connection, however, is inadequately appreciated, and it needs to be spelled out.

We note something curious right away. Immanuel Kant, one of the greatest of the modern philosophers and a thinker generally unsympathetic with the medieval theological tradition, is in essential agreement with the consequences and, up to a point, even the mode of argumentation that characterizes Thomas Aquinas's account of natural law. Neither Thomas nor Kant bases his natural law teaching on theological presuppositions.[58] Both argue, though in somewhat different ways, that a transcendent, binding law exists in human nature, as rational nature. Neither Thomas nor Kant would say that, for example, we should refrain from intentionally killing the innocent simply because God has forbidden our doing so. They agree in holding that reason itself — man's reason no less than God's — forbids intentional killing of innocent human beings. Doing such a thing is unjust; it is murder, by definition. When one murders, one offends, maximally. One thereby acts irrationally, no matter what ends, including moral ends, murder might be envisioned to further.

We cannot rehearse here the complex arguments that Thomas and Kant put forward for the existence and rationality of a trans-political, even supra-international, law that is morally and categorically binding on the finite will of human beings. We need to recognize, however, that although such a conception of law does not derive its evidence from theological *pre-suppositions*, it is not without theological *consequences*. The dictates of transcendent law are morally obligating; they are not naturally necessitating. These dictates do not compel, but instead call for voluntary — that is, free — compliance. It is from our awareness of transcendent moral law, then, that we infer freedom of the will.[59] And since freedom of the will cannot be deduced from, or even comprehended within, natural causality, we are led to infer that it owes its existence to supernatural causality, more precisely, to the free creative agency of a divine being. This theological inference nicely complements — it does not presuppose — Thomas's natural (rational) theology, and it is essential to his revealed theology.

For Kant, the case for transcendent moral law, the consciousness of which he calls a "fact of reason," gives rise to — it does not presuppose — "postulates of pure practical reason," one of which is the existence of God while the other is the immortality of the soul. The awareness of natural law predisposes one to take religion seriously, even if it is only a "religion within the limits of reason alone."

Thomas Aquinas is a canonized saint and a theologian of unsurpassed authority in the Roman Catholic Church; he is the *Doctor Angelicus*. Kant is a freethinking philosopher who in his most famous work makes a sustained argument to the effect that the human mind itself constitutes the only reality of which we have experience. Different as they are, both men agree that human beings are morally bound by a transcendent law as intrinsic to reason as is the principle of noncontradiction. Neither Kant's religion within the limits of reason alone nor Thomas's natural theology is based on revelation. And neither is based on the discredited cosmology of Aristotelian and medieval natural science.

One would think that the contemporary just war theorist would be reassured to discover that the concept of natural law is not derived from revealed religion, since he can base his understanding of just war on it without making sectarian commitments of any kind. But the contemporary theorist is not reassured. For his difficulty is not with the claims of revelation. These claims are alleged, by those who hold them to be true, to surpass everything that man can know on his own. That the believer understands them to be supra-rational only confirms the nonbeliever in his conviction that they are sub-rational. The real difficulty for the contemporary theorist is that the concept of natural law grounds (as in the case of Kant) or reinforces (as in the case of Thomas) a theology that appeals to no authority other than unassisted reason.

But with few exceptions, modern philosophy, from which contemporary just war theory inherits its premises, defines itself in opposition to theology of every kind, by argument against it and, failing that, by ridicule. Rational theology, however, is as impervious to ridicule as it is unimpressed by specious reasoning. It is rational theology — not revealed theology — that vexes modern philosophy. Consequently, the concept of natural law is seldom invoked by contemporary theorists.

And yet, without the concept of natural law or some variant of it, contemporary theorists cannot make a compelling case that the targeting of noncombatants is *intrinsically* wrong. To be sure, they can say that doing this sort of thing is not in keeping with "Western values." But they cannot say why we should continue to feel committed to these values, any more than they can explain why we should feel bound by what we have stipulated. Like their contemporaries who feel a need to mimic quotation marks by twitching the middle and index fingers of both hands whenever they speak of right and wrong, good and bad, and even truth and falsity, today's just war theorists are haunted by the fear that a commitment to moral absolutes, or absolutes of any kind, entails a commitment to theological absolutes. Thus, natural law is today a specifically Christian concept only by default.

The predicament in which contemporary just war theory finds itself is illuminated by the "supreme emergency" doctrine of Michael Walzer, one of the most well-known writers in the field. According to Walzer, human beings possess fundamental rights. Walzer follows the usage of the times in not calling them "natural rights," which suggests a possible association with natural law, but "human rights." Where these human rights come from is not so clear (apparently, it's neither nature nor nature's God), but they are supposed to transcend political divisions, and they appear to be infinite in number, if not infinite in kind.[60] Walzer says that they must be respected in the conduct of war, but only up to a point. If a country's existence or communal way of life is imminently and gravely threatened, it is confronted with a supreme emergency and may waive the *jus in bello* criteria. In a supreme emergency, a country may ignore the basic human rights of enemy noncombatants and deliberately target them.

One problem with this reasoning is that what constitutes supreme emergency is a matter of interpretation, since gravity and imminence cannot be precisely calculated. It also raises the awkward question of why a developing threat should be permitted to become grave and imminent before the *jus in bello* criteria may be waived. In any war, a country's existence or communal way of life is at least implicitly threatened. The *jus ad bellum* criterion of last resort implies that war itself is an extreme situation — so much so that it may not be entered into unless all other options have been tried and found wanting. If it is permissible for a country to waive the *jus in bello* criteria in a supreme emergency, prudence would seem to dictate waiving them much earlier, precisely so as to avoid being confronted later with a supreme emergency. After all, extreme measures may be rendered ineffective by the imminence of catastrophic defeat, when their effectiveness might have been considerable had they been employed sooner. Additionally, the targeting of enemy noncombatants when defeat is imminent is likely to be less discriminate than it would have been early in a conflict when urgency was less critical. If a country is going to abandon the *jus in bello* criteria *in extremis*, why not do so earlier, in the interest of forestalling situations *in extremis* altogether?

The answer to this question seems to be that we have agreed not to do such a thing. And we shall abide by our agreements, unless things get *really* bad for us, for our community and way of life — liberal democratic, militant communist, national socialist, theocratic — whatever our communal life happens to be. The wobbly foundation on which Walzer erects his doctrine of supreme emergency cannot support a principled moral argument against the targeting of noncombatants when doing so might enhance the prospects of victory in a just cause. What is needed is a solid foundation but, apparently, not so solid that theological arguments can be erected on it.

Contemporary just war theory has drawn fire from both the left and the right. To a certain kind of pacifist, all war is unjust.[61] It is not sometimes a necessary evil, the least bad of several bad options. It is always an unnecessary evil, the worst of all options. Neither self-defense nor defense of the innocent justifies the use of deadly force by one human being against another, however murderous his past actions and present intent may be. The deliberate killing of another human being, regardless of his guilt or innocence, is murder in all cases. It is not, however, sufficient for the pacifist simply to *declare* these things. He has to *argue* that self-defense and defense of the innocent are unjust and violate a rational and, therefore, publicly recognizable standard of justice.

The most obvious standard of justice is, as we noted, to give each person his due — that is, to give him what he deserves. The pacifist has to claim that a murderer does not deserve to meet with forceful resistance from the person he is trying to murder. He has to claim, as well, that enemy forces, wrongfully invading a country and determined to destroy its population, do not deserve to encounter a vigorous defense. These claims obviously deprive the concept of desert — and thereby, justice — of all meaningful content.[62] The pacifist's solemn insistence, dogmatic and unsupported, that it is *unjust* to defend oneself and one's fellows, employing lethal force if necessary, against wrongful assault with murderous intent, is typically met with incredulity (if not with hilarity) by those who do not share his faith.

The so-called realist takes a different aim at just war theory. In distinguishing his position from what he considers to be the naïve moralism that gives rise to the concepts of just war in particular, and of natural law in general, he asserts that obligations, if they exist at all, are one and all conditional.[63] We most definitely do not have unconditional obligations to the enemy, either to combatants or to noncombatants. Even if the enemy is abiding by the principles of *jus in bello* and is beating us fair and square, we might have to target his civilian population. And we should do so, if that's what it takes to achieve military success — a fortiori if the enemy is not abiding by the principles of *jus in bello*. Against an absolutely unscrupulous opponent who is resolved on our destruction and has made it clear that he will use our moral scruples against us, we have no choice but to abandon these scruples.

To reinforce his point, the realist draws attention to the increasing number of conflicts in which at least one of the belligerent parties sees no utility at all in abiding by the principles of just war. Terrorists, as nonstate actors, have unquestionably violated the *jus ad bellum* principle of right authority, and they have publicly rejoiced over their successful violations of the *jus in bello* principle of noncombatant immunity. That is to say, they have violated the two principles that are least open to interpretation, and they have violated most, if not all, of the remaining just war principles as well. Terrorists cannot realize their ends — which they are convinced, or have convinced themselves, are good—without abandoning these principles. The good end justifies whatever means are needed to realize it.

Interestingly, the terrorist's defense of his action is indistinguishable from that put forth by the realist. In the view of both, the value of the just war criteria resides in their utility exclusively. Once the utility, whether of the rule or of the act, is no longer apparent, the principles may be discarded, to be reasserted only in changed circumstances when they become useful again. According to the realist, these principles are not natural, as Thomas taught. They are conventional. And they remain conventional in spite of their enshrinement in customary international law. Terrorists concede that they cannot win a war fought according to conventional standards. They must adopt unconventional standards.

Terrorists and realists are right on one point at least: there is no compelling reason to hold that the conventional is intrinsically more just than the unconventional. In the light of developments unforeseen by earlier generations, contemporary just war theorists need to revisit and perhaps revise the standard just war criteria. Regarding *jus ad bellum*, an increasing number of theorists say that intervening militarily in the internal affairs of another state is justifiable if that state is practicing outright genocide against a segment of its own population. Assuming that genocide is unjust — as one must if the term is to have any meaning — humanitarian intervention is implicitly sanctioned by the *jus ad bellum* principle of just cause. It is, to be sure, at odds with the presumed inviolability of state sovereignty, the notion of which was a product of the Peace of Westphalia. But there is no reason to regard the inviolability of state sovereignty as absolute. It is not so much as mentioned by Thomas Aquinas in his treatment of just war. Because of the misery that war necessarily inflicts, military intervention on humanitarian grounds should be limited to such extreme cases as the halting of genocide in progress, lest it be a violation of the *jus ad bellum* principle of proportionality of ends. It would be a violation of this principle to invade another country solely in order to, say, replace a non-democratic government with a democratic one or to secure voting rights for women and ethnic minorities.

An increasing number of just war theorists say that *preemptive* war is justifiable when the threat of being on the receiving end of an attack is imminent. The classic case is that of the Six Day War in 1967, when Israel stole a march on the Arab forces that were massing on its borders with professed belligerent intent and anticipatory celebrations of the destruction of Israel. Quite different from a preemptive war is a *preventive* war. In the latter, the threat is envisioned as real and growing but not imminent. Whereas preventive war is viewed with much more suspicion than preemptive war, it should be remembered that the United Nations reserves the option of initiating military operations of a preventive nature. It explicitly grants itself the authority to "determine the existence of any threat to peace" and to take measures to "maintain or restore international peace and security."[64] It may take not only enforcement measures but preventive measures as well.[65]

The possibility of a surprise attack against civilian population centers, an attack with weapons of massive destructive potential that can be delivered too rapidly for effective defense, was not envisioned by Thomas Aquinas, nor was it envisioned by other classical theorists. Nonetheless, the criterion of just cause could plausibly be invoked to justify a preventive, and not merely preemptive, war against a country that has publicly announced its determination both to acquire such weapons and to use them in order to destroy another country, particularly if it has given every indication that it will not be deterred from doing so by fear of retaliation.[66]

Regarding *jus in bello*, the criterion of noncombatant immunity admits of no modification whatsoever. It is what distinguishes the conduct of war from murder.[67] The criterion of proportionality, however, might have to be relaxed, though certainly not abandoned, when fighting an enemy who deliberately and systematically uses civilians as a shield, both in the literal sense and by positioning military targets such as artillery batteries in hospitals, schools, places of worship, and the like, so that it becomes virtually impossible for soldiers to discriminate between enemy combatants and noncombatants. Adherence to the criterion of proportionality in combat against such an enemy may not entail as much as it does in combat against a more rational and less barbarous enemy.

The realist will counter that an enemy who does not abide by the principles of *jus in bello* is not irrational if he is convinced that adherence to these principles will lead to his defeat. Rather than luxuriate in a riot of indignation, we need to recognize that at some point we ourselves may be forced to do the same thing. Better to own up to that now and act accordingly, before it is too late and we find ourselves at the mercy of an enemy both more rational and more ruthless than we have hitherto been willing to be.

To this weighty objection we can only state that the principles of just war, like the principles of natural law generally, do not exist solely or even primarily for the preservation of life, but for the preservation of a rational life. These principles are rooted in the *nature* of man as a *rational* animal. Only in that way are they principles of *natural* law — not because apes, baboons, and other irrational primates act according to them.[68] From the perspective of natural law, a life that has been preserved by means of committing an injustice so extreme as the intentional killing, or acquiescence in the killing, of innocent human beings, is a life hardly worth living. It is a life worse than that of an irrational animal because it is chosen by a rational animal in an act of abrogating his rationality.

It must be admitted, however, that this perspective — which is the perspective of both Thomas and Kant — comes with a price. And because of the awesome destructive potential of current weapons, the price is higher than it was in previous periods. It is only reasonable, then, to take a closer look at the price tag before buying into it.

Consider the following variation on the familiar ticking-bomb scenario. We have every reason to believe that a captured and certified terrorist knows the location of a number of nuclear devices, timed to detonate simultaneously in the major metropolitan areas of our country. Nothing we have done to him has compelled him to reveal where the nuclear devices have been placed. But the terrorist has young children. May we torture and kill them one by one before his eyes so as to force him to reveal information that we have good reason to believe would save millions of American lives, and perhaps even the terrorist's own life and the lives of his remaining children as well?[69] With this question we abstract from marginal issues, such as how we can be sure that the person we have captured really is a terrorist, how we can be sure that he knows the location of the nuclear devices, and so forth. We focus solely on the moral issue.

Let us be clear that, in this case, we do not have a conflict merely between duty and pleasure, or between duty and the avoidance of pain, or between duty and the avoidance of an extreme amount of pain for a vast number of people. If that were all that were at stake, we would be considering a conflict between the precepts of natural law and the precepts of utilitarianism, and to abandon the former in favor of the latter would be simply to give up on the concept of *jus in bello*, except when prudence suggests that the consequences of invoking its criteria are more advantageous than the consequences of ignoring them. The conflict in the case under consideration is between duty and duty. For just as there is a duty to refrain from murder, so there is a duty to protect the innocent, including the millions of innocent human beings who would be killed if the nuclear devices were to detonate. Murdering the terrorist's children is bad, but not protecting the innocent, particularly one's innocent fellow countrymen, is bad too.

Now, if two courses of action are, from a moral perspective, equally bad, then utilitarian considerations may enter the picture. A genuine moral dilemma, in which we are faced with an irreconcilable conflict of duties, so far from tying our hands, actually lets us off the hook. We may pick the course of action that entails the least disadvantageous consequences in the realization that we have done our duty just as fully as had we picked the opposed course of action. Or we can flip a coin. Morally it makes no difference. The question in the case under consideration, then, is the following: Do we have an absolutely irreconcilable conflict of duties?

We do not. We may not fulfill our duty to protect the innocent by murdering the innocent. The murder of the terrorist's innocent children — for murder is what it is — is unequivocally prohibited by natural law and by its instantiation in the *jus in bello* criterion of noncombatant immunity. From the perspective of natural law, the murder of children — even just one of them — is an offense so grievous that it cannot be justified by any end, however so urgent or even moral. The *jus in bello* criterion of noncombatant immunity would be fully abrogated were we to admit the false principle that protecting the innocent justifies murdering the innocent. For any country that understands itself to be fighting for a just cause could construe all its citizens, combatant no less than noncombatant, as innocent and deserving protection at any cost to the enemy, combatants or noncombatants.

It is a tenet of natural law that some acts are so evil that it would be better for an individual to perish than commit them. It is not much of a leap to infer from this that some acts are so evil that it would be better for a number of individuals — even a nation — to perish than commit them. Such is the high price of a genuinely principled conception of just war, one that does not *in extremis* disclose its Hobbesian or decisionist foundations, as much of contemporary just war theory does. The stand that one takes on this matter — indeed, the stand that a country takes on this matter — is a defining stand. This is not to deny that government and military authorities, charged with protecting the lives of their fellow citizens and forced to make the choice sketched in the above scenario, might well decide to murder the terrorist's children.

The moral question, however, is not so much what will happen, or is likely to happen, as what *ought* to happen. If our answer is that they ought not to commit the murder, whatever the consequences, we have committed ourselves to the ethics of natural law. If our answer is that they ought to commit the murder, we have committed ourselves to so-called realism.[70] We can hope — we can pray as well — that our country is never faced with the choice we have just sketched or with one like it.[71] But we need to be clear in our minds about what we ought to do should such a choice ever be forced upon us.

The conservative who places love of his own country, love of his own fellow citizens, and, last but not least, love of his own life and pleasure above all principle is exasperated by the rigors of natural law — as is the liberal, for different reasons. And yet there is a kind of conservatism, a specifically Christian pessimism, supporting and supported by the recognition that we are often faced with choices between alternatives all of which are bad in themselves.[72] But the alternatives are rarely if ever all equally bad, and practical reason demands a say in how they should be ranked.

According to both Thomas Aquinas and Kant, reason sets down certain nonnegotiable limits to what one may do in the interest of preserving life, even innocent life. Among these limits is the prohibition against murder. It will be objected that it is not so much reason that leads to such a view as it is the religious belief in an afterlife, and that religious belief cannot guide policy in a secular state. Even nonbelievers, however, will usually concede that some acts are so evil, or at least so shameful, that it would be better to die than to commit them. The moral fiber of a man can be gauged by what he is willing to die for, and the same is true of a nation.[73]

Only someone who holds that there is nothing at all worth dying for can consistently call the absolutism of natural law — because of the ultimate consequences that must be drawn from it — romantic, asinine, or nihilist. Yet he, too, must argue for his position, not just for its consistency but for its truth as well, and in doing so he must declare his premises. Rather than speculate idly about the structure and rhetoric of an argument that would need to show, among other things, why men and women in the military should risk their young lives defending the lives of their fellow citizens when the *good* is essentially one's *own* good — narrowly conceived as one's own life and pleasure — let us turn, instead, to the scenario sketched above, and consider another feature of natural law that is pertinent to it.

As we noted earlier, the theory of natural law is bound up with the claim that man has free will. The existence of free will is not demonstrable beyond the shadow of a doubt. Consequently, this theory, like any ethical theory, carries with it a measure of uncertainty, which eases one in evading the exactions of natural law, especially when great sacrifice is called for. This evasion, which is a form of self-deception, can proceed from momentarily overlooking one's obligations all the way to alleging, gravely but without argument, a "rule of necessity" in human affairs so all-encompassing as to preclude any moral freedom whatsoever.

Now, although the principal concern of ethics is indeed what one ought to do, what one would be strongly tempted to do in certain circumstances must also be taken into account in the course of ethical deliberations. If it can be surmised that one would be strongly tempted to transgress an ethical principle in a particular situation, then it is a sound judgment of practical reason that, to the extent possible, such a situation should be avoided or rendered unlikely to occur.[74] As we have conceded, the argument that reason absolutely prohibits murder of the innocent is unlikely to find a sympathetic hearing among political and military authorities who understand their charge to be the protection of the lives of their fellow citizens at any cost. In the hypothetical situation we have been considering, they would be strongly tempted to break free of the obligations of natural law. Accordingly, this situation and others like it should be rendered unlikely to occur. In practice, what this means is that the war on actual terrorists should be prosecuted with unremitting vigor in order to forestall, among other things, the occurrence of a situation in which murdering the children of terrorists is the only way to prevent the murder of our own children.

There is something salutary, not to say providential, about having to think our moral principles all the way to their foundations, even if we are induced to do so by the emergence of a resourceful enemy so hell-bent on our destruction that he is willing to destroy himself if that's what it takes to destroy us. For we are compelled to engage in a long overdue reevaluation of the easygoing and widespread relativism that renders us incapable of rationally criticizing even murder on any grounds other than that it is "unacceptable" or at odds with our "value preferences." It is high time to reject this relativism and, along with it, both the reveries of pacifism and the postures of a "prudential realism" that cannot definitively distinguish itself from ignorant cynicism.

The practical question that must be confronted today by the West is whether officially secular regimes can fight a principled war against an unprincipled enemy. This question can be answered in the affirmative only on the presupposition that there is a natural law transcending all merely positive law, international as well as national, and that this natural law is at the same time fully rational, even if it has received its most profound exposition within the theological tradition of the Catholic Church. We do not pretend to have grounded this presupposition here.[75] We have only tried to show that a principled just war theory relies ultimately on the concept of natural law, whether called by this name or by another. We urge a reconsideration of natural law disburdened of the misconception that it derives its evidence from Christian revelation or from any other revelation. For, absent an acknowledgment of natural law, it makes no sense at all to criticize our current enemies for ignoring the principles of just war when, on their assessment, adherence to these principles will lead straight to their defeat. Indeed, absent an acknowledgment of natural law, it makes no sense at all *not* to follow the path our current enemies have so vividly blazed.

NOTES:

1. I realize that use of the name *Christ* outside of a church building is increasingly viewed as religiously incorrect, insensitive, and even offensive to non-Christians. Since this paper will represent the perspective of Catholic Christianity, however, I shall stay with the name *Christ*, rather than *Jesus*, the latter being the name preferred by Fundamentalists and other liberal Christians who deny the authority of a Church magisterium, and instead, reserve to themselves the prerogative of interpreting Scripture. See 2 Peter 1:20.

2. Matthew 5:39; 5:43; and 26:52. Roland Bainton, *Christian Attitudes toward War and Peace* (Nashville, TN: Abingdon, 1960) is a good source for the controversial texts. Bainton's treatment is relatively even-handed, but not entirely so; he typically gives the pacifist perspective the last word.

3. Luke 22:36; Matthew 22: 21.

4. Matthew 8:5–13.

5. Luke 3:14. Since John does not tell the soldiers, who have sought his counsel, to leave the military, his admonition, "shake no one violently" (*mēdena diaseisēte*), can be construed as demanding moderation even in combat, and therefore to anticipate the just war teaching of later Catholic theologians.

6. Romans 13:1–7.

7. John 15:26–16:13; Acts 2:1–4. By *Catholic* I do not mean Roman Catholic exclusively, but Orthodox and Anglo-Catholic as well. (In reflecting on 2 Peter 1:20, compare the first-person singular in 1:14–15 and the first-person plural in the remainder of the chapter. At 1:18, Peter is clearly not referring to himself alone, so there is no reason to think that he is referring to himself alone in 1:19.) According to ancient Catholic ecclesiology, the responsibility for defining doctrine falls to the bishops assembled in council who, guided by the Holy Spirit, evaluate theological opinions in light of Holy Tradition.

8. *Summa Theologiae* I, Question I, Article I, Reply to Objection I. (Hereafter, *Summa Theologiae* citations will note the part, where *1*, *1-2*, and *2-2* stand for "First Part," "First Part of the Second Part," and "Second Part of the Second Part," respectively; the question, where *q.* is followed by the appropriate number; the article, where *art.* is followed by the appropriate number; and the reply to objection, where *ad* is followed by the appropriate number. Unless otherwise noted, the citation *art.* by itself, refers to the body or *corpus* of an article.) Ibid. q. 2, art. 2, ad 1.

9. It should be obvious, though it isn't, that when one insists that a moral precept derives its binding character from divine authority, one inadvertently gives those who do not acknowledge that authority a dispensation from abiding by it.

10. 1–2 q. 94, art. 2: "*bonum est faciendum et prosequendum, et malum vitandum.*" I have discussed Thomas's claim (that the natural law is rational) in a paper, "Prudence, *Synderesis*, and Natural Law in the *Summa Theologiae*," which was presented at the 41st International Congress on Medieval Studies.

11. We have an inclination to know the truth about God, whether he exists or not. Whether there is a God is a matter about which it is not possible for a rational being to be indifferent.

12. 1–2 q. 94, art. 2. The whole phrase is, ". . . *inest homini inclinatio ad bonum secundum naturam rationis, quae est sibi propria: sicut homo habet naturalem inclinationem ad hoc quod veritatem cognoscat de Deo, et ad hoc quod in societate vivat. Et secundum hoc, ad legem naturalem pertinent ea quae ad huiuusmodi inclinationem spectant: utpote quod homo ignorantiam vitet, quod alios non offendat cum quibus debet conversari, et cetera huiusmodi quae ad hoc spectant.*"

13. To be sure, attorneys, family, and friends might claim that awarding the death penalty to a convicted murderer constitutes an offense against him. But the criminal, assuming he really is guilty, knows better. He may even find a plea of mental incompetence advanced on his behalf itself offensive. For, however well intended, such a plea implies that his humanity, of which rationality is an essential element, is not fully intact.

14. See Genesis 4:1–10; 23.

15. "*Iustitia est constans et perpetua voluntas ius suum unicuique tribuens.*" 2-2 q. 58, art. 1 and 8. The standard of giving a person his due, or his right, may be difficult to determine and apply in a particular place. Nonetheless, it is generally workable. It is the standard a teacher uses in grading a student's work, and it is the standard a judge uses in passing sentence on a convicted criminal. On the relation between mercy and justice, see I q. 21, art. 4, ad 2. Thomas treats justice (*iustitia*) as a virtue, and therefore a settled disposition of the soul, rather than as a certain state of affairs. The latter he calls *right* (*ius*), in the singular.

16. By what means an invaded country may and may not rightfully defend itself is a question we shall consider shortly. It is, however, distinct from the question of whether an invaded country may rightfully defend itself at all.

17. *Utrum bellare semper sit peccatum.* 2–2 q. 40, art. 1. See 1–2 q. 71, art. 4. Sin is an evil act, whereas vice is an evil habit. Compare Thomas's treatment of the criteria for just war with the parallel but different treatment by Franciscus de Victoria, *On the Law of War*, Section 60 (in *Classics of International Law*, New York: Oceana, 1964, Vol. 7). Victoria relies greatly on Thomas, but he blurs the distinction between what reason teaches and what Scripture teaches. Thomas Pangle, in his essay, "The Moral Basis of National Se-

curity: Four Historical Perspectives," in *Historical Dimensions of National Security Problems*, edited by Klaus Knorr (Lawrence: University Press of Kansas, 1976), speaks of "the problematic dependence of the Thomistic doctrine of just war on divine revelation" (p. 329). But he says this at the conclusion of his treatment, not of Thomas, but of Victoria and Suarez and their concern with a problem that Thomas was not aware of, namely, the Spanish treatment of the native inhabitants of the new world. Pangle does not show how Thomas's own treatment of just war, or natural law more generally, depends on divine revelation, though he leaves his readers with the impression that he thinks it does.

18. Thomas is concerned with the criteria for a just war, not with what is sometimes called a holy war. Unlike the former, the latter, if it exists at all, is clearly based on appeal to something other than what is accessible to unassisted reason and ordinary human experience. On Thomas's lack of sympathy with the crusading spirit, cf. J. Daryl Charles, *Between Pacifism and Jihad* (Downers Grove, IL: InterVarsity Press, 2005) pp. 45–47. There is, so far as I know, not one contemporary thinker working in the Catholic tradition who does not decry the atrocities committed by the Crusaders and by the hangers-on accompanying them. Nor did Christian clerics and theologians at the time of the Crusades uniformly refrain from denouncing the excesses they gave rise to either.

19. 2–2 q. 40, art. I, c. "*illi qui impugnantur propter aliquam culpam impugnationem mereantur.*"

20. I–2 q. 57, art. 4 and 5; q. 94, art. 4.

21. Natural law is known by reason alone. Divine law is not; it presupposes revelation. I-2, q. 92, art. 2 and 4.

22. 2–2 q. 40, art. 3; q. 110, art. 2 and 3. It is worth noting that prisoners of war are *not* told to lie to their captors. They are told, instead, to give name, rank, and serial number only.

23. 2–2 q. 110, art. 3; but compare art. 4. Kant's stance on the impermissibility of lying was not always as inflexible as he presents it in *On a Presumed Right to Lie because of Philanthropic Concerns*. See Kant, *Lectures on Ethics*, translated by Peter Heath (Cambridge: Cambridge University Press, 1997) pp. 204 and 427–28.

24. The rigors of the traditional natural law teaching on lying can, in my opinion, be mitigated, though only slightly. Refraining from lying is an obligation of justice. But protecting the innocent is an obligation of justice as well. It is bound up with the obligation to give each person his due, even if, as Kant would point out, it is an obligation characterized by latitude rather than narrowness. Lying to a person who exhibits murderous intent in order to prevent him from killing an innocent human being is not only permissible but obligatory, assuming that no other means are at hand to prevent the murder. If lying to

such a person in such circumstances is an injustice at all, it is a slight injustice only. I shall argue in the sequel that an injustice as grievous as murder is never permissible, much less obligatory.

25. *The Rudder of the Orthodox Church* (Chicago: The Orthodox Christian Educational Society, 1957) pp. 801–2.

26. Victoria, *On the Law of War* (see note 17 above) section 52.

27. Ibid., sections 31–33.

28. I use the term *realist* with misgivings. It implies a narrow conception of reality, according to which moral principles are not quite real. This conception of reality needs to be argued for rather than acquiesced in. But, like *realpolitik*, the term *realist* is frequently employed by contemporary theorists, and its meaning is widely recognized. Following contemporary usage, I mean by a *realist* someone who thinks that morality should be granted a rhetorical but not a constitutive role in the conduct of foreign policy. By this term I do *not* mean someone whose approach to foreign policy is governed by modest rather than grandiose expectations. Such a person may also hold that moral principles are real, every bit as real as our desire for self-preservation and pleasure.

29. James Turner Johnson, "The Just War Idea and the Ethics of Intervention," *Moral Dimensions of the Military Profession* (Cincinnati, OH: Thomas Learning, 2001) p. 121.

30. 2–2, q. 40, art. 1, c; see also ibid., ad 1.

31. In 1939–40, Finland fought the Soviet Union against what appeared to be hopeless odds. After a spirited defense, Finland was forced to yield some of her territory to Soviet control. But she still maintained her political independence and hence achieved at least a measure of success.

32. Victoria spells this out, while noting that ignorance can lead soldiers to think that they are fighting a just war that has in fact been unjustly entered into. Victoria, *On the Law of War* (see note 17 above) section 32.

33. *Aquinas: Selected Political Writings*, ed. A. P. d'Entr`eves; trans. J. G. Dawson, with the Latin text facing (Oxford: Blackwell, 1974) pp. 174–79. Thomas agrees with Paul that all political authority comes from God. But Thomas also has arguments in favor of political obedience that do not rely on theological premises. See, for example, 1-2, q. 96, entire.

34. 1–2 q. 90, art. 4 c, ad 3.

35. Ibid.

36. Such was the reasoning of the German officers who on July 20, 1944, unsuccessfully attempted to assassinate Hitler and replace his tyranny with something better. Among the many accounts of their efforts, two of the best are by Walter Görlitz, *History of the German General Staff*, trans. Brian Battershaw (New York: Praeger, 1955) chapters 11–16; and Roger Manville, *The Conspirators* (New York: Ballantine, 1971). See Thomas Aquinas, "On Princely Government," *Aquinas: Selected Political Writings*, pp. 30–35. In the *Commentary on the Sentences of Peter Lombard*, Dist. 33, q. 2, art. 2 (Ibid., pp. 180–85), Thomas explicitly concurs in Cicero's judgment that in certain circumstances tyrannicide is not only to be praised but rewarded as well. See also *ST* 1–2 q. 93, ad 2; q. 95, art. 2, c.

37. A consideration of the problematic cases, real and hypothetical, that combat can give rise to is a worthwhile endeavor, so long as the goal is that of clarifying principles and sharpening the faculty of judgment. It is futile, however, to expect that such an endeavor could elevate, or reduce, just war theory or any other part of ethics to the status of an exact science like mathematics. Cf. Aristotle, *Nicomachean Ethics*, 1094b13–27.

38. It has been remarked that if the distinction between war and murder, which relies on a distinction of intention, is denied because of the identity of the end result, namely, killing, then the distinction between pacifism and cowardice must also be denied on the same grounds. There, too, the end result—namely, not fighting—is identical, whatever intention may lie behind it.

39. The distinction between merely foreseeing (the likelihood of) the bad consequences of a voluntary action and actually intending them is central to the doctrine of double effect. There is a current dispute as to whether this distinction can be maintained. However, though one often both foresees and intends the consequences of a certain action, foreseeing and intending are not identical. For example, when a physician performs a necessary but painful medical procedure, he intends only its beneficial effects for his patient, though he foresees both the benefits and the pain. Something similar happens when a parent punishes a child. There may be situations in which foreseeing the secondary consequence of an action cannot be easily distinguished from intending it. And there are surely situations in which the principle of double effect can be abused. The existence of such situations, however, hardly justifies rejecting this principle across the board.

40. Technological advances in weaponry carry with them more exacting moral standards. See Martin Cook, *The Moral Warrior* (Albany: State University of New York Press, 2004) p. 34.

41. This language derives from the second version of Kant's categorical imperative: "*Handle so, dass du die Menschheit, sowohl in deiner Person, als in der Person eines jeden*

andern, jederzeit zugleich als Zweck, niemals bloss als Mitttel brauchest." (Act so that you treat humanity, both in your own person and in the person of anyone else, always as an end and never merely as a means.) Grundlegung zur Metaphysik der Sitten (*Groundwork of the Metaphysics of Morals*), in Immanuel Kant, *Schriften zur Ethik and Religionsphilosophie*, edited by Wilhelm Weischedel (Darmstadt: Wissenschaftliche Buchgesellschaft, 1981) p. 61.

42. The unqualified ban on the use of incapacitating but nonlethal gas may not be a sound application of the principle of proportionality.

43. Thomas, whose knowledge of Aristotle was profound, cites him as an authority in the *Summa Theologiae* repeatedly. But he cites Aristotle only once in the question "On War" and then only as an authority for the truisms that a variety of things need to be done for the good of society and that many things can be done more effectively by many people than by one alone; 2–2 q. 40, art. 2, c. We can infer that Thomas found little in Aristotle to support his own theory of just war.

44. See, for example, Plato, *Republic* 351 b; Aristotle, *Politics* 1333a31–1334b4; Leo Strauss, *Natural Right and History* (Chicago: University of Chicago Press, 1953) p. 157.

45. Leo Strauss, "On Natural Law," *Studies in Platonic Political Philosophy* (Chicago: University of Chicago, 1983) pp. 139–40; Ernest Fortin, "Augustine, Thomas Aquinas, and Natural Law," *Mediaevalia* 4 (1978): pp. 181–82; and, above all, Plato, *Statesman* 294 a–c.

46. The analogy that Socrates makes in the *Republic* between justice *within* the city and justice *within* the soul does not help in giving an account of how justice might hold sway *between* cities. For that, some concept of natural law needs to be invoked if any advance is to be made beyond conventionalism.

47. See, however, *Peloponnesian War* 7.29.4. It is worth remembering that Plato does not speak in his own name either, except in his letters. See *Epistle* VII 341 c.

48. See Plutarch, "Life of Alcibiades," xvi, 5; Plato, *Gorgias* 481 d; 519 b; *Alcibiades Major* 103 a ff. Xenophon, *Memorabilia* 1.2.

49. *Republic* 469b–471. Consider also *Laws* 627e–630c; *Timaeus* 19 c–d.

50. Cicero, *De Re Publica* 3.33–35; *De Legibus* 2.8–16; *De Officiis* 1.34–40, 2.26–27, 3.46–49, and 3.107–08.

51. As if the international community had any moral authority at all, distinct from the dubious moral authority of the individual nations that make it up.

52. 2-2 q. 110, art. 3 and 4; q. 40, art. 3, c. That agreements are morally binding is a secondary tenet of the natural law, and it can admit of occasional exceptions. 1–2 q. 94, art. 4, c; 2–2 q. 51, art. 4 c; q. 57, art. 2, ad 1.

53. "Injury or injustice, in the controversies of the world, is somewhat like to that which in the disputations of scholars is called absurdity. For as it is there called an absurdity to contradict what one maintained in the beginning, so in the world it is called injustice and injury voluntarily to undo that which from the beginning he had voluntarily done. The way by which a man either simply renounceth or transferreth his right is a declaration, or signification by some voluntary and sufficient sign or signs, that he doth so renounce or transfer, or hath so renounced or transferred the same, to him that accepteth it. And these signs are either words only, or actions only; or, as it happeneth most often, both words and actions. And the same are the bonds, by which men are bound and obliged: bonds that have their strength, not from their own nature (for nothing is more easily broken than a man's word), but from fear of some evil consequence upon the rupture." Thomas Hobbes, *Leviathan*, edited by Edwin Curly (Indianapolis: Hackett, 1994) p. 81.

54. Ibid., p. 84.

55. Ibid., pp. 82, 87.

56. Ibid., pp. 76–78; compare the first sentence of Chapter 17 (p. 106).

57. We moderns have a way of trying to solve problems by introducing learned words that seem to mean more than they do. One occasionally hears, for example, that alteration in the genetic material of a species is due to *mutation*, which is only a synonym for *alteration*, or that the heaviness of bodies is due to *gravity*, which is only a synonym for *heaviness*.

58. Thomas calls this law "the natural law" and Kant calls it "the moral law." For simplicity's sake, we shall continue to call it natural law even when speaking of Kant. There are significant differences in the way this law is conceived by these two quite different thinkers, but the differences can be ignored in light of the remarkable similarities. Thomas interprets natural law as the participation of eternal law in the rational creature. The eternal law is expressed in the rational structure of the world as a whole and its intelligibility to rational creatures. Thomas traces this rational structure to God, the supreme lawgiver. The first principles of natural law are as intrinsic to human reason as are the laws of logic, such as the principle of noncontradiction. Thomas distinguishes between the divine law, which is revealed, and the natural law, which is not. 1–2, q. 90, art. 1–2, 3; q. 93, art.1; q. 94, art. 2; q. 99, art. 2–3. See also Romans 2:14–15 and Deuteronomy 4:6.

59. This is a weak inference, as even Kant saw. (See Kant, *Critique of Practical Reason*, Preface, first footnote.) There is a possibility, which cannot be conclusively ruled out, that

practical reason (and even reason in general) might be totally at odds with reality, commanding voluntary compliance from a being who lacks the freedom to comply voluntarily. It is thinkable, but only from a theoretical, as opposed to a practical, perspective, that we might be incapable of freely choosing between alternative courses of action. Man *acts*, however, as though he thinks he has this freedom even when he is committed to determinism as a theory.

60. "I have a right that [workmen for the gas company] observe very strict safety standards." Michael Walzer, *Just and Unjust Wars* (New York: Basic Books, 1977) p. 156. Why Walzer does not say, more simply, that the workmen have a *duty* to observe strict safety standards — which is the way nonacademics would put the matter — is puzzling. Perhaps he realizes that the concept of duty presupposes the concept of law. When Walzer appeals to a "theory of rights" (p. 133) in support of his account of just war, he does not attempt to ground this theory, nor does he even suggest how it might be grounded. He imports the contemporary conception of rights into his exegesis of a passage from Deuteronomy that says nothing about rights, and he speaks of prohibitions in general as "properly conceived in terms of rights" (p. 135) without a trace of an argument as to why prohibitions are properly conceived that way (p. 54). To his credit, Walzer does note a trenchant objection made by Simone Weil to what Walzer himself calls "rights talk" (p. 134 fn.). But his brief response does not go beyond pointing out that such discourse has "played a significant part in the struggle against oppression, including the sexual oppression of women."

61. I am not speaking here of the religious pacifist who practices nonviolence as part of what he recognizes as a personal and essentially particular vocation. I am speaking, rather, of the pacifist, typically secular, who recognizes no distinction at all between war and murder. See n. 38 above.

62. In the *Republic*, Socrates redefines justice in such a way as to sever it from the concept of desert (368 b ff.). Whether the concerns expressed by Glaucon and Adeimantus (ibid., 358 e–367 e) justify this redefinition is disputable.

63. When pressed, the intelligent realist will concede that our animal nature has ends, which are (minimally) life and (maximally) pleasure, but he will deny that our rational nature has ends different in kind from these and of higher rank. The sole function of reason is instrumental. It is in the service of life and pleasure. The realist does not intend to rank *feeling* good higher than *being* good. He is more likely to equate the two: pleasure (including pleasure of the mind) *is* the good. As far as goodness is concerned, how one *feels* is how one *is*.

64. *Charter of the United Nations*, Chapter VII, Article 39. See also Article 42, where the language of "maintain or restore" reappears.

65. Ibid. Article 50. If a league or union of nations is justified in initiating military

operations for preventive reasons, why this would not be true for a federation or alliance of nations as well, or even for just one nation, is hard to explain.

66. In the early years of the twenty-first century, one looks back with something approaching nostalgia to the good old days of "mutually assured destruction," when neither of the contestants in the Cold War would risk, much less accept, its own destruction solely in order to destroy the other. Not all parties on the contemporary scene are similarly self-restrained.

67. Whereas, in the targeting of enemy combatants, one intends not their death but their capitulation, in the targeting of enemy noncombatants, one intends their death, albeit as a means to the good end of victory and a just peace. (The capitulation of enemy *non-combatants* is, of course, not a possible end, but a contradiction in terms.) This consideration underscores the fact that the targeting of noncombatants, particularly innocent children, unlike the targeting of combatants, cannot be meaningfully distinguished from murder.

68. This is an elementary but all too common misunderstanding. See *Ethics and the Military Profession*, ed. George Lucas and Rick Rubel (Boston: Pearson, 2006) p. 206. Only in our time would one suppose that the nature of man could be illuminated by a trip to the zoo.

69. The question naturally arises here as to whether it is ever morally justifiable to inflict acute physical pain — as distinct from causing death, mutilation, or permanent bodily injury — on a terrorist who has participated in the murder of a number of innocent people and who also possesses information the discovery of which would avert the murder of yet more innocent people. I am unaware of a credible argument to the effect that such a thing cannot be justified morally. In the scenario under consideration, our obligations to the terrorist himself, assuming he really is a terrorist and not an ordinary prisoner of war, are much more limited than our obligations to his children. I speak here, of course, from a natural law perspective, disregarding whatever the transient law of the land may happen to say (or be interpreted as saying).

70. Note that by telling us that we *ought* to murder the terrorist's children, the realist inconsistently makes use of the language of morality, the practical inescapability from which he pays insufficient attention to.

71. Brian Orend, *The Morality of War* (Peterborough, Ontario: Broadview, 2006) construes supreme emergency as a "moral tragedy" in which "each viable option . . . involves a severe moral violation" (p. 155). If the moral violations really are equally severe, then no alternative is morally superior to another and, to repeat, settling the matter on utilitarian grounds is altogether rational and permissible. But Orend does not show that in a supreme emergency the alternatives involve *equally* severe moral violations. Instead, he complicates

matters by asserting that a country "*will* do whatever it can to prevail" (p. 155, Orend's italics; cf. ibid., pp.151–52). Orend is probably right if he intends to be speaking about a matter of likelihood simply, but he seems to be speaking about a matter of necessity. If he means to say that in a supreme emergency a country necessarily loses its moral freedom and simply *cannot* refrain from murdering the innocent, then he owes his readers an argument for exactly how this loss of moral freedom necessarily occurs. His reference to an "interpersonal analogy" that he has offered earlier in his book does not help, since he did not show that a loss of moral freedom necessarily occurred there either (p. 155; cf. p. 150). If, on the other hand, Orend means to say that in a supreme emergency a country really *can* refrain from murdering the innocent, then he owes his readers an argument as to why it is not *obliged* to refrain, since he commendably aspires to offer concrete, nonparadoxical advice instead of hand-wringing (pp. 154, 157).

72. Romans 8:22.

73. "The city may and must demand sacrifice from its citizens; the city itself however cannot sacrifice itself; a city may without disgrace accept even under compulsion the overlordship of a another city which is much more powerful; this is not to deny of course that death or extinction is to be preferred to enslavement proper." Leo Strauss, *The City and Man*, (Chicago: Rand McNally, 1964) p. 189. The final clause in this complex sentence undercuts the second clause. A city, or nation, can accept extinction, which is apparently what Strauss means by "sacrifice itself," rather than accept shameful enslavement. There is no reason to think it could not also accept extinction rather than commit shameful injustice. On sacrifice, see also Leo Strauss, *What is Political Philosophy?* (Glencoe, IL: The Free Press, 1959) p. 33, line 14 from the bottom; and "Why We Remain Jews," *Jewish Philosophy and Crisis of Modernity*, edited by Kenneth Hart Green (Albany: State University of New York, 1997) pp. 322–23. Strauss speaks in the latter essay with what certainly appears to be approbation, of "the heroic act of self-dedication of a whole nation to something which it regarded as infinitely higher than itself." The context is voluntary martyrdom.

74. In the language of the Church, one should "avoid the near occasion of sin." Deliberately and unnecessarily placing oneself in a situation where the temptation to sin is all but irresistible is itself a sin.

75. Cf. note 10 above.

COMMENTS ON JAMES CAREY'S ESSAY
(WITH A REPLY TO CAREY'S COMMENTS ON CRAIG NICHOLS'S ESSAY)

CRAIG NICHOLS

Professor Carey provides a strong and compelling argument in favor of natural law theory in ethics and for the concept of a just war in particular. I am in substantial agreement with his position and am appreciative of his profound analysis and defense of this under-appreciated position in the modern ethical milieu. Although I have little direct criticism to offer, perhaps a critical dimension can be gained nevertheless by bringing Professor Carey's essay and my own into dialogue.

We are describing two different, but potentially complementary, areas: (apophatic) theology and (rational) ethics. Aquinas (standing at the center of the Roman Catholic dogmatic tradition) and traditional Christian orthodoxy, generally speaking (including Eastern Orthodoxy, and some branches of Protestantism) would be in essential agreement that the two areas can be wedded together into a coherent worldview. Modern fundamentalist-postivist theology, however, seems to be barred (or bars itself) from adopting a natural law position in either ethics or theology. In his essay, Prof. Carey has not established a specific link between Christian theology (or any other theology) and just war theory — quite the opposite, in fact. He specifically dissociates the two realms, leaving open the question of the possible relation between theology and ethics as well as the issue of a possible link between violence and any specific theology.

Any theology (or religious orientation to Transcendence) among the world religions that explicitly makes room for — or at least does not explicitly preclude — a link with the "perennial philosophy" of natural revelation through reason could potentially be shown to be compatible with the just war theory described by Professor Carey. Consider Krishna's counsel to Arjuna in the Bhagavad Gita, for example. Orthodox Christianity, while drawing upon its liturgical and dogmatic roots, has traditionally made an explicit connection with the natural light of reason, although ultimately culminating in an apophatic orientation to the human relation to God (thus, traditional Christianity has typically understood itself as *fides quarrens intellectum* — "faith seeking understanding"). Theological apophaticism, connected with a full acceptance of the use of reason as part of the goodness of creation, makes room not only for internal ecumenical dialogue within the branches of Christendom, but opens Christian theology to "the other" in a radical way — not by giving up its theological distinctiveness, but precisely *through* it, as hinted at by, among other doctrines, the *perichoresis* of the Trinity, which suggests a constant outward movement of love toward otherness.

A fundamentalist-positivist approach to other faith traditions, however, closes the possibility that God might speak through the other. If we think we *know* the absolute truth as an objective datum, we are likely to have no "ears to hear" anything but our own stock of revealed truths. What is more, we may no longer listen to the ongoing revelation in nature either, but seek to impose upon nature — and others — the truth that we think we possess a priori. Hence, a strictly kataphatic (that is, inherently gnostic) approach to divine revelation would make an integration of Christian theology (or any other theology) with natural law theory either merely accidental or simply incoherent.

My essay may be read as a complement to Professor Carey's, insofar as I have attempted to provide an explanation of how one might set a fence around theology to withhold it, in its very principle, from turning to violent and aggressive modes of thought and behavior toward nonbelievers. For example, when unbelievers in "our" theology become a threat to "our" way of life (which is perceived to be absolutely ordained by the Absolute), then the conditions of a just war may *appear* to have been met. But have they? Maintaining a healthy apophaticism in one's theology is a way of preserving theology as a means of participating in the higher levels of the human experience of truth while providing a strong check against the forcible advance of one's faith against "the other." A middle ground between pacifism and aggression can be established.

Reasons are thereby established to explain why the advance of a faith tradition should only be done through reasonable means — for instance, through the persuasive example of an exemplary life ("be like me because I am showing what the good life looks like") and through the persuasive use of reason ("think like me because my description of reality explains the whole range of possible human experience more coherently than your world-view does"). Conversion by the sword is thus neither theologically nor morally permissible. However, if I claim to have direct and immediate access to God's will — not mediated through the collective refining of faith and reason, each infusing the other with meaning over a long period of reflection — then there is no reason why I should check with reason (or natural law, or sacred tradition, both of which imply the use of reason over time) before imposing God's supposed will on others.

I further agree with Professor Carey's description of the lack of grounds for the claims of modern pacifists and so-called realists (a rather unfortunate name, considering the dissociation with the Platonic tradition the term carries in this context). But how might an effective turnaround in modern thinking take place on this matter? Again, Professor Carey has argued that natural law — *in principle* — need not be tied to a specific theology, even though it is historically associated with Thomism, and hence Roman Catholicism. Thus, one might develop a natural law theory within a traditional Western pagan paradigm, using Aristotle as a base, or perhaps in a non-Christian Asian paradigm, using Confucius as a base. But it seems unlikely to expect that the modern Western, secular-progressive frame of mind will be able to change its view and recognize reason as the solid ground of thought and action that it was traditionally held to be via the perennial philosophy. Modern thinking clings to positivism as the ground for "scientific" epistemology, while confining theology and philosophy — including ethics — almost completely to the private sphere, where nothing but emotivist assertions remain (shifting sands, upon which are built the occasional stipulated agreements in the public sphere).

Alasdair MacIntyre identifies this as the reason why so much ethical and political discourse today takes in a rather shrill tone.[1] Professor Carey does not here attempt an explanation for how the many modern thinkers who are blind to the tradition might regain their sight (or how they lost it in the first place). MacIntyre's *After Virtue* might prove helpful in this regard, insofar as he locates what was lost, and needs to be restored, as the dimensions of hierarchy and teleology.[2] The gradual excision of these two dimensions of human thought have brought about the modern loss of meaning (nihilism) with respect to the concepts of tradition, God, collective human purposes, and the exercise of reason as a whole. In short, everything that transcends human individuality becomes dubious. I wonder whether it is possible to recover a meaningful ethical discourse that transcends emotivism (including, under this banner, utilitarianism, pragmatism, and contemporary "realism"), without embracing a healthy human acceptance of Transcendence, in general, and a specific tradition that cultivates Transcendence, in particular.

Jaspers, whose philosophy I have used to make this general point (although I have gone beyond him to argue for the need to embrace a particular tradition), contends rather convincingly that the collective human use of reason in ethics depends on *philosophical faith* — hence, *faith* in *reason*. And reason itself must then be seen — generally, at least — to have a ground in Transcendence (however it is conceived, whether Being-as-a-whole, or God, or Brahman, or the Dao, or something else). But this is the very faith that moderns — qua moderns — have lost.

The modern West, to a large extent, has lost *both* its philosophical *and* its theological faith. Jaspers believes it possible to recapture a philosophical faith in the perennial philosophy (another way of describing the natural law, the *Logos*, or the Dharma that permeates the cosmos) simply through reflection. But such faith involves embracing a mystery at the very heart of being, a mystery that traditional religions have made it their business to cultivate. For moderns, nothing is sacred, nothing mysterious — at least not in the sense that calls forth reverence. Positivism has desensitized modern thought to an apophatic approach to ultimate reality. Peace is maintained — when it is — largely as a result of the desire to avoid pain. But emotivism is no basis for a lasting peace, just a temporary avoidance of the problem of the human condition. Is it possible to embrace traditional natural law theory on a large scale without an equally large revitalization of religious tradition in the hearts and minds of modern people? The sense of the sacred, which is cultivated by religion, seems to be a necessary support for the *faith* in reason.

Which sort of religious tradition should we then embrace? And should we look to ancient or modern forms? As Professor Carey points out, the Christian tradition is not the only viable option vis-à-vis the acceptance of natural law. Without digressing into apologetics, I would affirm here merely that, regardless of which faith tradition one uses to revitalize a sense of the sacred, we should be very careful not to seek the grounds of natural law in fundamentalism, nor to expect support for natural law theory in any form of theological positivism. For if we do, we are likely to end up with exactly the situation that we find today in contemporary Protestantism: liberal fundamentalism on the left and conservative fundamentalism on the right. And if either end is pushed beyond the constraints of reason (with which tradition has gifted them), then, due to the remaining emotivist impulses, the result can be an aggressive stance toward "unbelievers." This can lead to violence in the struggle for God's — or a god's, or simply "my" *übermenschliche* — will; or for "the greatest good for the greatest number." It all ends up the same.

Such (e)motive forces operate both within and without organized religious institutions, but show the same religious impulses — as the twentieth-century standoff between capitalism and totalitarian fascism and communism has shown, and as the contemporary struggle of Western egalitarianism with radical Islamic fundamentalism is violently demonstrating in the twenty-first century. What sort of religious orientation should thus be promoted in order to further promote the faith in reason necessary to embrace Professor Carey's vision of natural law? I answer that we should promote involvement in a particular kind of faith tradition — a mode of human involvement that restores, preserves, and cultivates the dimensions of teleology and hierarchy that were lost in the modern era (resulting in nihilism). But the promotion of such a faith must be rooted in a profound apophaticism, a deep embracing of mystery, of truth as non-knowledge that is nevertheless not relativism or perspectivism. A form of theology is needed that will not abandon the meaningfulness of absolute Truth, and yet will leave open at least the possibility for communication, tolerance, and respect between traditions stemming from such different figures as Socrates, Buddha, Confucius, and Jesus.[3] Such an orientation may even provide the ability to own up to that hardest of human choices that Professor Carey describes: the capacity to sacrifice oneself for the sake of something truly worth dying for — something that transcends oneself. And with an apophatic dimension of faith in place — whether it is philosophical, theological, or both — we are then in a position to fundamentally exclude any sense of "martyrdom" that involves killing to promote one's faith.

NOTES:

1. See Alasdair MacIntyre, *After Virtue: A Study in Moral Theory*, 3rd. ed. (Notre Dame, IN: University of Notre Dame Press, 2007) p. 8.

2. See especially Chap. 5: "Why the Enlightenment Project of Justifying Morality Had to Fail," and Chap. 6: "Some Consequences of the Failure of the Enlightenment Project"; ibid., pp. 51–78.

3. Jaspers describes these four as the "paradigm individuals" of world history. See Karl Jaspers, *Socrates, Buddha, Confucius, Jesus* [from *The Great Philosophers*, Vol. I], trans. Ralph Manheim (New York: Harcourt Brace, 1962).

James Carey's Reply

Professor Nichols makes a number of interesting remarks concerning my essay, "Christianity and Force: The Just War Tradition." He recognizes that my central intent was to argue that, though Thomas Aquinas provides us with the classic statement and most impressive grounding of the concept of just war, he does not base his treatment on specifically Christian principles but on reason and ordinary human experience, that is, on what is accessible to man as man. I fully share Professor Nichols's doubts as to whether "the modern Western, secular-progressive frame of mind will be able to change its view and recognize reason as the solid ground of thought and action." But since the likely alternative is increasing and increasingly destructive irrationalism, in both thought and action, it seemed worthwhile to restate the case for reason. I limit myself here to saying a bit more about the relation between reason and religious faith, particularly as Thomas Aquinas understands this relation.

I am not a Roman Catholic, and Thomas is not for me a final authority on philosophical or theological matters. But having studied his works off and on for several decades I have reached the conclusion that it is all but impossible for him to comment on any problem without shedding at least some light on it, usually a lot of light. In framing and arguing for his theses, Thomas takes pains to address the weightiest objections of those who disagree with him. He tries to find common ground with his opponents so as to see exactly where he and they part ways. He is not interested in knocking down straw men. Moreover, he assumes as self-evident that every human being acknowledges the authority of reason. If there is a weakness in Thomas's approach, it is that he seems to have anticipated neither the extent nor the intensity of the passion with which human beings would come to embrace irrationalism.

Thomas holds that it is simply impossible to believe what one recognizes to be a bald contradiction in terms. The sentence, "A quadrilateral is a figure having only three sides," is grammatically coherent. The subject agrees with the verb, and so forth. But it is conceptually so incoherent that, though it can be uttered, it cannot be thought. It cannot even be thought vaguely or, for that matter, mystically. The opposition between the concepts "quadrilateral" and "a figure having only three sides" is so stark that nothing conceptually corresponds to the sentence as a whole. The same is true of the sentences, "God, who is only one God, is actually three Gods," and "Christ, who has two natures, actually has only one nature."

Although opponents of Christianity have often accused Christians of embracing such contradictions, the impossibility of doing so was recognized by almost all Christian theologians from the Patristic period at least up to the Protestant Reformation. Catholic theologians, East and West, invested intellect and energy in demonstrating that a Trinity of *persons* is logically compatible with the oneness of *God*, and that the oneness of Christ's *person* is logically compatible with his having two *natures*, along with other similarly paradoxical but not logically contradictory doctrines. Of course, many theologians have emphasized paradox, and some have even labeled absurd what is not, strictly speaking, contradictory — but only paradoxical. One is hard pressed, however, to find a theologian prior to the Reformation who maintained what he himself believed was a frank and irreconcilable contradiction. Thomas Aquinas adheres to the spirit that led to the letter of the dogmatic decrees of the early Church in its ecumenical councils, where logical contradiction was systematically shunned.

Now, though revelation does not violate reason, what it discloses does transcend anything that reason could find out on its own. God is not just the Supreme Being, or even the creator of the world *ex nihilo*, but has acted — indeed, has intervened—in history. At his own initiative, he established the Covenant with Israel and, somewhat later on, he became incarnate in the world — so Christians believe, at any event. That God has done these things, and has performed many other miracles that have to count as divine interruptions into, and interruptions of, the natural order of things, cannot be proven beyond the shadow of doubt. His miracles must be taken on faith. They cannot be proven to have happened, but they cannot be proven *not* to have happened either. The possibility of divine interruptions of the natural order does not in the least violate reason — *reason* being traditionally understood as simply the logical canon that any assertion must agree with in order to be taken seriously by a rational being.

The possibility of divine interruptions of the natural order might, however, be said to violate natural science, to the extent that science adopts as its guiding architectonic principle the notion that a worldly, physical event can have only another worldly, physical event as its cause. But this principle is not a purely logical principle. Natural science, unlike logic and unlike mathematics as well, is *empirical* science. Natural science makes use of logic and mathematics, to be sure. It also makes use, and must make use, of particular empirical observations. On the basis of such observations, it makes empirical generalizations, which it then calls *laws* (leaving rather vague the issue of who the lawgiver is). Such generalizations are always characterized, however, by at least a little bit of uncertainty. It is no surprise, then, that what is held to be a law of nature at one point in history can be held at a later point in history to be merely a false, even if ingenious, opinion.

This limitation of natural science, that its proclamations always carry with them some measure of uncertainty, was recognized until recently, not only by theologians and believers generally, but by unbelieving philosophers and scientists as well. Today, however, the uneducated public, dazzled by the extent of natural science's "mastery of nature" (Descartes) and the largesse of its benefactions "for the relief of man's estate" (Bacon) in the interest of "commodious living" (Hobbes) thoughtlessly attributes to science a certainty and indubitability that it constitutionally does not and cannot possess. Many contemporary scientists, who must know better, have shamelessly encouraged the public to buy into the demonstrably false opinion that the empirically based pronouncements of natural science possess the epistemic evidence proper to laws of logic.

Now, given that modern natural science defined itself from the outset in opposition to Medieval philosophy and theology, the excessively high estimation in which science is held in our times makes having recourse to a Medieval thinker like Thomas Aquinas to get a fresh perspective on contemporary problems seem pointless, even when he is speaking on a matter that lies outside the concerns of science. Going against the grain, I argued in my essay that contemporary just war theorists need to reconsider Thomas's teaching if they hope to navigate their way through the moral dilemmas currently posed by terrorism, dilemmas that make a mockery of the conventionalist and ultimately relativist language of "stipulation" and "customary international law." Nowhere in ethics is the need for a return to reason *as an absolute* more patent than in contemporary just war theory.

Of course, the reference to an absolute of any kind offends contemporary sensibilities, especially contemporary academic sensibilities, not least because it conjures up associations with religion. But taking reason as an absolute, that is, inviolable, canon for thought and action does not imply any kind of religious commitment. For, as Thomas himself insists, though reason and genuine faith are not in conflict, reason is not a substitute for faith, nor can specifically religious doctrines be deduced from what we know by virtue of our reason alone. And yet, though reason is not a substitute for faith, it does lead to the threshold of faith. What Thomas did not anticipate is how far an uneasy recognition of this fact would lead modern man — not to look at the claims of faith more closely, but instead — to deny the authority of reason itself and thereby repudiate his own humanity.

FINAL COMMENTS ON RELIGION, FUNDAMENTALISM, AND VIOLENCE

ANDREW L. GLUCK

After reading all of the chapters, writing one, commenting on one, and reading the comments and replies from the various authors, I think it might be valuable to discuss the general topic again. I am sure that many readers will be forming their own final impressions of the book, and perhaps they may want to compare theirs with mine.

One thing stood out rather starkly to me, and that was the apparent difference in perspectives of the various religions. It may, however, tell us more in reality about the particular authors than about the religions themselves, but I think it is worth commenting on nonetheless.

The two authors who wrote specifically on Islam and Judaism (Dr. Ghaemi and myself) quite frankly acknowledged *fundamental* problems with violence in their respective religions, while also attempting to put them into a comprehensible context. This frankness regarding violence as a foundational factor was also a characteristic of the chapters by Professors Antoun and Delaney. It was far less apparent in the three chapters that dealt specifically with Christianity and Hinduism. Of course, Professors Carey, Nichols, and Ramani all acknowledged problems in their respective communities regarding violence, but my impression is that they view the essences of their religions to be pure, as regards the illegitimate use of force. I would like to attempt an explanation of this, recognizing, however, that it is just an impression and does not stem from a well-established theoretical position.

It seems to me that while all of the great religions have absorbed strong philosophical influences, these are much stronger in Hinduism and Christianity than they are in Judaism and Islam. Those philosophical influences seem to mitigate whatever violent tendencies might exist in the respective religions and to allow for a relatively nonviolent interpretation of the "essential" teaching. It is possible that Sufism played an analogous (but less influential) role in Islam, but I don't know of any similar traditional movement in Judaism (although, in practice, violence has traditionally been renounced by most Jews). That conjecture does not imply that those more philosophical religions are necessarily less violent than the others, but only that their ideology focuses on nonviolence — and perhaps they have the capacity to be nonviolent if conditions allow. This might be obvious, for example, from the teachings of Mahatma Gandhi, the Quakers, and Martin Luther King Jr. On the other hand, both Gandhi and King were assassinated by members of their own faiths, so this tells us little about how adherents of those religions actually behave.

I will not speak directly to the issue of Gnosticism, but it is interesting that the hallmark Gnostic doctrine of a supreme God who does not create is also found in Hinduism. How this doctrine impacts on violence is a subject that I feel incapable of discussing in a very fruitful way at this time, but perhaps it is something of interest for future research. Nevertheless, I would argue that the claim to possess esoteric knowledge is not necessarily linked to violence, but, when combined with the activist temperament of the Abrahamic religions, it might indeed result in violence. Professor Delaney is probably on to something there (even if I disagree with many of her particular conclusions).

As I wrote in the introduction, the Bible should not be blamed for human violence or blood sacrifices, but the emphasis in the Bible on Divine creativity and the notion of humans being created in God's image lends itself to activism, which might spill over into violence. And indeed there does seem to be some evidence for this. On the other hand, one might well ask whether human slavery or the caste system would ever have been abolished if not for the Abrahamic religions. It has been said that Gandhi only embarked on what became his mission after reading the Bible. Whether that is true or not, he was surely influenced by the Bible and Western civilization (despite his wonderful quip when asked about the latter that "it would be a good idea"). So perhaps the activism of the Abrahamic faiths is a double-edged sword, producing both good and evil.

I am still quite puzzled regarding the human penchant for animal (and even human) sacrifice. Without going into details here, it should be evident that this apparently primordial human need has been incorporated into all the religions discussed in this book. There seems to be a deeply held belief or feeling that for some to be redeemed something (or someone) must suffer, bleed, and die. Perhaps we must better understand this phenomenon if we are ever to get to the bottom of religiously inspired violence.

Finally, I am fascinated by the dispute between Professors Carey and Nichols. I wonder whether this dispute is largely confined to Christianity or whether (perhaps to a weaker extent) it is a fundamental problem for all religions. It seems to be spilling over into Judaism and Islam and probably always was a feature of those religions — even if to a lesser extent than in Christianity. Personally, I feel a greater affinity to Professor Nichols's position, but I must admit that Professor Carey's type of orthodoxy is what most religious people seem to want and perhaps need. That emphasis on dogmatic belief, as contrasted with the ancient rituals and myths, may even be a feature of all advanced religions. If that is the case, perhaps we should be very concerned about what people believe and not only about their core values. Beliefs that may seem charming and quaint may at other times lead to dangerous consequences. For that reason, we must be cautious in blaming reactive fundamentalism for all our problems regarding religiously inspired violence; we must continue to search the depths of our respective religious traditions. On the other hand, we must use judgment in criticizing religious beliefs and should attempt to distinguish the truly dangerous ones from those that are merely nonrational.

I happen to believe that the only way to a dynamic and lasting peace between peoples is through the capacity for rational belief and action. That does not mean that we must always be rational, but only that, in times of crisis, we must have the ability to revere reason and follow its dictates — just as, in times of illness, we go to a doctor. You may recall that in my introduction I conjectured that many people seem to need some kind of orthodoxy, but the borderline between orthodoxy and fundamentalism was left somewhat blurry. Despite the fact that all religions have some nonrational beliefs, I suspect that the great reverence for reason — embodied, for example, in Proverbs 8–9 and Job 28 — serves as an antidote to irrational fundamentalism. I am sure that similar intellectual phenomena exist in other traditions as well (for example, in Mutazilite theology and Hindu philosophy).

There is this blurry line between the nonrational and the irrational in religious faith, and I strongly suspect that it impacts upon violence. I don't believe that our discussions have eliminated that blurriness, but I hope they will aid in further exploration and analysis.

INDEX

299

women in, 61, 62, 63
Christianity and Liberalism (Machen), 237n35
Christmas story, 58
Church Dogmatics (Barth), 229
Cicero, 262
City and Man, The (Strauss), 284n73
civitas terrenae/civitas dei, 19
clan violence, 7
Clement, 237n34
clergy members, wartime role of, 251
Cloninger, C. Robert, 195–196, 205n52
coercion in religion, 39, 46–47, 62, 218
Cohen, Richard, 31n14
Cohn, Norman, 4
communion, 224
Communism, 11
community, need for, 211–213, 218–225
Comte, Auguste, 236n24
conformity in society, 22
conversion, 13, 17, 39, 46–47, 62
Cook, Martin, 279n40
I Corinthians, 61
cosmic war, 37
Council of Constantinople, 213
Council of Nicea, 239
creation stories, 54–55, 69
creativity, 64
creed, need for, 216–220
"Creed of Sadat's Assassins, The" (Faraj), 43n11
criminal terrorism, 36
cross-cultural research, 40
Crusades, 277n18
cultural climate as deterrent for violence, 21–22

Cultural Heritage of India, The (Bhattacharya), 114n2
cultural relativism, 65

D
Daat Emet, 167n13
Dalai Lama, 230–231, 242
Dalits (untouchables), 94, 97–105, 120n75
damnation, 16
Daoism, 232
dar al-harb/dar al-islam, 19
Darwish, Noni, 68n13
Dawkins, Richard, 197
De l'esprit des lois (Montesquieu), 31n15
death instinct *(Thanatos),* 5
Defenders of God (Lawrence), 42n3
Defenders of the Faith (Heilman), 42n5
defining beliefs of orthodoxy/fundamentalism, 9–12
Delaney, Carol, 53, 55, 67n2, 68n7, 69, 73, 74, 177, 181
Dennett, David, 197
Deobandi School, 47–48
descending Savior figure, 213–216
Deuteronomy, 36
devadasi system, 90
dharma, 80–81
dialogue with fundamentalists, 40–42
doctrinal belief *versus* attitude, 13
double effect principle, 257–258

E
economic libertarianism, 35
Economy and Society (Weber), 176n90
education, 64–65, 66